HARRY'S BAR
FIRENZE

Zum weißen Rössl

Menu and Cocktail List

CASA CARIOCA
GARMISCH · RECREATION AREA

CAFE DE LA RAMBLA

RESTAURANT

RAMBLA ESTUDIS
14 — CANUDA, 2
TELEFON 18321

31 DESEMBRE 1933
REVEILLON
DE——LA
— RAMBLA —

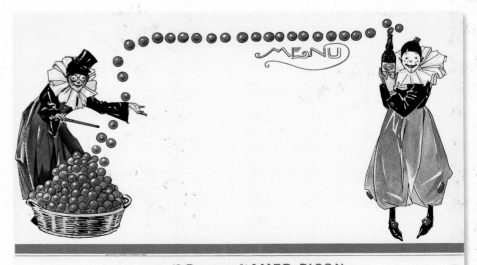

MENU

Offert par l'AMER PICON

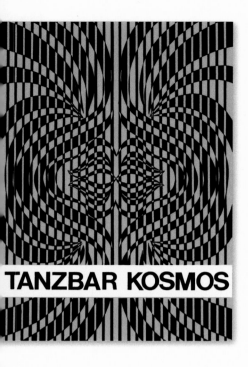

TANZBAR KOSMOS

Berliner Bierstube

N.V. STOOMVAART MAATSCHAPPIJ „NEDERLAND"

Notre devise est
TOUJOURS A MIEUX
comme notre nom

Menu

IMP. ERA. ROBERT FRÈRES-NANTES-PARIS

SWEDISH AMERICAN LINE

WINES
COCKTAILS &
DRINKS
ETC. ETC.
FROM THE
KUNGSHOLM bar

DÉSILINE Tonique
Stomachique
Digestive

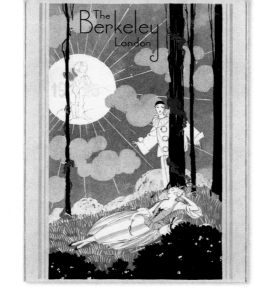

Menu Design
In Europe

Patrick Fulgraff

Jim Heimann [Ed.]
Steven Heller
Marc Selvaggio

Menu Design
In Europe

A Visual and Culinary History of
Graphic Styles and Design 1800–2000

TASCHEN

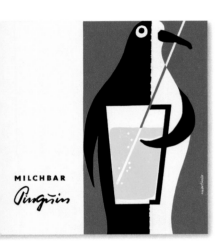

menu

IMP. V. VIDOUX OF MAN:

Menus

The European Menu

by Jim Heimann

As the printed menu slowly recedes from the culinary experience, menus of the past have increasing value and are becoming the domain of serious collectors and institutions.

Being the source of culinary development, Europe provided the blueprint for menu design, which blossomed for several centuries. Delectable as the cuisine being served, menus and their design followed a pragmatic course: from a verbal recitation of a restaurant's meal to a simple bill of fare written on a board. As meal preparation and serving became more sophisticated, increasingly elaborate *cartes,* or cards, with a printed or handwritten list of the items, became available.

France, the fountainhead of many gastronomical traditions, initiated the earliest paper menus starting in the mid-1700s. Chefs were newly liberated from their ties to aristocratic families via the French Revolution (1789–1799) and began preparing meals for private diners. Enter fine dining. Other aspects of this new eating experience included meals being served at private tables and not in a communal space, the reserving of tables, and the introduction of table accessories, tablecloths, fine china, and cutlery. With these restaurant changes, the details of the paper menu also evolved, becoming more elaborate and illustrative. The *carte* became an integral and celebrated companion to the meal as an experience.

More affordable travel and the proliferation of restaurants around the continent and Great Britain expanded the use of printed menus. As the 1800s progressed, the marvelous graphics of many European menus were unparalleled, prompting many diners to retain them as souvenirs, thus commencing the practice of collecting them. As the decades advanced, color began to be implemented into menus with more fervor. The illustrative component also flourished as reproduction techniques progressed. Eventually, photography, both color and black-and-white, could be seen on the cover.

Special occasions and unique events in pre-20th-century Europe underscored an elite customer base that was strikingly absent in the social structure of their American counterparts. Royal weddings, state visits, and celebrity tributes were more common in a monarchy, thus eliciting exuberant and specialized graphics. Hotel, ship, and, later, airline menus were another category in which European menu design flourished. Over time the menu became associated as an emotional adjunct and positive memory to an event.

The variety of comestibles available throughout Europe complemented the diversity of artistic styles employed on menu covers. From the late 1800s through the turn of the century, the popularity of Art Nouveau knew no borders. Spanish, Dutch, Belgian, Swiss, Italian, and, of course, French menus applied exquisite swirls and organic forms to paper, and the female form was liberally used on many covers. The 20th century saw many design movements applied equally to menu covers—from Art Deco, Streamline Moderne, and Bauhaus to abstraction and graphic realism. The appropriation of fine art photography and humor, along with the occasional risqué menu cover, could also be found. As information passed more quickly, technology was shared, and ideas became borderless. Menu design eventually evolved to be more common with an international community rather than being unique to a specific region. Yet it can be argued that a distinctive style associated with menus of individual countries could still be found. Ultimately, though, the overlapping global influences of menu design helped to democratize the look of the menu.

As the restaurant world evolves and the paper menu is being replaced by QR codes via personal phones or computer printouts, the beauty and tactile experience of a tangible and unique menu is slowly diminishing. Citing cost, along with the flexibility of altering food and beverage items and prices, restaurant owners see the menu, especially one that is unique and engineered, as an economic burden. As the printed menu slowly recedes from the culinary experience, menus of the past have increasing value and are becoming the domain of serious collectors and institutions.

One hopes that this book, a record of several centuries of gustatory elation, will be a reminder that this common object was once a key element of a meal. In many instances, the menu elevated dining to an art, reflecting, in turn, its purpose as an essential part of graphic and culinary history to be retained for posterity.

Le Relais
Café Royal

Die europäische Speisekarte

von Jim Heimann

Während gedruckte Speisekarten nach und nach aus der kulinarischen Welt verschwinden, werden jene aus der Vergangenheit immer wertvoller und zur Domäne ernsthafter Sammler und Institutionen.

Europa war die Wiege der kulinarischen Entwicklung, und so kamen die Speisekarten, die über mehrere Jahrhunderte hinweg eine Blütezeit erlebten, ebenfalls aus Europa. Ihr Design, das so ansprechend war wie die servierte Küche, verfolgt einen pragmatischen Ansatz: von der mündlichen Aufzählung der Speisen eines Restaurants bis zum einfachen Angebot auf einer Tafel. Als die Mahlzeiten immer raffinierter zubereitet und serviert wurden, kamen auch kunstvolle *cartes* bzw. Speisekarten in Gebrauch.

In Frankreich, dem Ursprungsland vieler gastronomischer Traditionen, stellte man ab Mitte des 18. Jahrhunderts die ersten Speisekarten auf Papier her. Infolge der Französischen Revolution (1789–1799) begannen Köche, Mahlzeiten für bürgerliche Privatpersonen zuzubereiten. Dies war die Geburtsstunde der gehobenen Gastronomie. Zum neuen kulinarischen Erlebnis gehörte auch, dass Mahlzeiten an privaten statt an Gemeinschaftstischen oder sogar in Privaträumen serviert wurden, dass man Tische reservieren konnte und diese kunstvoll gedeckt wurden. Außerdem entwickelten sich auch die Details auf Papierspeisekarten weiter. Die *carte* wurde zu einem wichtigen und hochgeschätzten Bestandteil des Esserlebnisses.

Als das Reisen erschwinglicher wurde und zahlreiche Restaurants in Europa eröffneten, erfreuten sich gedruckte Speisekarten immer größerer Beliebtheit. Im Lauf des 19. Jahrhunderts wurden unzählige von ihnen von wunderschönen, einzigartigen Grafiken geziert. Viele Gäste nahmen sie als Souvenir mit, und so wurde es üblich, sie zu sammeln. In den folgenden Jahrzehnten verwendete man mit wachsender Begeisterung Farben für das Design. Mit den verbesserten Reproduktionstechniken entwickelte sich auch die illustrative Komponente weiter. Schließlich waren auf den Titelseiten sowohl Schwarz-Weiß- als auch Farbfotografien zu sehen.

Vor dem 20. Jahrhundert entwickelte sich ein elitärer Kundenstamm in Europa, wie er im sozialen Gefüge Amerikas nicht zu finden war. In den europäischen Monarchien waren Hochzeiten, Staatsbesuche und Ehrungen von Berühmtheiten häufiger an der Tagesordnung. Zu diesen Anlässen wurden überaus aufwendige Grafiken erstellt. Auch die Speisekarten von Hotels, Schiffen und später von Fluggesellschaften bildeten eine Kategorie für sich, die das europäische Speisekartendesign aufblühen ließ.

Die Vielfalt der in Europa erhältlichen Speisen ging Hand in Hand mit den zahlreichen künstlerischen Stilen, die bei der Gestaltung von Speisekarten zum Einsatz kamen. Um die Wende zum 20. Jahrhundert war der Jugendstil äußerst beliebt. Auf spanischen, niederländischen, belgischen, schweizerischen, italienischen und natürlich französischen Speisekarten brachte man elegante Schnörkel und organische Muster zu Papier. Weibliche Formen wurden auf Titelseiten abgebildet. Auch die zahlreichen Designströmungen des 20. Jahrhunderts fanden sich auf den Titelseiten wieder – von Art déco über Stromlinienmoderne und Bauhaus bis hin zu Abstraktion und realistischen Grafiken. Man ließ auch die eine oder andere gewagte Titelseite entwerfen. Mit der Beschleunigung des Informationsflusses wurden Technologien und Ideen über Grenzen hinweg geteilt. Das Design von Speisekarten entwickelte sich weiter und richtete sich vor allem an eine internationale Gemeinschaft. Zwar gab es weiterhin unverwechselbare Stile, die die Speisekarten einzelner Länder prägten. Letztlich haben jedoch die sich weltweit überschneidenden Einflüsse dazu beigetragen, das Aussehen der Speisekarten zu vereinheitlichen.

Während sich die Welt der Restaurants weiterentwickelt und es statt Papierspeisekarten immer mehr QR-Codes für Mobiltelefone oder Computerausdrucke gibt, nimmt die Zahl von schön gestalteten, einzigartigen Speisekarten zum Anfassen stetig ab. Unter dem Hinweis auf die Kosten betrachten Restaurantbesitzer Speisekarten als wirtschaftliche Belastung – insbesondere wenn sie einzigartig und individuell gestaltet sind. Während gedruckte Speisekarten nach und nach aus der kulinarischen Welt verschwinden, werden jene aus der Vergangenheit immer wertvoller.

Es bleibt zu hoffen, dass dieses Buch, in dem mehrere Jahrhunderte der Gaumenfreude festgehalten sind, daran erinnert, dass dieser gewöhnliche Gegenstand einst das Schlüsselelement einer Mahlzeit war. Oftmals erhob die Speisekarte das Essen zu einer Kunstform und wurde ein essenzieller Bestandteil der grafischen und kulinarischen Geschichte, der für die Nachwelt erhalten werden sollte.

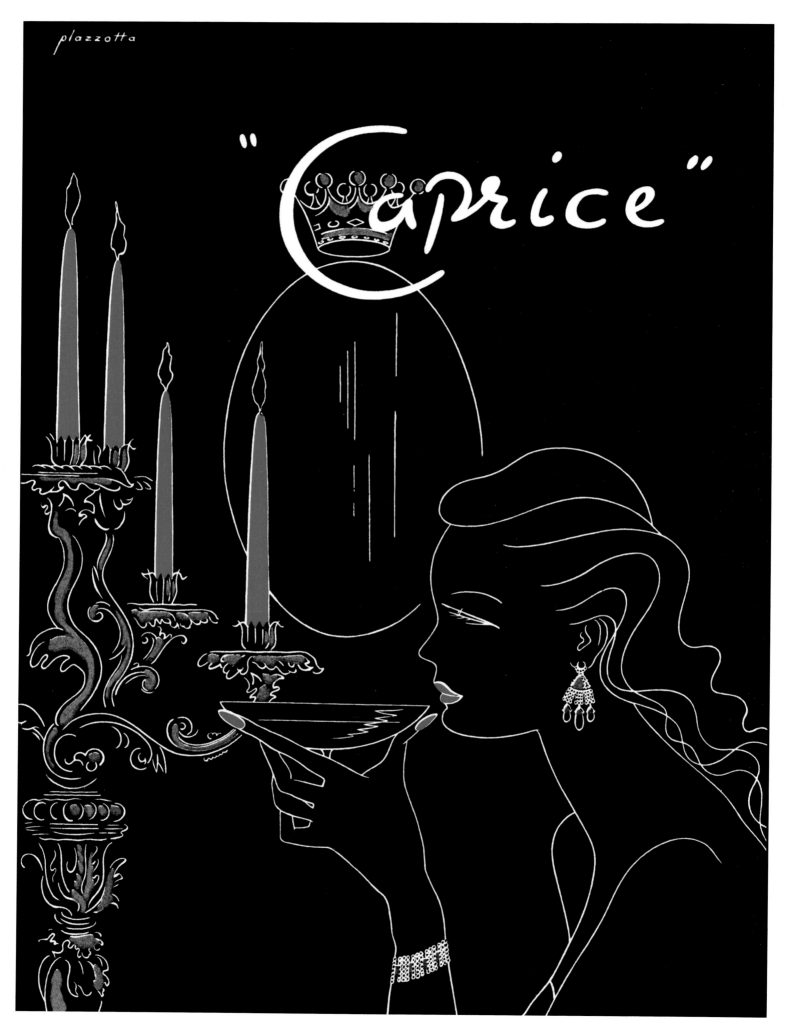

Le menu à l'européenne

par Jim Heimann

À mesure que cartes et menus disparaissent du moment gastronomique, les exemplaires du passé prennent de la valeur et font leur entrée dans le domaine des collectionneurs sérieux et des institutions.

Source originelle du développement de la gastronomie, l'Europe a donné le ton de la forme graphique qu'ont adoptée les menus et les cartes. Aussi délectable que les plats proposés, l'aspect visuel du menu a évolué de façon très pragmatique, de la description orale du repas d'un restaurant à la simple énumération des mets, inscrite sur un tableau. À mesure que la préparation et le service gagnent en raffinement, des cartes de plus en plus élaborées, comportant la liste manuscrite ou imprimée des plats, sont présentées aux convives.

C'est en France, où sont nées bien des traditions gastronomiques, qu'apparaissent les premiers menus en papier au milieu du XVIIIᵉ siècle. Libérés des chaînes qui les liaient aux familles aristocrates grâce à la Révolution française (1789–1799), les chefs peuvent désormais préparer des repas pour des particuliers. C'est le début de la gastronomie. Cette nouvelle manière de manger suscite aussi l'apparition de la table individuelle qui remplace la table commune, la pratique de la réservation et l'introduction d'accessoires : nappes, vaisselle en porcelaine et couverts. Au fil des évolutions du restaurant, les détails qui figurent sur le menu en papier changent aussi et se font plus sophistiqués et explicatifs. Dès lors, la carte est un élément à part entière, et apprécié, du repas.

Grâce au développement des voyages moins onéreux et à la prolifération des restaurants sur le continent européen et en Grande-Bretagne, le menu imprimé est de plus en plus employé. Tout au long du XIXᵉ siècle, de nombreux menus s'ornent de prouesses graphiques sans pareilles que les convives s'empressent de garder en souvenir. Ainsi naît la pratique des collectionneurs de menus. Au fil des décennies, la couleur est convoquée avec une ferveur grandissante. À mesure que les techniques de reproduction se perfectionnent, les illustrations s'imposent par leur présence. Enfin, la photographie, en noir et blanc et en couleur, vient orner la couverture du menu.

Avant le XXᵉ siècle, grandes occasions et événements exceptionnels mettent en évidence une clientèle d'élite qui n'a aucun équivalent dans la structure sociale de l'Amérique. Mariages royaux, visites d'État et hommages à des personnalités sont plus fréquents dans les monarchies et, par là même, suscitent des créations visuelles spéci-fiques et exubérantes. Les menus d'hôtel, de paquebot et, plus tard, d'avion constituent une autre catégorie ayant permis à la forme des menus de se donner libre cours. Avec le temps, le menu devient le compagnon sentimental et le souvenir heureux d'un événement.

La diversité des denrées comestibles de l'Europe ajoute à la variété des styles artistiques qui ornent les couvertures de menu. Au tournant des XIXᵉ et XXᵉ siècles, la popularité de l'Art nouveau ne connaît pas de frontière. Les menus espagnols, hollandais, belges, suisses, italiens et, bien sûr, français s'illustrent d'arabesques et de formes inspirées de la nature. Les silhouettes féminines sont également présentes sur plus d'un menu. Les couvertures de menu se font aussi l'écho des styles artistiques du XXᵉ siècle : Art déco, style international, Bauhaus, abstraction, réalisme. Cartes et menus accueillent également la photographie artistique et l'humour, voire l'illustration osée. Avec l'accélération des moyens de communication, la technologie est partagée, les idées n'ont plus de frontière. La conception graphique des menus n'est plus attachée à une région donnée et se fait davantage internationale. S'il reste possible de déceler un style particulier selon le pays d'origine du menu. les multiples influences internationales amènent l'aspect visuel des menus à s'uniformiser.

L'univers de la restauration change. Le menu en papier est remplacé par les codes QR présents sur les smartphones ou que l'on imprime soi-même. Le plaisir visuel et tactile qu'on tirait d'un menu palpable et unique en son genre disparaît peu à peu. Parce qu'il coûte cher et ne facilite pas la modification de la liste des plats, des boissons et des prix, les restaurateurs considèrent le menu comme un fardeau économique, surtout quand il ne sert qu'une fois. À mesure que cartes et menus disparaissent du moment gastronomique, les exemplaires du passé prennent de la valeur et font leur entrée dans le domaine des collectionneurs sérieux et des institutions.

J'espère que les pages de ce livre, témoignages de plusieurs siècles de plaisirs gustatifs, prouveront que cet objet courant fut l'un des ingrédients essentiels du repas. En faisant de l'acte de manger un art véritable, la carte et le menu font partie intégrante d'une histoire graphique et gastronomique pour les générations futures.

INTRODUCTION

From Anticipation to Excitation

by Steven Heller

A beautiful menu will not make a dish taste better,
but it will make the dining experience a total experience.

Hungry? Crave variety? Try Europe! Europe is arguably the largest food court in the world. Comprising haute cuisine and common repast—most of it delicious—the continent is a mecca for star chefs and a cornucopia of gustatory delights. One might say that Europe is an immense smorgasbord-cum-moveable feast, continuously changing its fare while pledging allegiance to the historic and modern as well as its national, regional, and provincial culinary heritages. Despite centuries of wartime devastation—repeated occupations, annexations, and dislocations of land and people—European food culture flourished throughout the 20th century and into the 21st century. One reason is the continuous shift of ethnic populations from around the globe; with each of these migrations, new gastronomic cultures emerge as venerable cooking traditions of various cultures are infused with native flavors. During the 18th and 19th centuries, increased travel by ship and train from country to country accounted for novel cooking and eating habits too.

How each dish is prepared and what ingredients are used distinguish one culture (or class) from another. For much of European history, preparation and consumption occurred mostly in the home —whether it was a palace, farmhouse, or hut. Aristocrat or peasant, everyone has to eat. Eventually public eateries were created for those who could afford to or had no other option than to eat out. As these eateries evolved, they were called by various names that suggested a range of status and quality: restaurants, cafés, bistros, taverns, brasseries, inns, and bars, etcetera.

The most popular of these terms, restaurant, is reported to have been coined in France . . . where else but the birthplace of cuisine? In French, *restaurant* means "food that restores," a derivation of *restaurer*, "to restore or refresh." An eatery with tables and chairs is where such restoration occurs. In fact, from the Middle Ages, the word *restaurant* translated as rich bouillons made with chicken, beef, roots, onions, herbs, and, according to some recipes, spices, crystallized sugar, toasted bread, barley, butter, and other ingredients. In 1765 an entrepreneur named Monsieur Boulanger opened a shop in Paris where he featured *restaurants* or *bouillons restaurants*, meat-based consommés intended

to restore health. Broths and stews were always at the boil, and mouthwatering scents filled the air. In order to entice customers into his shop, Boulanger had inscribed on his window a line from the Gospel of Matthew: "*Venite ad me omnes qui stomacho laboratis et ego vos restaurabo*" ("Come to me all who suffer from pain of the stomach and I will restore you"), as noted in *Food: A Culinary History from Antiquity to the Present*. Boulanger was, however, looking to provide more than bouillon to his clientele, so one day he announced that he had prepared a leg of lamb in white sauce, thereby infringing on the monopoly of the caterers' guild that prepared meals for those without kitchens. The guild filed suit, which to everyone's astonishment ended in a judgment in favor of Boulanger. Voilà! *Le premier restaurant à Paris*.

The objective of a restaurant was to satisfy the hunger that everyone experiences and to indulge in delicious victuals. Of course, not all restaurants were or are created equal in terms of deliciousness or atmosphere. Some satisfy the palate, some are a treat for all the senses. It comes down to taste and preference—and, ultimately, the talent of the chef or cook to wed nutrition and pleasure into a menu that addresses both needs and desires.

Speaking of the word *menu* . . . the *Online Etymology Dictionary* traces its layered derivation: a) "from French *menu de repas* 'list of what is served at a meal," b) "from French *menu* (adj.) 'small, detailed," c) "from Latin *minutus* 'small, literally 'made smaller, past participle of *minuere* 'to diminish, from root of *minus* 'to diminish." This original meaning notwithstanding, a menu can be a short, medium, or long list—annotated or not—of an eatery's comestibles. In fact, to read menu offerings over time is to consume the history of European gastronomy. (There was a lot of mutton to be had during the early days of restaurants, and lots of fermented beverages.) In the mid-19th century, signboards began to give way to graphically designed and ostensibly ephemeral cartes du jour (although both are still used). Paper menus, as this book shows, serve as records of which ingredients, recipes, and preparatory styles were popular at any given time and of what manner of gourmet or gourmand or average diner was targeted.

Although there is an infinite amount of choice for menu typography and illustration, there are at minimum two kinds of menu design: the first being the comparatively informal variety, usually a two-sided piece of paper with the daily fare either written in by hand, mechanically typeset, or pecked out on a typewriter. Some of these menus are ephemeral, highlighting the daily (blue-plate) specials, and are disposed of immediately. They may be clipped on to a larger menu, or slipped into a holder for easy access and protection, but are quickly obsolete. The second type of menu is a keepsake. Over the past two centuries, these menus have followed pretty much the same format: usually four pages (or more, depending on whether drinks are included) printed on stiff paper or board. They are either unadorned and utilitarian, like the single letter-sized page used at the Restaurant du Grand Hotel in Paris, or, as seen in most examples here, covered with artwork—in drawing or painting styles —that references anything from local scenery and grand feasts to strange but wonderful fantasies. Some are simply *l'art pour l'art*, because the image appeals to the restaurant's owner. Others are portraits, so to speak, of the establishment itself, perhaps done by a famous customer or erstwhile artist-relative of the proprietor. Of course, there are those that speak to the theme of the restaurant's fare, like images of classic seafood items or steak-house meats. Many of the most artful stock menus were produced with a blank space on the right-hand side filled in either by hand or typography to reflect current offerings. Some liquor distilleries and breweries printed them to advertise their respective products. Others were designed to establish a representative ambiance, identity, a brand by any other name for the eating establishment through the uniqueness of artwork or photography.

One of the most exquisite in this book is a color menu page for Quinzi & Gabrieli. With sublime elegance and a touch of the comic surreal, the menu is a gradient of blue to capture the view of the sea through the shape of a window or door. Two impish chefs bookended by red lobsters are seen above a small hanging curtain. As a kind of Pop Art, it is appetizing to the extreme.

The physical size of a menu is sometimes determined by how much food and the number of courses served on any given day, but its size and shape are mostly arbitrary or determined by the printer. Sometimes the entries are tightly packed, while others are an airy display of fine serif typography that exudes a sense of luxury. An oversized menu implies a certain level of status, especially when the waiter ritualistically hands it opened to the customer with a bow, as though presenting an official document. In movies this particular gesture signals that the guests are in a tony and expensive restaurant. But a small folder-type menu or one-pager does not necessarily indicate inferior or less expensive food.

Doubtless, there are psychological triggers used in designing modern-day menus regarding structure and where on the page the item is placed for maximum profit. Yet, as much as the industry would like to believe otherwise, menu design is not an exact (or any other kind of) science. The menu, though an essential tool, is not governed by strict rules but rather by intuition, taste, and predilection for certain colors, images, and letters. It is probably a good bet that late-19th-century or early-20th-century menus did not follow exacting standards, other than the convention in fine eateries of omitting prices on menus provided to women, so as not to discourage them from ordering freely.

Nonetheless, there was a classic menu format (based on the French tradition) of this period that followed an established format in terms of the cuisine it offered and the order in which it was presented. It listed seven to eight courses with a variety of items that generally followed this sequence: appetizer (hors d'oeuvre), soup, fish entrée, poultry or meat entrée, vegetable, salad, dessert, and finally an offering of cheeses or nuts—and an after-dinner liqueur.

The visual language of menus is not typically avant-garde, lest the menu be unreadable and deter their clientele. Yet there are some fine examples like the hand-lettered Restaurant Cattelin in Stockholm, Club 31 in Madrid, and Hotel St. Gotthard in Zurich that echo progressive mid-century modern art and lettering/type design of the times. Plenty of Victorian-inspired styles abound

Bérard

HOTEL
LUTETIA

RIGHT Salon de Thé de l'Ocel, c. 1935, Paris, France

The coffee shop that operated within the studio of an electrical appliance store on the tony Boulevard Haussmann included a selection of teas, pastries, cocktails, and beers. The name is an acronym of the firm *L'Office Centrale Électrique*.

Das Café, das in den Räumen eines Elektrogeschäfts am schicken Boulevard Haussmann untergebracht war, bot eine Auswahl an Tees, Gebäck, Cocktails und Biersorten. Der Name ist ein Akronym der Firma L'Office Centrale Électrique.

Le café qui occupe l'atelier d'un magasin d'appareils électriques situé sur le boulevard Haussmann propose un assortiment de thés, de pâtisseries et de bières. Son enseigne est un acronyme du nom du magasin, *L'Office central électrique*.

throughout this book, and the Art Nouveau illustration for Gran Casino in San Sebastian reflects an important global design style. A diner does not go to a restaurant for humor, but a comic style also has its place, as seen in the cartoon scribbles on the Mirabelle menu.

Menu design is not a direct-marketing tool for the establishment —what is served at the table is the draw. So, when menus are displayed in cases or vitrines directly outside the restaurant, the covers may have minimal information, but what's inside the menu is indeed part of the decor, and the decor is a key part of the dining experience. Therefore, when some restaurants put their "special" or "signature" offerings on the cover, as the Balkan-Grill in Vienna did with its meat specialties, they had better be photographed and styled in an extremely mouthwatering manner. Exquisite food photography depends on just the perfect lighting and composition.

Menus also have a life after the meal. It was common to save the menu before smart-phone-enabled "food porn" photography. Travelers frequently saved menus from luxury travel conveyances as souvenirs, like those from the grand dining rooms on the great ocean liners, the Red Star and White Star, with their first-class dining that included such selections as *consommé dubourg, halibut au gratin italienne, petites bouchées à la reine*. The posterlike special dinner menus for the Red Star Line, designed in an elegantly stylized early Art Deco to celebrate Saint Patrick's Eve (with the saint himself driving the snakes from Ireland) and other historical vignettes, were prized collectibles.

Another wellspring of menus was the elegant and cozy Wagons-Lits and other sleeper trains that crisscrossed Europe with well-stocked galleys to serve their dining cars. The Hindenburg, the famous and tragically incinerated airship, had a restaurant with its own menu. The restaurants of the *grand magasins* (department stores) produced menus as well.

Some restaurants pulled out the production stops with die-cut menus—see Smaa Hjem 7 Hotel for its distinctive menu cut like a soup tureen. Then there was the lithographic color printing with inks so saucy one could almost eat the menu—such is the case with the Carlton Restaurant's Gala Dinner of 1902, a banquet cancelled due to the guest of honor's appendicitis. In fact, "gala suppers" always were accompanied by celebratory menus, which used regal borders with flags, laurels, and emblems of empire. For receptions like the one for the president of the French Republic, Raymond Poincaré, in the early 1900s, the menu cover was embellished with gold ink.

Perhaps it is the tradition, maybe it's the language (food sounds so much better in another tongue), but European menus once seemed more refined than their U.S. counterparts. Today's American menus have taken their cue from across the pond. Yet one thing is certain: A beautiful menu will not make a dish taste better, but it will make the dining experience a total experience. It is the first encounter, the promise of what is to come. A menu triggers anticipation, which leads to excitation. Bon appétit!

Von der Vorfreude zur Gaumenfreude

von Steven Heller

Durch eine schöne Speisekarte wird ein Gericht zwar nicht leckerer, doch das Essengehen zu einem runderen Erlebnis.

Hungrig? Lust auf Abwechslung? Probieren Sie Europa aus! Der Kontinent ist der wohl größte Food-Court der Welt. Mit seiner Mischung aus Haute Cuisine und gewöhnlichen – meist köstlichen – Speisen ist er ein Mekka für Sterneköche und hält ein breites Spektrum an Gaumenfreuden bereit. Europa kommt einem riesigen, sich ständig verändernden Büfett kulinarischer Highlights gleich, das sowohl seinem historischen und modernen als auch seinem nationalen, regionalen und örtlichen kulinarischen Erbe treu bleibt. Obwohl im Lauf der Jahrhunderte immer wieder Kriege herrschten – mit ihren Zerstörungen, Besatzungen, Annektierungen und Vertreibungen – entwickelte sich die europäische Esskultur weiter, besonders im 20. und 21. Jahrhundert. Ein Grund dafür ist die kontinuierliche Zuwanderung von Bevölkerungsgruppen aus aller Welt. Mit jeder Migration entstanden neue gastronomische Kulturen, die die kulinarischen Traditionen verschiedener Länder mit den einheimischen Aromen vermischten. Als im 18. und 19. Jahrhundert immer mehr Menschen mit Schiff und Bahn von einem Land zum anderen reisten, entstanden ebenfalls neue Koch- und Essgewohnheiten.

Die einzelnen Kulturen (oder sozialen Klassen) unterscheiden sich durch die Zubereitungsart der Gerichte und die verwendeten Zutaten voneinander. Über weite Strecken der europäischen Geschichte wurde vorwiegend zu Hause gekocht und gespeist – in Palästen, Bauernhäusern und Hütten. Schließlich muss jeder etwas essen, ob er nun Adeliger oder Bauer ist. Mit der Zeit entstanden öffentliche Gaststätten für diejenigen, die es sich leisten konnten oder keine andere Möglichkeit hatten, als auswärts zu essen. Als sich diese Lokale weiterentwickelten, erhielten sie verschiedene Bezeichnungen, die auf ihren Status und ihre Qualität schließen ließen: Restaurants, Cafés, Bistros, Wirtschaften, Tavernen, Brasserien, Gasthäuser, Bars usw.

Der beliebteste Begriff, „Restaurant", soll in Frankreich entstanden sein … wo sonst als im Geburtsland der *cuisine?* Das französische Wort *restaurant* leitet sich von *restaurer* her, „wiederherstellen oder erfrischen". Diese Stärkung erfolgt in einem Lokal mit Tischen und Stühlen. Tatsächlich steht das Wort *restaurant* seit dem Mittelalter für

reichhaltige Suppen mit Huhn, Rindfleisch, Wurzelgemüse, Zwiebeln, Kräutern und, je nach Rezept, Gewürzen, kristallisiertem Zucker, geröstetem Brot, Gerste, Butter und anderen Zutaten. Im Jahr 1765 eröffnete ein Unternehmer namens Monsieur Boulanger in Paris ein Geschäft, in dem er *restaurants* oder *bouillons restaurants* anbot: Fleischbrühen, die das Wohlbefinden wiederherstellen sollten. Brühen und Eintöpfe köchelten unaufhörlich vor sich hin. Die Luft war von köstlichen Düften erfüllt. Um die Kunden in seinen Laden zu locken, hatte Boulanger eine Zeile aus dem Matthäusevangelium abgewandelt und auf sein Schaufenster geschrieben: *Venite ad me omnes, qui laboratis, et onerati estis, et ego vos restaurabo* („Kommt alle zu mir, deren Magen knurrt, und ich werde euch wiederherstellen"), wie es in *Food: A Culinary History from Antiquity to the Present* heißt. Boulanger wollte seiner Kundschaft jedoch mehr als nur Bouillon anbieten und verkündete eines Tages, er habe eine Lammkeule in weißer Soße zubereitet. Damit verstieß er gegen das Monopol der Gastronomenzunft, die Mahlzeiten für Menschen ohne Küche anbot. Die Zunft reichte Klage ein, doch zum Erstaunen aller fiel das Urteil zugunsten Boulangers aus. *Voilà! Le premier restaurant à Paris.*

In einem Restaurant sollten die Gäste ihren Hunger stillen und köstliche Speisen genießen. Natürlich waren – oder sind – nicht alle Restaurants gleich, was die Qualität des Essens oder die Atmosphäre betrifft. Manche verwöhnen den Gaumen, andere sind ein Genuss für alle Sinne. Es kommt auf den Geschmack und die Vorlieben jedes Einzelnen an – und letztlich auf das Talent des Küchenchefs oder Kochs, aus den Zutaten ein köstliches Menü zu zaubern, das Ernährung und Vergnügen in einer Speisekarte verbindet und die Erfordernisse und Wünsche der Gäste berücksichtigt.

Apropos Speisekarte … Zur komplexen Abstammung des französischen Wortes *menu*, das auch im Deutschen und Englischen gebräuchlich ist, heißt es im *Online Etymology Dictionary*: a) „von Französisch *menu de repas* ‚Liste dessen, was bei einer Mahlzeit serviert wird'", b) „von Französisch *menu* (Adj.) ‚klein, detailliert'", c) „von Lateinisch *minutus* ‚klein', wörtlich ‚verkleinert', Partizip Perfekt Passiv von *minuere* ‚verkleinern', vom Stamm von *minus* ‚verkleinern'".

PAGE 18 **Café de Paris**, 1936, Paris, France

LEFT **Maison Prunier**, 1939, Paris, France

OPPOSITE **Holland-America Line**, 1938

Neben dieser ursprünglichen Bedeutung bezeichnet der Begriff *menu* im Englischen und Französischen eine kurze, mittellange oder lange Auflistung der Gerichte eines Lokals, die mit Anmerkungen versehen sein kann, also der deutschen Speisekarte. Tatsächlich lässt sich die Geschichte der europäischen Gastronomie anhand von Speisekarten nachvollziehen, die aus verschiedenen Epochen stammen. (Zu Beginn der Restaurantära wurden jede Menge Hammelfleisch und vergorene Getränke aufgetischt). Ab Mitte des 19. Jahrhunderts nutzte man statt der Anzeigetafeln immer öfter die grafisch gestalteten *cartes du jour* (Tageskarten), die eine vorübergehende Erscheinung zu sein schienen. Beides wird jedoch bis heute verwendet. Wie dieses Buch zeigt, informieren die Speisekarten auf Papier darüber, welche Zutaten, Rezepte und Zubereitungsarten zu einem bestimmten Zeitpunkt beliebt waren und welcher Typ von Gourmet, Feinschmecker oder Durchschnittsgast angesprochen wurde.

Obwohl es unendlich viele Möglichkeiten für die Typografie und Illustration von Speisekarten gibt, lassen sich mindestens zwei Arten von Designs unterscheiden: Das erste ist eine vergleichsweise informelle Variante, in der Regel ein zweiseitiges Blatt Papier, auf dem die Tagesgerichte handschriftlich, maschinell gesetzt oder mit der Schreibmaschine getippt festgehalten wurden. Manche dieser Speisekarten sind nicht lange in Gebrauch, da sie über die (günstigen) Tagesgerichte informieren sollen und schnell wieder entsorgt werden. Sie werden an größere Speisekarten angeheftet oder in Menühaltern angebracht, um leicht zugänglich und dennoch geschützt zu sein. Allerdings veralten sie schnell. Die zweite Art von Speisekarten wird gerne aufbewahrt. Sie hatte in den vergangenen zwei Jahrhunderten fast immer dieselbe Form: in der Regel vier Seiten (oder mehr, je nachdem, ob Getränke enthalten sind), auf festes Papier oder Karton gedruckt. Sie ist entweder schlicht und zweckmäßig, wie die im Briefformat gestaltete Seite des Restaurant du Grand Hôtel in Paris, oder sie verfügt – wie die meisten Beispiele in diesem Buch – über Titelbilder mit gezeichneten oder gemalten Kunstwerken mit allen möglichen Bezügen, von der regionalen Landschaft über große Feste bis hin zu skurrilen, doch wunderbaren

Fantasien. Bei einigen handelt es sich einfach um L'art pour l'art, weil das Bild dem Restaurantbesitzer gefallen hat. Andere sind mehr oder weniger Porträts des Lokals selbst, die vielleicht von einem berühmten Gast oder einem mit dem Inhaber verwandten Künstler angefertigt wurden. Natürlich gibt es auch solche, die sich auf das Thema der Restaurantküche beziehen, z. B. Bilder von klassischen Meeresfrüchten oder Steakhausfleisch. Viele überaus kunstvolle Speisekartenvorlagen lassen auf der rechten Seite ein leeres Feld, auf dem das aktuelle Angebot entweder von Hand oder typografisch eingetragen wird. Sie wurden von Schnapsbrennereien und Brauereien als Werbung für ihre Produkte gedruckt. Andere Speisekarten sollten durch einzigartige Kunstwerke oder Fotografien ein repräsentatives Ambiente, eine Identität oder einen Markenamen für das Restaurant kreieren.

Eines der schönsten Exemplare in diesem Buch ist eine farbig gestaltete Speisekarte von Quinzi & Gabrieli. Mit ihrer erhabenen Eleganz und einem Hauch komischem Surrealismus ist sie in einem blauen Farbverlauf gehalten, der den Meerblick durch eine Fensteroder Türform einfängt. Über einem kleinen wehenden Vorhang sieht man zwei verschmitzte Köche, die von roten Hummern umrahmt werden. Dank ihres Pop-Art-Stils ist die Speisekarte an sich schon extrem appetitanregend.

Die eigentliche Größe einer Speisekarte richtet sich mitunter nach der Anzahl der an einem Tag servierten Speisen und Gänge, aber ihre Größe und Form werden meist willkürlich bestimmt oder vom Drucker festgelegt. Manche Beschreibungen sind dicht gedrängt, andere hingegen eine luftige Darstellung mit eleganter Serifen-Typografie, die einen Hauch von Luxus ausstrahlt. Eine übergroße Speisekarte impliziert einen gewissen Status, vor allem, wenn der Kellner sie feierlich aufschlägt und mit einer Verbeugung überreicht, als handelte es sich um ein offizielles Dokument. In Filmen signalisiert diese besondere Geste, dass sich die Gäste in einem noblen, teuren Restaurant befinden. Allerdings steht eine kleine Speisekarte in Form einer Mappe oder eines Blatts Papier nicht zwangsläufig für minderwertige oder günstige Gerichte.

THE SAPPHIRE

PRECIOUS STONES

E.G

Ristorante Giannino
Milano

RIGHT **AB Aerotransport, Swedish Air Lines, 1945**

Sweden's national airline reentered postwar commercial aviation with a trio of new Douglas DC-14s. An aerial fantasy depicts a plane with complete alfresco facilities. The flight crew seems to have found a stash of akvavit.

Schwedens nationale Fluggesellschaft stieg mit drei neuen Douglas DC-14 wieder in die kommerzielle Luftfahrt der Nachkriegszeit ein. Eine Fantasieszene zeigt ein Flugzeug mit komplett ausgestatteten Außenbereichen. Die Flugbesatzung scheint einen Vorrat an Aquavit gefunden zu haben.

Au lendemain de la guerre, la compagnie aérienne nationale de la Suède reprend ses vols commerciaux avec trois Douglas DC-14 flambant neufs. Dans cette illustration très inventive, les ailes sont des terrasses et l'équipage semble avoir déniché un stock de bouteilles d'aquavit.

Bei der Gestaltung moderner Speisekarten gibt es in Bezug auf die Struktur und die Platzierung der Speisen natürlich psychologische Trigger, die auf maximalen Gewinn ausgerichtet sind, doch so gern die Branche auch das Gegenteil glauben möchte: Die Gestaltung von Speisekarten ist keine exakte (oder überhaupt eine) Wissenschaft. Speisekarten sind zwar ein wichtiges Instrument, werden jedoch nicht von strengen Regeln bestimmt, eher von Intuition, Geschmack und der Vorliebe für bestimmte Farben, Bilder und Buchstaben. Wahrscheinlich folgte man bei den Speisekarten des späten 19. und frühen 20. Jahrhunderts keinen genauen Standards, abgesehen von einer speziellen Gepflogenheit gehobener Restaurants: Auf den Speisekarten, die man den Frauen reichte, wurden die Preise weggelassen, damit bei der Bestellung keine falsche Bescheidenheit aufkam.

Allerdings gab es in jener Zeit ein klassisches Speisekartenformat (in Anlehnung an die französische Tradition), das in Bezug auf die angebotenen Speisen und ihrer Reihenfolge einem festen Schema folgte. Es listete sieben bis acht Gänge mit verschiedenen Gerichten auf, in der Regel in dieser Abfolge: Vorspeise (Hors d'oeuvre), Suppe, Fischgericht, Geflügel- oder Fleischgericht, Gemüse, Salat, Dessert und zum Abschluss eine Auswahl an Käse oder Nüssen sowie einen Digestif.

Auf Speisekarten findet man in der Regel keine avantgardistische Bildsprache, da sie weder unleserlich noch abschreckend sein dürfen. Es gibt jedoch einige schöne Ausnahmen, darunter das Stockholmer Restaurant Cattelin mit seiner handgeschriebenen Karte, den Club 31 in Madrid und das Hotel St. Gotthard in Zürich, die an die fortschrittliche moderne Kunst der Jahrhundertmitte und das Schriftdesign aus jener Zeit erinnern. In diesem Buch sind zudem viele viktorianisch inspirierte Stile zu finden. Die Jugendstilillustrationen für das Gran Casino in San Sebastián stehen exemplarisch für einen wichtigen globalen Designstil. Auch wenn Restaurantbesucher ein Lokal nicht wegen seiner humorvollen Speisekarte betreten würden, findet auch ein komischer Stil Verwendung, wie die Cartoonskizzen auf der Speisekarte des Restaurants Mirabelle bezeugen.

Für ein Restaurant ist das Design einer Speisekarte kein direktes Marketinginstrument, da die Anziehung vielmehr von dem ausgeht, was serviert wird. Wenn eine Speisekarte in Schaukästen oder Vitrinen direkt vor dem Restaurant ausgestellt wird, enthält die Titelseite vielleicht nur wenige Informationen, doch sie gehört auf jeden Fall zum Dekor, welches wiederum ein wichtiger Bestandteil des Essengehens ist. Bilden Restaurants ihre „Spezialitäten" oder „Hausgerichte" auf der Titelseite ab, wie es der Balkan-Grill in Wien mit seinen Fleischspezialitäten getan hat, sollten sie auf jeden Fall gut fotografiert und auf äußerst appetitanregende Weise präsentiert sein. Ansprechende Essensfotografie lebt von einer perfekten Beleuchtung und Komposition.

Speisekarten bestehen auch nach dem Essen fort. Bevor es die „Foodporn"-Fotografie der Smartphone-Ära gab, war es üblich, Speise-

Restaurant
Raynaud

Nice - 59, Quai des Etats-Unis - Nice
Tél.: 892-90

karten zu sammeln. Reisende nahmen sie häufig von Luxustouren als Souvenirs mit, z. B. aus den vornehmen Speisesälen der großen Ozeandampfer der Linien Red Star und White Star, wo erstklassige Gerichte wie *Consommé Dubourg, Halibut au Gratin Italienne* und *Petits bouchées à la reine* serviert wurden. Begehrte Sammlerstücke waren neben anderen historischen Darstellungen auch die plakatgroßen Abendspeisekarten der Red Star Line, die im eleganten frühen Art-déco-Stil gestaltet und für den Vorabend des Saint Patrick's Day bestimmt waren (mit einer Abbildung des Heiligen, der die Schlangen aus Irland vertreibt). Eine weitere Fundgrube für Speisekarten waren die eleganten, gemütlichen *wagons-lit* und andere Schlafwagen, die als Teil von Zügen durch Europa fuhren und deren gut ausgestattete Bordküchen die Speisewagen mit Essen versorgten. In der *Hindenburg*, dem berühmten und tragisch verunglückten Luftschiff, gab es ein Restaurant mit eigener Speisekarte. Auch die Restaurants glanzvoller Kaufhäuser ließen Speisekarten herstellen.

Manche Lokale setzten mit gestanzten Speisekarten neue Maßstäbe, z. B. das Hotel Smaa Hjem 7 mit seiner unverwechselbaren Speisekarte in Form einer Suppenterrine. Lithografiefarben wiederum

konnten so saftig aussehen, dass man das Gefühl hatte, die Speisekarte essen zu können – wie beim Galadinner des Carlton Restaurants von 1902, einem Bankett, das wegen der Blinddarmentzündung des Ehrengastes abgesagt wurde. Bei Galaabendessen gab es tatsächlich immer festliche Speisekarten, die mit königlichen Bordüren sowie Fahnen, Lorbeeren und Emblemen des Kaiserreichs geschmückt waren. Bei Empfängen im frühen 20. Jahrhundert wie dem für Raymond Poincaré, den Präsidenten der Französischen Republik, wurde die Titelseite der Speisekarte mit goldener Tinte verziert.

Vielleicht liegt es an der Tradition oder der Sprache (in fremden Sprachen klingen Gerichte viel besser), aber europäische Speisekarten erschienen damals raffinierter als ihre amerikanischen Pendants. Mittlerweile hat man sich bei der Gestaltung der amerikanischen Speisekarten von der anderen Seite des Großen Teiches inspirieren lassen. Wie dem auch sei, eines lässt sich mit Sicherheit sagen: Durch eine schöne Speisekarte wird ein Gericht zwar nicht leckerer, doch das Essengehen zu einem runderen Erlebnis. Eine Speisekarte ist eine erste Begegnung, ein Versprechen auf das, was kommt. Sie erzeugt Vorfreude, die in Gaumenfreude übergeht. *Bon appétit!*

meniu

Restaurantul
Pescarul

De l'attente à l'excitation

par Steven Heller

*Un menu agréable à l'œil ne peut rendre un plat meilleur,
mais il contribue pleinement au plaisir du repas.*

Vous avez faim ? Faim de diversité ? Alors, essayez l'Europe ! Le continent européen offre sans doute le menu le plus varié du monde. Que ce soit pour la haute cuisine ou les repas du quotidien – délicieux, la plupart du temps –, l'Europe est la Mecque des chefs vedettes, une corne d'abondance de plaisirs gustatifs. Autant dire que l'Europe est un immense buffet ou une table tournante qui se renouvelle constamment, tout en restant fidèle à ses patrimoines historiques et modernes, nationaux, régionaux et provinciaux. Malgré des siècles de destruction due aux guerres, avec leur lot répété d'occupations, d'annexions, de déplacements des personnes et des frontières, la culture gastronomique européenne a prospéré tout au long du XXᵉ siècle et continue de bien se porter au début du XXIᵉ. Cela tient notamment aux mouvements permanents de populations dans le monde entier. Chaque migration provoque l'émergence de nouvelles cultures culinaires, les traditions vénérables des unes se nourrissant des saveurs propres aux autres. Au cours des XVIIIᵉ et XIXᵉ siècles, l'intensification du transport maritime et ferroviaire international s'accompagne de nouvelles manières de faire la cuisine et de manger.

Les civilisations (et les classes sociales) se distinguent par la façon dont elles préparent leurs plats et par les ingrédients qu'elles emploient. Durant une grande partie de l'histoire de l'Europe, préparation et consommation avaient principalement lieu au sein du foyer, qu'il s'agisse d'un palais, d'une ferme ou d'une cabane. Aristocrate ou paysan, chacun doit manger. Petit à petit sont nés des lieux publics où l'on mange, destinés à ceux qui en ont les moyens ou n'ont pas la possibilité de manger chez eux. Au fil de leur évolution, ces lieux prennent différents noms, chacun synonyme d'un statut et d'un niveau de qualité : restaurant, café, bistrot, taverne, brasserie, auberge, bar, etc.

Le terme le plus couramment employé, y compris dans de nombreuses langues, est restaurant, mot de la langue du pays de naissance de la gastronomie, bien sûr ! Participe présent du verbe *restaurer* (« rétablir la vigueur par la nourriture »), il signifie comme adjectif « qui nourrit, fortifie ». Un lieu meublé de tables et de chaises sert de cadre à ce phénomène de restauration. D'ailleurs, à partir du Moyen Âge, un *mets restaurant* désigne un bouillon riche, composé de poulet, de bœuf, de racines comestibles, d'oignons, d'herbes et, selon certaines recettes, d'épices, de sucre candi, de pain grillé, d'orge, de beurre et autres ingrédients. En 1765, un certain Boulanger, entrepreneur de son état, ouvre à Paris une échoppe où il propose des restaurants ou des bouillons restaurants, consommés à base de viande destinés à restaurer la santé. Bouillons et ragoûts y cuisent en permanence, l'atmosphère est parfumée de senteurs qui font saliver. Afin d'y attirer les clients, Boulanger a inscrit sur sa vitrine un verset de l'Évangile selon saint Matthieu : « *Venite ad me omnes qui stomacho laboratis et ego vos restaurabo* » (« Venez à moi, vous tous que l'estomac fait souffrir et je vous restaurerai »), comme le rapporte l'*Histoire de l'alimentation*. Pourtant, Boulanger veut offrir à sa clientèle davantage que des bouillons. Mais lorsqu'il annonce, un jour, avoir préparé un gigot d'agneau dans une sauce blanche, il marche sur les plates-bandes de la guilde des traiteurs, qui préparent des repas pour ceux qui ne disposent pas de cuisine. La guilde poursuit Boulanger en justice, laquelle rend, contre toute attente, un jugement qui lui est favorable. Voilà donc institué le premier restaurant de Paris.

Le but d'un restaurant est d'apaiser la faim de ceux qui l'éprouvent et de jouir d'exquises victuailles. Bien entendu, tous les restaurants ne sont pas égaux du point de vue des délices ou de l'ambiance. Certains ne satisfont que le palais, d'autres comblent tous les sens. Question de goût ou de préférence. Mais, en dernier ressort, tout dépend du talent du chef, du cuisinier ou de la cuisinière qui sait ou non marier alimentation et plaisir dans un menu qui réponde aux besoins comme aux désirs.

Puisque le mot est lâché, *menu* vient, nous apprend le *Dictionnaire historique de la langue française*, du latin *minutus*, participe passé du verbe *minuere* (amoindrir, diminuer). On le trouve dans l'expression *par le menu*, présente dans le sens qu'a acquis menu en tant que substantif : « Liste détaillée, par le menu, des plats composant un repas ». Quelle que soit sa longueur, le menu est donc bien la liste, annotée ou non, des mets que l'on peut manger dans un restaurant. La lecture des repas proposés dans les menus au fil du temps revient même à

PAGE 26 **Restaurantul Pescarul, c. 1953, Bucharest, Romania**

LEFT **Smaa Hjem 7 Hotel, 1954, Copenhagen, Denmark**

OPPOSITE **Steigenberger Frankfurter Hof, c. 1967, Frankfurt, Federal Republic of Germany**

appréhender l'histoire de la gastronomie européenne (le mouton et les boissons fermentées sont très présents dans les premiers temps de la restauration). Au milieu du XIXe siècle, les pancartes commencent à être remplacées par des cartes du jour théoriquement éphémères, au graphisme soigné. Les menus imprimés, comme on le voit dans cet ouvrage, rendent compte des ingrédients, recettes et préparations qui connaissent le succès à telle ou telle époque, ainsi que des clients – gourmets, gourmands ou consommateurs ordinaires – auxquels ils sont destinés.

Si les variétés typographiques et iconographiques des menus sont infinies, il y a au moins deux types de format. Le premier, relativement informel, se compose d'une feuille de papier où le repas du jour est détaillé au recto et au verso dans une écriture manuscrite ou en caractères d'imprimerie, ou encore dactylographié avec deux doigts. Certains menus, éphémères, mettent en valeur la spécialité du jour, avant d'être aussitôt mis au rebut. Ils peuvent être attachés à la carte générale ou glissés dans une chemise de protection où ils sont facilement consultables. Mais ils sont vite caducs. Le deuxième format relève du souvenir à emporter. Depuis deux siècles, cette catégorie garde à peu près la même forme, couramment composée de quatre pages (ou plus, selon que les boissons y figurent ou non) imprimées sur un papier épais ou un carton. Ils sont sans fioritures et strictement utilitaires, comme celui du restaurant du Grand Hôtel à Paris, imprimé sur une seule page de papier à lettres, ou bien – c'est le cas de la plupart des exemples présentés ici – recouverts de dessins ou de peintures évoquant des paysages locaux, de grands festins ou des inventions étranges mais merveilleuses. D'autres sont purement artistiques et ne doivent leur existence qu'au fait que l'image plaît au propriétaire du restaurant. D'autres encore sont, pour ainsi dire, le portrait de l'établissement, peut-être dû à un client célèbre ou à un ancien artiste, parent du tenancier. Il y a, bien sûr, des menus qui vantent les repas proposés grâce à des images classiques de fruits de mer ou de steaks, par exemple. Nombre des menus standards les plus artistiques disposent d'un espace vide sur la droite, que l'on remplit à la main ou sous forme typographiée pour décrire les repas du moment. Certaines distilleries et brasseries en font imprimer pour faire la publicité de leurs produits. D'autres menus sont conçus afin de créer une ambiance représentative, une identité, une marque pour l'établissement, grâce à des illustrations ou des photographies uniques en leur genre.

Le menu d'une page en couleur de Quinzi & Gabrieli est l'un des plus raffinés de cet ouvrage. Avec une élégance sublime et un soupçon d'humour surréaliste, ce menu présente un dégradé de bleu qui suggère un paysage marin vu à travers une fenêtre ou une porte. Au-dessus d'un petit rideau suspendu, deux chefs malicieux sont flanqués de homards rouges. Voilà du pop art qui met sérieusement en appétit.

Si l'aspect d'un menu est parfois conditionné par la quantité de nourriture et le nombre de plats servis, sa taille et sa forme sont généralement arbitraires ou bien définis par l'imprimeur. Il arrive que la liste des mets soit très dense, tandis que certains menus sont très aérés en recourant à une fine police de caractères à empattement, d'où émane une impression de luxe. Un menu de très grande taille est l'expression d'un certain statut, surtout quand le serveur le tend au client en s'inclinant rituellement, comme s'il lui remettait un document officiel. Dans les films, ce geste indique que les invités se trouvent dans un restaurant chic et onéreux. Pourtant, un petit menu dépliable ou sur une seule page n'est pas nécessairement synonyme de plats de moins bonne qualité ou meilleur marché.

Il ne fait aucun doute qu'il existe des ressorts psychologiques employés pour organiser la structure des menus d'aujourd'hui et la disposition des plats afin de maximiser les bénéfices. Toutefois, quoi qu'en pense le secteur de la restauration, la conception de menus n'est pas une science, et encore moins exacte. Il a beau être essentiel, cet outil n'est pas régi par des règles strictes, mais par l'intuition, le goût et une prédilection pour certaines couleurs, images et lettres. On peut sans doute parier qu'au tournant des XIXe et XXe siècles, les menus ne répondaient pas à des critères très exigeants, si ce n'est l'usage, dans les établissements chics, de ne pas faire apparaître les prix sur les menus destinés aux femmes, afin de ne pas les décourager de choisir selon leurs désirs.

Restaurante Finisterre

Barcelona

Toutefois, on trouve à cette époque un format classique (inspiré de la tradition française) qui suit une structure bien établie dans la présentation et l'ordre des mets. Sept à huit plats aux compositions variées sont généralement répertoriés dans l'ordre suivant : hors-d'œuvre, soupe, poisson, volaille ou viande, légumes, salade verte, dessert et, pour finir, un plateau de fromages ou un choix de noix, repas que conclut un digestif.

Le vocabulaire visuel des menus n'a rien d'avant-gardiste, de peur d'être illisible et de dissuader la clientèle. On trouve pourtant de très beaux exemples, comme les menus rédigés à la main du restaurant Cattelin à Stockholm, du Club 31 à Madrid et de l'Hôtel Saint-Gotthard à Zurich, qui rappellent l'art moderne et les lettrages novateurs du milieu du XXᵉ siècle. Le présent ouvrage regorge d'images d'inspiration victorienne, tandis que les illustrations Art déco du Gran Casino à Saint-Sébastien, en Espagne, témoignent de cet important mouvement artistique international. Bien qu'on n'aille pas au restaurant pour y trouver l'humour, le style comique a aussi sa place, comme le montre le gribouillage façon bande dessinée qui orne la couverture du menu du restaurant Mirabelle.

L'aspect du menu n'est pas un outil de marketing pour l'établissement. C'est ce qu'il y a dans l'assiette qui attire le client. Lorsque le menu est affiché ou en vitrine à l'extérieur du restaurant, il ne présente parfois que l'essentiel sur sa couverture. Ce que ses pages contiennent fait partie du décor, et le décor joue un grand rôle dans les plaisirs de la table. Par conséquent, lorsqu'un restaurant met en avant ses spécialités sur la couverture de son menu, comme le Balkan Grill à Vienne et ses plats de viande, celles-ci doivent être photographiées et mises en scène de manière à susciter l'envie de les déguster. Pour obtenir une photographie culinaire réussie, la perfection de l'éclairage et de la composition s'impose.

Les menus ont une vie après les repas. Il était courant de conserver les menus avant la débauche de photographies gastronomiques que permet le smartphone, ce qu'en anglais on appelle *food porn*. Souvent, les voyageurs gardaient en souvenir les menus des repas servis à bord de trains ou de navires luxueux, comme ceux des somptueuses salles de restaurants des paquebots des compagnies Red Star et White Star, dont les excellents mets comprenaient notamment un *consommé Dubourg*, un *halibut (flétan) au gratin à l'italienne, de petites bouchées à la reine*. Semblables à une affiche, les menus de dîners spéciaux, illustrés dans un style élégant des débuts de l'Art déco pour la veille de la Saint-Patrick (où l'on voit le saint homme chasser les serpents d'Irlande), et autres tableaux historiques, étaient des pièces de collection très recherchées. Autres sources de menus, la Compagnie des wagons-lits et les différents trains de nuit grand style et confortables qui sillonnaient l'Europe avec des cuisines fort bien achalandées au service de leurs voitures-restaurants. Le célèbre zeppelin *Hindenburg*, qui finit tragiquement en flammes, avait à son bord un restaurant et son propre menu. On trouvait aussi des menus spécifiques dans les restaurants des grands magasins.

Certains restaurants ne reculent devant rien et vont même jusqu'à faire fabriquer des menus découpés à l'emporte-pièce, comme par exemple l'hôtel Smaa Hjem 7 et son menu en forme de soupière. Et lorsque les encres de la lithographie en couleur prennent l'allure de sauces, on pourrait presque manger le menu : c'est le cas du dîner de gala du restaurant de l'hôtel Carlton en 1902, banquet annulé à cause de la crise d'appendicite de l'invité d'honneur. Les dîners de ce genre s'accompagnaient d'ailleurs presque toujours de menus souvenirs, aux bordures royales ornées de drapeaux, de lauriers et d'emblèmes impériaux. Pour une réception comme celle donnée en 1902 en l'honneur de Raymond Poincaré, président de la République française, le menu s'ornait d'encre à l'or.

C'est peut-être une question de tradition, ou bien de langue (les mets semblent toujours meilleurs dans une autre langue), mais les menus européens ont jadis paru plus raffinés que leurs homologues des États-Unis, lesquels s'inspirent aujourd'hui de ceux du Vieux Continent. Une chose est sûre : un menu agréable à l'œil ne peut rendre un plat meilleur, mais il contribue pleinement au plaisir du repas. Il en est l'invitation, la promesse. Le menu suscite l'attente, dans l'antichambre des délices. Bon appétit !

BELOW Les Frères Troisgros, 1976, Roanne, France

From their family-owned restaurant, the celebrated Troisgros brothers, Jean and Pierre, presented nouvelle cuisine with a graceful conviviality. Food writer Robert Low remembered them as "a Gallic version of the Laurel and Hardy Team."

In ihrem Familienrestaurant boten die berühmten Troisgros-Brüder Jean und Pierre eine gelungene Mischung aus Nouvelle Cuisine, Eleganz und Geselligkeit. Der Kochbuchautor Robert Low bezeichnete sie als „die gallische Version des Teams Laurel und Hardy".

Dans leur restaurant familial, les célèbres frères Troisgros, Jean et Pierre, présentent leur nouvelle cuisine avec une convivialité élégante. Pour le critique gastronomique Robert Low, ils étaient les « Laurel et Hardy français ».

OPPOSITE Restaurant Galaxis, Hotel Kosmos, 1990, Erfurt, German Democratic Republic

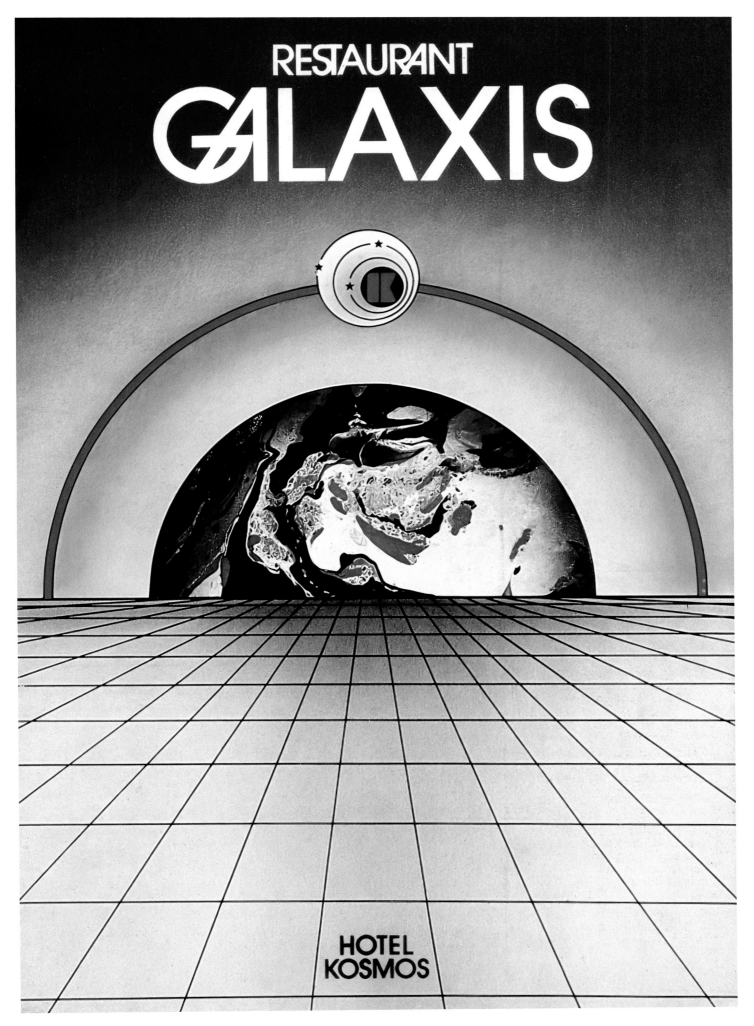

1800–2000
The Menus

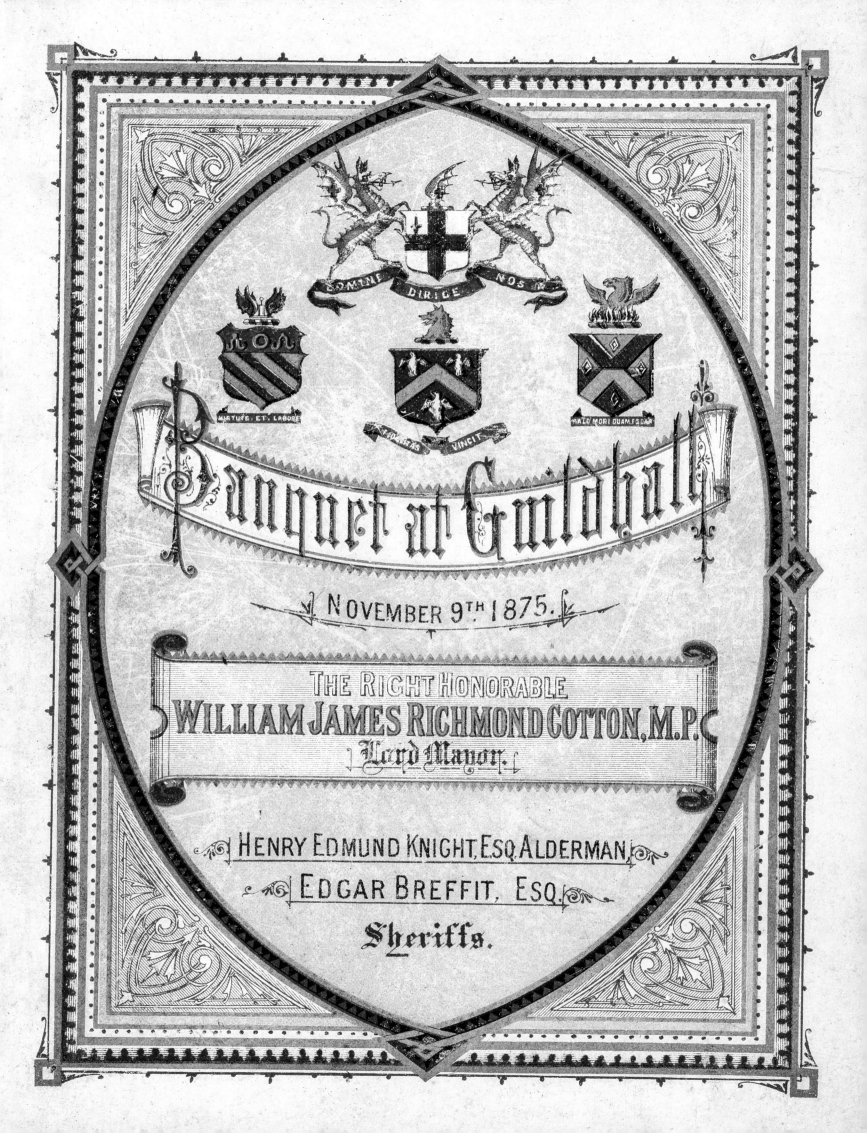

Banquet at Guildhall

NOVEMBER 9TH 1875.

THE RIGHT HONORABLE
WILLIAM JAMES RICHMOND COTTON, M.P.
Lord Mayor.

HENRY EDMUND KNIGHT, Esq. ALDERMAN

EDGAR BREFFIT, Esq.

Sheriffs.

PAGES 34–35 **Les Frères Troisgros,
c. 1989, Roanne, France**

OPPOSITE **Banquet for the new Lord
Mayor, Sir William Cotton, Guildhall,
1875, London, England**

BELOW **Restaurant du Boeuf à la
Mode, c. 1836, Paris, France**

Menu
1800–1899

Le Goût du Jour.

Restaurant du Boeuf à la Mode.

8, Rue de Valois.

A BILL OF FARE FOR BAILEY EPICURES!!
2/3 DUKE STREET, DUBLIN

ABOVE **The Bailey, c. 1808, Dublin, Ireland**

What was George Moutard Woodward satirizing in a print produced for an Irish grocer in 1808? Was it British cuisine, British fashion, or the body types of British women? With that heavy dish, the baron of beef (a double sirloin) taking center stage, it may have been all three.

Was wollte George Moutard Woodward mit dem Druck verspotten, den er 1808 für einen irischen Lebensmittelhändler anfertigte? War es die britische Küche, die britische Mode oder der Körperbau britischer Frauen? Da das schwere Gericht *Baron of Beef* (Braten aus ungeteilten Lendenstücken) im Mittelpunkt steht, waren es vielleicht alle drei.

Dans cette gravure réalisée pour un épicier dublinois en 1808, que tourne donc en dérision George Moutard Woodward? La cuisine ou la mode de Grande-Bretagne, ou bien le corps des femmes de ce pays? Peut-être bien les trois, si l'on en juge par la place de choix qu'occupe la « baronne de bœuf» (double aloyau).

OPPOSITE **Hôtel du Commerce, 1844, Bruges, Belgium**

Hôtel du Commerce
à BRUGES,
7 Février 1844,
Turbot sauce hollandaise.
Petits pâtés aux rognons de veau.
4 Entrées.

Poularde en demi deuil. | Tête de veau en tortue.
Pieds de porcs aux truffes. | Côtelettes de chevr l aux champ

4 Pièces Froides.

Buisson de homards. | Jambon d'Anvers.
Mayonnaise de saumon. | Pâté de foies gras de Strasb.

4 Rots.

Filet de chevreuil piqué. | Perdreaux truffés.
Bécasses. | Bécassines.

2 Légumes

Petits pois à la française | Croutes aux champignons.

2 Entremets de Douceur.

Pouding à la diplomate | Gelée au kirsch.

Fromage glacé, Fruits, & Dessert,

Lith. Daveluy, Bruges.

KAT-JOO

MENU

2 Novembre   1865.

Huîtres fraiches
Potage à l'Anglaise
Potage au Macaroni
Poissons
Bouchées à la Parisienne
Croquettes au Salpicon
Filet de boeuf à la Baÿonne
Légumes
Tête de veau à la Financière
Bécassines aux Champignons
Pouding de Cabinet.— Sauce au Rhum
Viande de Chevreuil marinée.— Sauce groseille
Dindon aux Truffes
Bécasses
Faisan
Coq de Bruÿère
Aspic d'Homards.— Sauce Maÿonnaise.
Gélatine aux truffes de Perigord
Terrine aux Perdraux rouges
Bavaroise à la Vanille
Petits Nougats
Pièce   Gelée au Punch
    montée.   Glace panachée.

DESSERT

Lith: de F.Böger.   à Utrecht.

OPPOSITE **Nederlandsche Handel-Maatschappij, 1865, Amsterdam, Netherlands**

RIGHT **Private dinner menu, 1879, Wiesbaden, Germany**

BELOW **Private dinner menu, 1876, Wiesbaden, Germany**

Five years after Germany's victory in the Franco-Prussian War, guests at a private dinner were served a French menu. The dessert was *Pouding à la Wellington*. As the saying goes, "Keep your friends close, but your enemies' cuisine closer."

Fünf Jahre, nachdem die Deutschen den Deutsch-Französischen Krieg gewonnen hatten, wurde den Gästen eines privaten Essens ein französisches Menü serviert. Das Dessert war *Pouding à la Wellington*, frei nach dem Motto: „Halte deine Freunde nahe bei dir, aber die Küche deiner Feinde noch näher."

Cinq ans après la victoire allemande dans la guerre franco-prussienne, les convives d'un dîner privé ont droit à un repas français avec, au dessert, un «pouding à la Wellington». Comme le dit le proverbe: «Soigne tes amis, mais plus encore la cuisine de tes ennemis.»

DINER

MENU.

Wiesbade, le 5 Juin 1879.

Oxtailsoup.
Rissoles de salpicon.
Saumon du Rhin,
sauce Victoria.
Jambon de York au vin
de Madère.
Grenadins de chevreuil.
Dindonneaux truffés rôtis.
Salade. Compote.
Asperges en branches.
Pouding à la diplomat.
Glaces panachée.

Dessert.

Wiesbaden, den   25e April 1876.

Potage julienne.
Truites au bleu.
Fricandeau de veau à la provençale.
Poulets à la Villeroi.
Céleri à la moëlle.
Bécasses rôties, salade.
Pouding à la Wellington.
Compote, biscuits.
Dessert.

BANQUET TO H.R.H. THE PRINCE OF WALES, K.G.

Fishmongers' Hall.

Saturday,   *June 10th, 1865.*

PRIME WARDEN—JAMES SPICER, Esq.

WARDENS.

WALTER CHARLES VENNING, Esq.   WILLIAM KYNASTON, Jun Esq.
FRAZER BRADSHAW HENSHAW, Esq.   JOSEPH TRAVERS SMITH, Esq.
GEORGE MOORE, Esq.
FF   W. B. TOWSE, Esq. CLERK.

PREMIER SERVICE,

Tortue à l'Anglaise.   Tortue Claire.
Truites de Spey à la Tartare.   Cotelettes de Saumon à la Milanaise.
Filets de Soles à la Provencale.   Char à la Beaufort.   Saumon de Gloster aux Capres.
Turbot Sauce d'Homard.

SECONDE SERVICE.

Reés Contis à la Napolitaine.   Ortolans en Petits Caisses aux Pois d'Asperge.
Cailles en Croustade de Truffes.   Petites Croquettes à la Princesse.
Ris d'Agneau à la Villeroi.   Cotelettes d'Agneau à la Regence.

Chapons Braises aux Truffes.   Jambon Sauté au Vin de Maderè.   Pâtes à la Maitre d'Hotel.
Vol au Vent de Quenelles de Volaille.   Petits Poulets à la Zingara.
Pâté de Perigord à l'Anglaise.

QUARTIERS D'AGNEAU ROTIS.   HANCHES DE VENAISON.

TROISIEME SERVICE

Cailles piques.   Oisons.   Canetons.   Dindonneaux piques.

Œufs de Pluviers en Bouquets.   Crevettes en Buissons.s.   Maionaise d'Homard.

Poudin à la Windsor.   Gelées claires aux Conserves.   Suedoise aux Millefruits.
Croquettes aux fraises en Caramel.   Patisserie à la Florentine.
Meringues de Pommes à la Seville.   Gateau de Genoise glacé à la Danoise.
Crème à la Vanille.   Feuilletage à l'Imperiale.

Petites Soufflées glacées aux Macarons.   Poudins à la Nesselrode.
Caviare à la Russe.

GOLDSMITHS' HALL.

March 31st, 1853.

| PRIME WARDEN. | PERCIVAL NORTON JOHNSON, Esq., F.R.S. |
| WARDENS. | RICHARD DAVIS, Esq.
GEORGE SMITH HAYTER, Esq.
JOHN MASTERMAN, Jun. Esq. |

1ᴱᴿ SERVICE.
LA TORTUE.

Le Potage au riz à l'Indienne. La Brunoise au Consommé.

RELEVES.

Le Saumon et sauce d'Homard. Les Turbots garnis d'Eperlans.
Les Filets de Merlans au fumet. Les Cabillauds sauce d'Huîtres.
Les Truites à la Genevoise. Les Filets de Soles à l'Orlie.

ENTREES.

2ᴱ SERVICE.

Les Filets de Pluviers aux Truffes.
Les Mauviettes en Surprise aux Truffes.
Les Cotelettes d'Agneau au Soubise. Les Ris de Veau à la Tomate.
Les Petits Grenadines aux Epinards. Le Boudin d'Homard au fumet.
Les Supremes de Poularde à l'ecarlotte et aux truffes.
Le Dindon au sauce de Truffes. Le Chapon au sauce d'Huîtres.
Les Chapon aux Champignons. Les Poulets rôtis.
Les Pates à la Française. Les Langues de Bœuf.
Le Jambon de York au Madere. Les Boudins de Becassines.

RELEVES,——Bœuf róti, et Echines de Mouton.

3ᴱ SERVICE.

Les Becasses. Les Canetons. Les Gallienés.
Les Gelées de Marasquin. Les Cremes de Noyau.
Les Salicoques en Boquets. Le Croque en Bouche à l'Orange.
Les Petits Brioches. La Suedoise d'Oranges.
Le Gateau à la Napolitane.
Les Gelées d'Orange. Les Cremes d'Anana. Les Petits Nouilles.
La Maionnaise d'Homard. Les Fanchonettes.
Les Tourtes de Peches,
La Corne d'Abondance garnie de Fruits.

RELEVES,——Le Boudin d'Abricots.

Le Boudin de Nesselrode. Le Fondeau.

DESSERT. ICES. &c.

RING & BRYMER,
Successors to BIRCH, BIRCH, & Co.
15, Cornhill, and 62, Cannon-street.

PAGE 42 **Banquet for the Prince of Wales, Fishmongers' Hall, 1865, London, England**

The Worshipful Company of Fishmongers gave a banquet for Queen Victoria's 24-year-old son, the future King Edward VII. Representative of the duke's famous appetite, the rich multicourse feast began with an all-marine selection followed by the presentation of one of the duke's favorites, roasted ortolans.

Die Worshipful Company of Fishmongers veranstaltete ein Bankett für den 24-jährigen Sohn von Königin Victoria, den zukünftigen König Edward VII. Um dem berüchtigten Appetit des Herzogs gerecht zu werden, begann das reichhaltige, mehrgängige Festmahl mit einer Auswahl an Meeresfrüchten, gefolgt von einem seiner Lieblingsgerichte: gebratenen Gartenammern.

La Vénérable Compagnie des Poissonniers donne un banquet en l'honneur du fils de la reine Victoria, le futur roi Edward VII, alors âgé de 24 ans. Reflet de l'appétit fameux du duc, ce festin aux mille mets s'ouvre par un choix de poissons et de crustacés, suivi d'ortolans rôtis, un de ses plats préférés.

PAGE 43 **Goldsmiths' Hall, 1853, London, England**

LEFT **Bénédictine, Café-Restaurant du Bel-Air, c. 1900, Paris, France**

BELOW RIGHT **Galliard, c. 1840, Bordeaux, France**

OPPOSITE **High Constables Dinner, London Hotel, 1877, Edinburgh, Scotland**

LONDON HOTEL
St. ANDREW SQUARE.

HIGH CONSTABLES OF EDINBURGH.

CAPTAIN'S DINNER.

28th JUNE. 1877. 6 o'Clock.

Captain J. Small Chairman.
Captain Alexander Thomson Croupier.

RECEPTION OF H.R.H THE PRINCE OF WALES K.G &c.

BY

THE CORPORATION OF THE CITY OF LONDON

BALL

IN THE GUILDHALL

Friday   May 19th 1876

MENU

Boar's Head.

Salmon en Mayonnaise.   Truite à la Danoise.

Roast Chickens.   Capons à la Crême.
Capons à la Princesse.   Larded Turkey Poults.

Langues de Bœuf à la Moderne.   Hams.

Perigord Pies.   French Pies.
Galantines à la Royale.   Ribs Lamb.

Lobster Salads.   Chaudfroids de foie gras.
Trifles.

Gateau de Savoy à la Royal.
Meringues à la Crême.   Compôtes d'Ananas.

Clear Jellies.   Noyeau Jellies.   Pine Creams.

Suedoises aux Fruits.   Charlotte à la Russe.

Ices.

Wines.

Sherry—Claret, Château Léoville.
Champagne—Piper's Carte Dorée, Roederer.

THE RT. HON. WM. JAMES RICHMOND COTTON, M.P.
LORD MAYOR.

HY EDMUND KNIGHT ESQ. ALD.   HENRY AARON ISAACS, ESQ.
EDGAR BREFFIT, ESQ.   SHERIFFS   CHAIRMAN.

GUILDHALL,

... 9TH 1874

THE RIGHT HON...

DAVID HENRY STONE

LORD MAYOR.

JOHN WHITTAKER ELLIS, ESQ. ALD^N
JAMES SHAW, ESQUIRE,
SHERIFFS.

MENU

Turtle Soup

Poulardes rôties.

Jambons ... York.   Pâté ... Order à la Française
Petits Poulets rôtis.   Pâtés de Pigeons à l'Anglais.
Galantines de Volaille à l'Aspic.   Côtelet de Homard

Barons of Beef

Dindons à l'Ivoire.   Faisans.   Perdreaux.

Gateaux à la Napolitaine.   Gelées au Vin.
Mince Pies.   Crêmes Françaises à la Royale.
Compotes d'Abricots.   Patisserie à la Reine.
Gelées à la Moderne

Ananas.   Raisins de Serres.   Poires
Cerises à l'Eau de Vie.   Noix, &c., &c.

Glaces variées

Wines.

Sherry—Amontillado.
Hock—Hockheimer, Marcobrunner.
Champagne—Perrier Jouet's Dry
Creaming, Giesler.
Port—Choice old.
Claret—Haut Brion.

The Albion,   Aldersgate S...

MANSION HOUSE

POSSUNT QUIA POSSE VIDENTUR

THE RIGHT HONOURABLE

ROBERT NICHOLAS FOWLER M.P.

LORD MAYOR

BANQUET TO THE

BEAUFORT HUNT

WEDNESDAY JUNE 4th

1884

MUTARE VEL TIMERE SPERMO

WATERLOW BROS. & LAYTON, LONDON

Upon the Prince of Wales's return from an eight-month tour of India and other parts of the empire, there was the requisite banquet. The prince spoke forcefully in support of the local population over the often harsh and prejudicial treatment dealt out by British officials. For this honesty, his mother, Queen Victoria, was given the title Empress of India.

Nachdem der Prinz von Wales von einer achtmonatigen Reise durch Indien und andere Teile des Empires zurückgekehrt war, fand wie zu diesen Anlässen üblich ein Bankett statt. In seiner Rede setzte sich der Prinz nachdrücklich für die ursprünglichen Bewohner der Kolonien ein, die von den britischen Behörden oft schlecht und voreingenommen behandelt wurden. Für dieses Bekenntnis erhielt seine Mutter, Königin Victoria, den Titel „Kaiserin von Indien".

Au retour d'un voyage de huit mois en Inde et dans d'autres pays de l'Empire britannique, le prince de Galles a droit au banquet de rigueur. Il s'y exprime clairement en faveur des populations locales, en butte au traitement sévère et aux préjugés des fonctionnaires britanniques. Sa franchise vaudra à sa mère, la reine Victoria, le titre d'impératrice des Indes.

The proprietor of Hotel de la Ville boasted of its delightful palm garden and "superb French restaurant." *Bradshaw's Guide* of 1864 agreed that the hotel, close to the cathedral, possessed "good rooms and excellent cuisine."

Der Besitzer des Hôtel de la Ville war stolz auf den herrlichen Palmengarten und das „hervorragende französische Restaurant" seines Hauses. Auch dem *Bradshaw's Guide* von 1864 zufolge zeichnete sich das Hotel in der Nähe der Kathedrale durch „schöne Zimmer und ausgezeichnete Küche" aus.

Le propriétaire de l'Hôtel de la Ville s'enorgueillit de sa magnifique palmeraie et de son «superbe restaurant français». Le *Bradshaw's Guide* de 1864 confirme que cet hôtel, voisin de la cathédrale, possède «de bonnes chambres et une cuisine excellente».

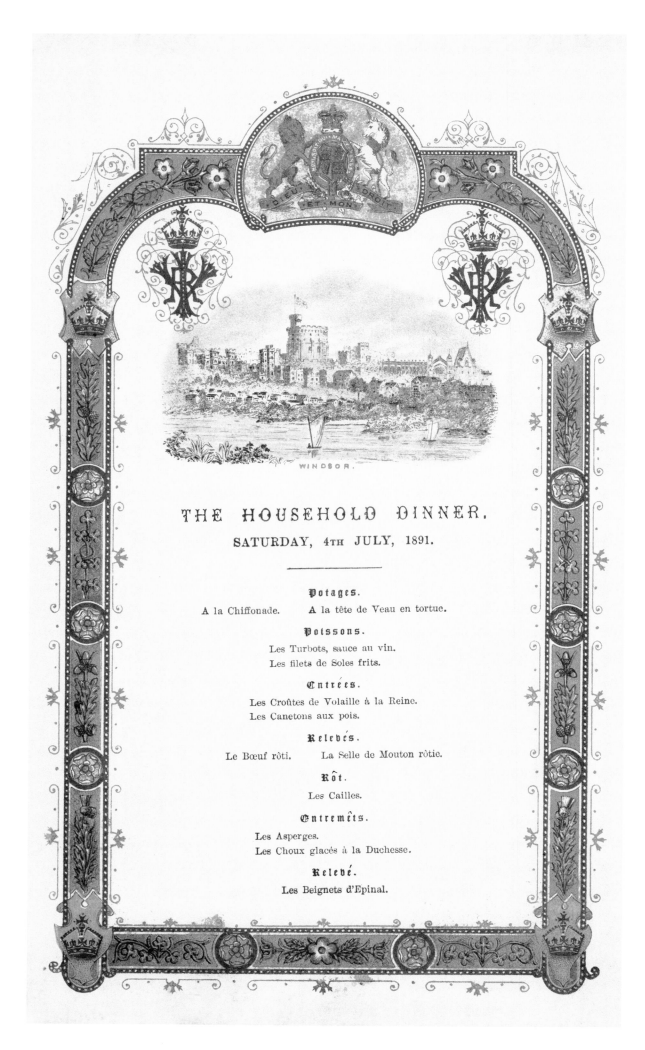

WINDSOR.

THE HOUSEHOLD DINNER.

SATURDAY, 4TH JULY, 1891.

Potages.

A la Chiffonade.   A la tête de Veau en tortue.

Poissons.

Les Turbots, sauce au vin.

Les filets de Soles frits.

Entrées.

Les Croûtes de Volaille à la Reine.

Les Canetons aux pois.

Relevés.

Le Bœuf rôti.   La Selle de Mouton rôtie.

Rôt.

Les Cailles.

Entremêts.

Les Asperges.

Les Choux glacés à la Duchesse.

Relevé.

Les Beignets d'Epinal.

J. F. Menzer

Weingroßhandlung

Neckargemünd.

SANTORIN

IN VINO VERITAS

FILIALEN:
FRANKFURT ª/M., BERLIN W
& PATRAS.

Lith. Anst. v. Wilh. Hawerbier, Heidelberg.

Menu.

DU

16 NOVEMBRE

HORS-D'ŒUVRE

Beurre, Saucisson, Crevettes

Les Filets de Soles normandes
Quartier de Chevreuil sauce poivrade
Poulets sautés Chevalière
Bécasses rôties sur croustades

Cardons à la moëlle
Babas glacés

Fruits assortis, Petits Fours
Mathilde glacée

VINS

Saint-Izan   Corton 1876
Châblis   Champagne

CAFÉ — LIQUEURS

Imp. G. Krastz

PAGE 50 **Household dinner, July 4, 1891, Windsor Castle, Windsor, England**

PAGE 51 **Julius Menzer, Weingroßhandlung, 1888, Neckargemünd, Germany**

OPPOSITE **Baptism lunch menu, c. 1890, France**

RIGHT **Private dinner menu, 1892, Wiesbaden, Germany**

BELOW **Stock menu cards, c. 1895, France**

Two stock illustrated cards for the same party arouse conflicting emotions: one is whimsical and harmless, the other cruel and diabolical; one moonstruck…the other, literally, striking.

Die beiden illustrierten Karten für ein und dieselbe Gelegenheit rufen widersprüchliche Gefühle hervor: Die eine ist drollig und harmlos, die andere grausam und diabolisch; die eine will den Mond vom Himmel holen … die andere zeigt die Hölle auf Erden.

Deux menus illustrés d'une même réception suscitent des sentiments antagonistes: l'un est onirique, inoffensif et lunaire; l'autre, cruel, diabolique et, littéralement, assommant.

WIESBADEN
den 4. Juni 1892.

Gebrüder Petmecky, Wiesbaden.

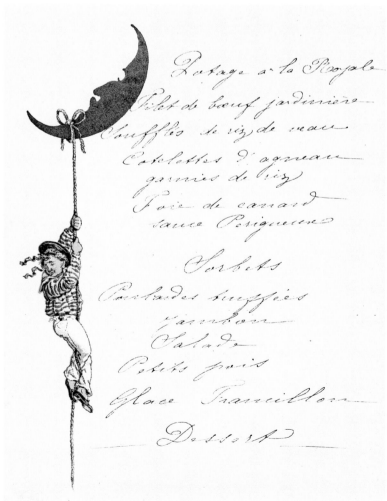

BELOW LEFT *SS Algeria*, Cunard Steam
Ship Company Limited, 1887

BELOW RIGHT Le Grand Véfour, 1891,
Paris, France

OPPOSITE Royal wedding breakfast
menu, 1893, London, England

THE
ROYAL WEDDING BREAKFAST.

THURSDAY, 6TH JULY, 1893.

POTAGES.
Bernoise à l'Impératrice.
Crême de Riz à la Polonaise.

ENTRÉES (CHAUDES).
Côtelettes d'Agneau à l'Italienne.
Aiguilettes de Canetons aux Pois.

RELEVÉS.
Filets de Bœuf à la Napolitaine.
Poulets Gras au Cresson.

ENTRÉES (FROIDES).
Chauds Froids de Volaille aux Légumes.
Salades de Homard et Saumon.
Galantines de Volaille à l'Aspic.
Filets de Veau à la Gelée.

Haricots Verts.   Epinards.

Kälte Schaale von Früchten.
Pâtisserie assortie.

SIDE TABLE.
Cold Fowl.   Cold Beef.
Tongue.

172ᵉᵐᵉ DINER DU BON BOCK.

C'est le Bon-Bock entier
Qui monte chez Vantier.
Carjat, le patriarche (1),
De son pas de rentier
Ouvre la marche.

L'esprit fol et dispos,
Il songe à Galipaux
Et sa cervelle appète,
En de joyeux propos,
La galipette.

B. M.

(1) Lire les œuvres complétes de Moussat.

GEORGES GRELLET.

PARIS. — Glyptographie SILVESTRE & Cᵉ, 97, rue Oberkampf.

OPPOSITE 172ᵉ Dîner du Bon-Bock, 1891, Paris, France

RIGHT 225ᵉ Dîner du Bon-Bock, 1897, Paris, France

Bon-Bock was an unusual dining club of artists, poets, and other creatives, who gathered from 1875 to around 1925. Meetings were a movable feast at various places such as Chez Vantier on Avenue de Clichy. The menus were movable, too, with a different artist and poet contributing each time. Before a scheduled meeting, members received a specially engraved menu. The separate mailing envelope functioned as the evening's admission ticket.

Bon-Bock war ein ungewöhnlicher Dinnerklub von Künstlern, Dichtern und anderen Kreativen, die sich von 1875 bis etwa 1925 trafen. Die Zusammenkünfte fanden immer an einem anderen Ort statt, z. B. im Chez Vantier in der Avenue de Clichy. Auch die Speisekarten änderten sich stets, da jedes Mal ein anderer Künstler oder Dichter einen Beitrag zu ihrer Gestaltung leistete. Vor den vereinbarten Treffen erhielten die Mitglieder eine speziell gravierte Speisekarte. Der separate Briefumschlag diente als Eintrittskarte für den Abend.

Le dîner du Bon-Bock est un club de peintres, poètes et autres artistes, qui se réunissent de 1875 jusqu'aux environs de 1925. Ce banquet itinérant se tient en différents lieux, comme chez Vantier, avenue de Clichy, à Paris. Les menus aussi sont itinérants puisqu'à chaque édition, un nouveau peintre ou poète y contribue. Avant la date prévue, les convives reçoivent un menu orné d'une gravure pour l'occasion. L'enveloppe d'expédition sert de billet d'entrée.

ALLAH!

Amis, une grave nouvelle
Vient de nous arriver d'Alger :
Du bon Marteroy la cervelle
Semble vouloir se déranger.

La nuit, syllabe par syllabe,
Il trace sur un pur vélin
Le nom du docteur, faux Arabe,
Elu du Franc-Comtois malin.

Depuis qu'il sait que dans la Chambre
On peut siéger ceint d'un burnous,
Il fume la pipe à bout d'ambre
Et ne mange que du couscous.

Ses pieds bien lavés dans la bière,
Il chevauche sur un croissant,
Admire en pacha la moukère
Et lui fait de l'œil en passant.

Suivi du commandant de Berlhe
Entraînant Valbert, Durocher,
Yann, Troimaux, Roumanille perle
D'éloquence, il s'en va prêcher,

Conférencier des plus habiles,
Dans Constantine et dans Oran,
Commentant pour les fiers Kabyles
Les divins versets du Coran.

Il vient de m'écrire : « A cette heure,
Pour moi tous voteront en bloc.
Donc, à bientôt l'assiette au beurre !... »
Qu'Allah veille sur le *Bon-Bock!*

Etienne CARJAT

CAFÉ GLACIER NAPOLITAIN

1, Boulevard des Capucines

BUFFET DE L'OPÉRA

FÊTE MILITAIRE DU 17 DÉCEMBRE 1892

MENU DU SOUPER

6 Fr. sans les Vins

Consommé de Volaille
Saumon sauce à l'Amiral
Filet de Bœuf à la gelée
Jambon d'York
Poulets froids
Salade Russe
Mandarines
Petits Fours variés
Café - Fine Champagne

Soupers servis par la MAISON CHARVIN
22, Passage Choiseul

VOIR AU DOS LA CARTE DES VINS

OPPOSITE Kraft's Grand Hôtel, c. 1895,
Turin, Italy

Located opposite the railroad station, the
Grand Hotel was a sister operation to
Kraft's hotels in Bern, Switzerland, and
Nice, France.

Das gegenüber dem Bahnhof gelegene
Grandhotel war ein Schwesterbetrieb von
Krafts Hotels in Bern in der Schweiz und
Nizza in Frankreich.

Situé face à la gare de Turin, le Grand
Hôtel appartient à la chaîne internationale Kraft, également implantée à Berne
et à Nice.

Kraft's Grand hôtel TURIN

MENU

le 14 Mai 1891

Potage à la Reine

Turbot bouillé

Beurre claire

Gigot de mouton

Pommes croquettes

Haricots verts

Tournedos à la Béarnaise

Poulets d'Hambourg

Salade

Croute d'orange

Dessert

Fruits.

LIT P. CASSINA - TURIN

OPPOSITE **American Bar du Restaurant Royal, c. 1891, The Hague, Netherlands**

BELOW **Banquet for the new Lord Mayor, Sir Joseph Renals, Guildhall, 1894, London, England**

Banquet for the new Lord Mayor, Sir Joseph Renals, Guildhall, 1894, London, England

ABOVE & RIGHT Great Nordic Telegraph Society dinner, 1894, Copenhagen, Denmark

This Danish telegraph company celebrated its silver anniversary with a grand evening of food and music. Each course was set on telegraph wires emanating from an allegorical figure to various locations across Europe and Asia.

Diese dänische Telegrafengesellschaft feierte ihr silbernes Jubiläum mit einem musikalischen Abendessen. Die Gänge waren über Telegrafenleitungen platziert, die von einer allegorischen Figur zu Orten in Europa und Asien verliefen.

Cette compagnie télégraphique danoise fête ses 25 années d'existence en donnant un grand banquet musical. Chaque plat est disposé sur l'un des fils télégraphiques qui rayonnent depuis une allégorie vers l'Europe et l'Asie.

OPPOSITE Banquet for the new Lord Mayor, Sir Walter Wilkin, Guildhall, 1895, London, England

MENU.

BANQUET
AT
GUILDHALL

on Saturday, November, 9th 1895.

The Right Hon.
Sir Walter Wilkin, Kt.
Lord Mayor.

John Pound, Esq., Aldn.

John Robert Cooper, Esq.,

Sheriffs.

Florence le 28 Février 1890

GRAND HOTEL
PORTA ROSSA
FLORENCE
MENU

DINER

Vermicelle
Filets de merlan
Gigot de mouton
bretonne
Fenouil
Poulet rôti
Salade

Glace
Fruits assortis

OPPOSITE Grand Hôtel Porta Rossa, 1895, Florence, Italy

Publicists have mused that this 12th-century building with the red door "is thought to be Italy's oldest hotel." Today, it is a five-star boutique hotel conveniently located on Via Porta Rossa.

Die Presse vermutet in dem Gebäude mit der roten Tür aus dem 12. Jahrhundert „das älteste Hotel Italiens". Heute ist es ein Fünf-Sterne-Boutiquehotel in günstiger Lage an der Via Porta Rossa.

Les publicitaires avancent que ce bâtiment du XIIᵉ siècle à la porte rouge est «considéré comme le plus ancien hôtel d'Italie». Aujourd'hui, c'est un hôtel chic, avantageusement situé via Porta Rossa.

A quartet of chromolithographed menu cards, two in a commercialized *Japonisme* style, document the progression of courses served in a first-class dining salon. Sailing out of Marseille, the *Sydney* charted a regular course to the French colonies in the Indian and Pacific Oceans and to Australia.

Auf vier Speisekarten, die als Farblithografien erstellt wurden, zwei davon im kommerzialisierten Japonisme-Stil, steht die Abfolge der Gänge, die in einem erstklassigen Restaurant serviert wurden. Von Marseille aus nahm die *Sydney* regelmäßig Kurs auf die französischen Kolonien im Indischen und Pazifischen Ozean sowie auf Australien.

Quatre menus en chromolithographie, dont deux dans un style japonisant commercial, rendent compte des plats servis au restaurant de la première classe d'un paquebot. Au départ de Marseille, le *Sydney* offre une ligne régulière vers les colonies françaises des océans Indien et Pacifique et vers l'Australie.

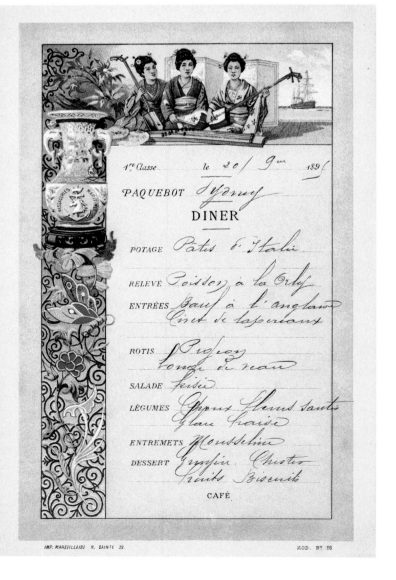

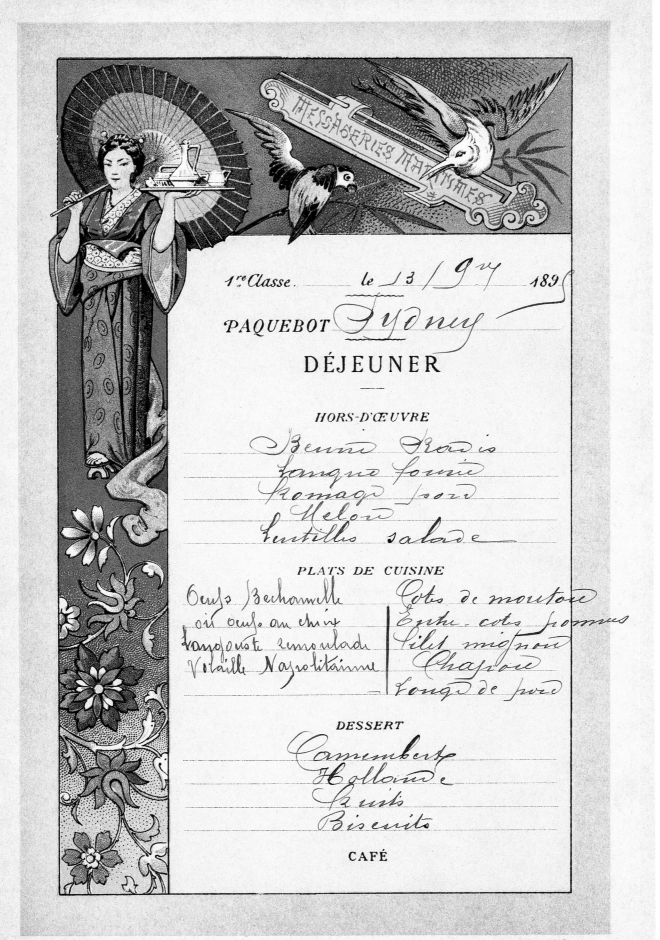

1re Classe.   le 13 / 9re   189

PAQUEBOT *Sydney*

DÉJEUNER

HORS-D'ŒUVRE

Beurre Radis
Langue fumée
Fromage ...
Melon
Lentilles salade

PLATS DE CUISINE

Oeufs Béchamelle   Côtes de mouton
ou oeufs au chou   Entre-côtes pommes
Langouste remoulade   Filet mignon
Volaille Napolitaine   Chasseur
                          Longe de porc

DESSERT

Camembert
Hollande
Fruits
Biscuits

CAFÉ

IMP. MARSEILLAISE. R. SAINTE, 39.   MOD. N° 5

Assortiment de Patés,
chauds et froids, Voles-au-vent,
Volailles fines,

N°. 10bis

PH. CAU

Marcha

AU PÂT

St. Jean
...froi,
...RLIER
Comestibles

AU PATÉ
ROULANT.

Gibier et tout ce qu
concerne la cuisine
Fait les Diners en ville.

...ROULANT

Lith. de T & D Hemelsoet   Gand

EMPIRE OF INDIA

1896

OLD WELCOME CLUB

·MENU·

Du 23 Juillet, 1896:

DÎNER.

HORS D'ŒUVRE.

Consommé Rachel.
Crème Egyptienne.

Suprême de Turbot à la Ambassade.
Blanchaille.

Crépinette de Caneton à la Dubarry.
Noisette de Pré-Salé à la Mascotte.

Poulet de Surrey au Cresson.
Salade de Saison.

Petits Pois à la Paysanne.

Crème Caramel.

Parfait Nélusko.

Petits Fours.

DESSERT. CAFÉ.

7/6 PER HEAD.

SPIERS & POND LD. REFRESHMENT CONTRACTORS.

Designed in England

Printed in Bavaria.

14 Septembre 1896.

Hors-d'œuvre,
Viande froide à la gelée,
Matelote d'Anguilles,
Veau santé au Kari,
Abatis de Volaille aux Pommes,
Côte de Porc frais grillée,
Artichaux sauce au beurre,
Dessert.

PROCHAINEMENT: LA TABLE D'HÔTE & LE RESTAURANT
seront descendus au rez-de-chaussée.

LEFT **Grand Hôtel, 1896, Angers, France**

BELOW **Bénédictine, c. 1900, France**

The producers of Bénédictine liqueur issued dozens of sets of illustrated menu blanks gratis. These cards were perfect for the small café with a limited menu or budget.

Die Hersteller des Likörs Bénédictine gaben Dutzende kostenlose illustrierte, aber unbeschriftete Speisekarten heraus. Die Karten eigneten sich ideal für kleine Cafés mit kleiner Speisekarte oder begrenztem Budget.

Les producteurs de la liqueur Bénédictine envoient gratuitement des dizaines de jeux de menus illustrés et vierges, parfaitement adaptés aux petits établissements dont le menu ou le budget est limité.

PAGES 68–69 Au Pâté Roulant, Philippe Caudierlier, 1843, Ghent, Belgium

In 1843 Belgian chef Philippe Caudierlier opened a shop specializing in pâtés, jellies, fine chickens, and other foodstuffs. He also offered his services as a banquet organizer. By 1859 a successful and richer Caudierlier closed shop and became a full-time writer of gastronomic works such as *L'Économie Culinaire*.

1843 eröffnete der belgische Koch Philippe Caudierlier ein Geschäft, das auf Pasteten, Sülzen, zartes Hühnerfleisch und andere Speisen spezialisiert war. Er bot seine Dienste auch als Bankettveranstalter an. 1859 schloss Caudierlier,

erfolgreich und reich geworden, sein Geschäft und widmete sich hauptberuflich dem Verfassen gastronomischer Werke wie *L'Économie Culinaire*.

En 1843, le chef belge Philippe Caudierlier ouvre un magasin spécialisé dans les pâtés, les gelées, les poulets fins et autres plats. Il propose aussi ses services d'organisateur de banquets. En 1859, riche et célèbre, Caudierlier ferme sa boutique et se consacre à plein temps à l'écriture d'ouvrages gastronomiques comme *L'Économie culinaire*.

OPPOSITE Old Welcome Club, 1896, London, England

LITH.F.APPEL.PARIS.

Amstel-Hotel
AMSTERDAM.

MENU.

Consommé purée à l'Italie
Saumon sce Câpres
Filets de boeuf aux petites carottes
Canetons en salmis
Noisettes de mouton aux pointes d'asperg
Poulet de grain à la broche
Compote. Salade
Glace plombière
Fruits
Desserts
le 8 Juin 1886

PAGES 72 & 73 Hôtel Continental,
c. 1895, Paris, France

LEFT Amstel-Hotel, 1886, Amsterdam,
Netherlands

BELOW The Grand Hotel, c. 1896,
London, England

OPPOSITE Le Grand Hôtel, 1896,
Paris, France

Both Jules Chéret and Alphonse Mucha,
celebrated as artists in the field of poster
design, created separate menu cards for a
dinner honoring the most famous actress
of the day. Mucha's was a masterwork
of Art Nouveau style; Chéret's reflected
his expertise in capturing a theatrical
performance. Although the feast did not
include *Consommé à la Sarah Bernhardt*,
it did serve *Gateaux Sarah*.

Sowohl Jules Chéret als auch Alphonse
Mucha, die als Künstler auf dem Gebiet
der Plakatgestaltung berühmt waren,
entwarfen jeweils eine Speisekarte für ein
Abendessen zu Ehren der berühmtesten
Schauspielerin der damaligen Zeit. Die
Karte von Mucha war ein Meisterwerk
des Jugendstils, die von Chéret fing
gekonnt eine Theateraufführung ein.
Das Festmahl enthielt zwar keine
Consommé à la Sarah Bernhardt, dafür
aber *Gateaux Sarah*.

Les célèbres affichistes Jules Chéret et
Alphonse Mucha créent chacun des
menus pour un dîner en l'honneur de
la plus célèbre actrice du moment. Si
Mucha signe un chef-d'œuvre de l'Art
nouveau, Chéret manifeste son savoir-
faire dans la représentation de l'art de
la scène. Le menu ne mentionne pas
de « *Consommé à la Sarah Bernhardt* »,
mais il annonce des « *Gâteaux Sarah* ».

Mercredi
9 Décembre 1896

Journée Sarah Bernhardt

Menu

Huîtres d'Ostende

HORS-D'ŒUVRE

Anchois, Beurre, Radis, Saucisson

RELEVÉ

Truite saumonée froide sauce verte

ENTRÉES

Côtelettes de Pré-salé aux pommes frites
Poulardes du Mans à la Sardou
Spoon au Georges Goulet

ROT

Faisans flanqués de perdreaux aux truffes
Pâté de foies gras Grand-Hôtel
Salade à la Parisienne

ENTREMETS

Gâteaux Sarah

GLACE

Bombe Tosca

DESSERTS

Compotes de fruits, Pâtisseries

VINS

Sherry Golden, Chablis Moutonne
Saint-Estèphe en carafes, Chambertin 1884
Champagne de Venoge frappé

Café, Liqueurs

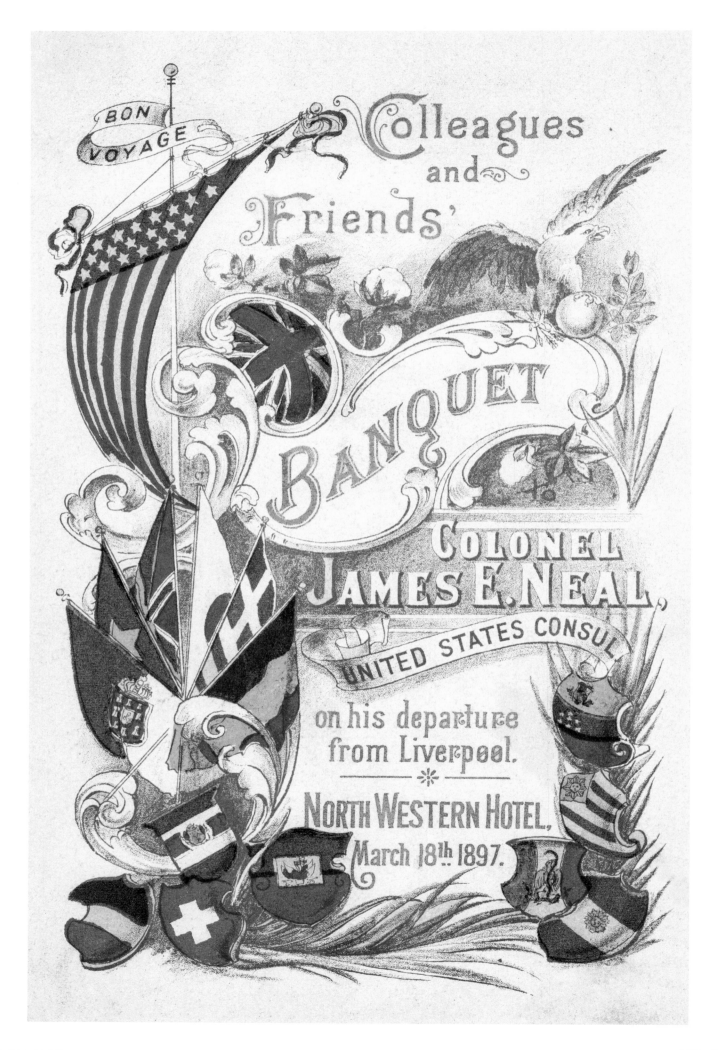

BON VOYAGE

Colleagues and Friends'

BANQUET

COLONEL JAMES F. NEAL,

UNITED STATES CONSUL

on his departure from Liverpool.

NORTH WESTERN HOTEL, March 18th 1897.

GRAND HÔTEL DES 3 COURONNES À VEVEY

GRAND HÔTEL VICTORIA INTERLAKEN

Dîner du 24 Avril 1896

CONSOMMÉ SANTÉ

SOLE D'OSTENDE A LA ·COLBERT

Gigot de Présalé à la bretonne

TÊTE DE VEAU A LA FRANÇAISE

Laitues au Jambon

Poulardes rôties Cresson

SALADE

Vacherin à la Suisse

FRUITS & DESSERT

HÔTEL DES ALPES & GRAND HÔTEL À TERRITET

LEFT **Grand Hôtel, 1896, Switzerland**

BELOW **Ye Olde Cheshyre Cheese, 1897, London, England**

The depiction of Charles Dickens and Anthony Trollope sharing a meal with some phantoms hints at the age of this establishment. Rebuilt after the Great Fire of London in 1666, Ye Olde Cheshyre Cheese continues to be a popular pub.

Die Zeichnung von Charles Dickens und Anthony Trollope, die mit einigen Phantomen am Tisch sitzen, lässt ahnen, wie alt dieses Lokal sein muss. Das Ye Olde Cheshyre Cheese wurde nach dem Großen Brand von London von 1666 wieder aufgebaut und ist nach wie vor ein beliebter Pub.

Le repas que partagent ici Charles Dickens et Anthony Trollope avec des fantômes renvoie à l'âge de l'établissement. Reconstruit après le grand incendie de Londres de 1666, Ye Olde Cheshyre Cheese reste aujourd'hui un pub apprécié.

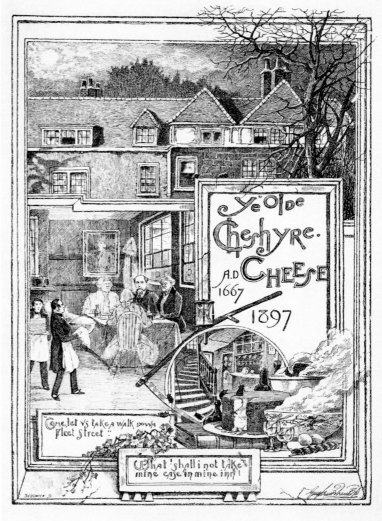

Ye Olde Cheshyre. Cheese A.D 1667 1897

Come let vs take a walk down Fleet Street

What shall i not like mine eye in mine inn!

OPPOSITE **Banquet for U.S. Consul James E. Neal, North Western Hotel, 1897, Liverpool, England**

When "Colonel" James Neal, a career politician from Ohio, lost his bid to become a U.S. senator, the incoming Cleveland administration awarded him the plum job of U.S. consul. When the political winds changed, Neal had to sail home, but his friends in the international crowd threw him a fitting send-off as this menu attests.

Als „Colonel" James Neal, ein Karriere-politiker aus Ohio, sich nicht als Kandidat für den US-Senat durchsetzen konnte, bot ihm die neue Regierung in Cleveland

den wichtigen Posten eines US-Konsuls in Großbritannien an. Als sich der politische Wind drehte, musste Neal die Koffer packen, aber seine internationalen Freunde bereiteten ihm eine gebührende Abschieds-feier, wie diese Speisekarte bezeugt.

Après la défaite à l'élection sénatoriale américaine du « colonel » James Neal, homme politique professionnel de l'Ohio, la nouvelle administration de Cleveland le nomme au poste convoité de consul des États-Unis en Grande-Bretagne. Quand le vent vient à tourner, Neal doit regagner les États-Unis. Ses amis des milieux internationaux fêtent son départ avec tous les honneurs, comme en témoigne ce menu.

RIGHT **Villa du Bois de Boulogne, 1897, Paris, France**

BELOW LEFT *SS Sydney*, **Messageries Maritimes, 1895, France**

BELOW RIGHT **Restaurant Voisin, 1897, Paris, France**

Julius Rossi's engraving of an elegant Belle Époque woman in her finery was most appropriate for a dinner held for executives of the French clothing industry involved with the Brussels International Exposition. The restaurant was not, as *Guide du Gourmand a Paris* (1925) noted, for philistines but for those who knew how to eat and drink well.

Julius Rossis Stich einer elegant gekleideten Frau aus der Belle Époque eignete sich hervorragend für ein Abendessen, das im Rahmen der Brüsseler Weltausstellung für Führungskräfte der französischen Bekleidungsindustrie ausgerichtet wurde. Das Restaurant war, wie der *Guide du Gourmand à Paris* (1925) fand, nichts für Banausen, sondern etwas für alle, die Wert auf gutes Essen und Trinken legten.

Cette gravure de Jules Rossi, représentant une élégante de la Belle Époque dans ses plus beaux atours, sied parfaitement au dîner des dirigeants de la confection française participant à l'Exposition internationale de Bruxelles. Selon le *Guide du gourmand à Paris* (1925), ce restaurant n'accueille pas les béotiens mais ceux qui savent bien boire et manger.

OPPOSITE **Union des Chambres Syndicales de la Bonneterie, 1897, Paris, France**

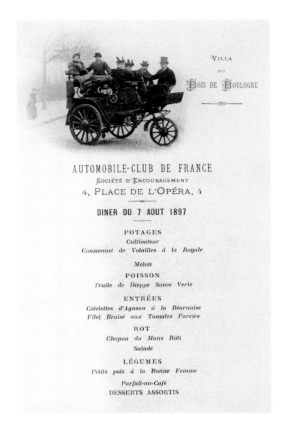

Mercredi 10 Février 1897

Union des Chambres Syndicales de la Bonneterie

25e Anniversaire

PARIS-TROYES

Menu

½ Douz. huitres

Potages

Bisque et Marmite

Relevé

Soles Marguery

Entrées

Selle Présalé avec Cépes et Tomates

Rôt

Poulardes de Houdan truffées

Salade

Paté de foies gras en gelée

Légumes

Pointes d'asperges au beurre

Entremets

Biscuits glacés

Gaufres

Fromages, Fruits, Desserts

Vins

Graves vieux,

Bordeaux, Médoc,

Volney Hospice

Champagne frappé

Café, Liqueurs

ROMA 1897

GRAND
hôtel

PISTOIA, 3 APRILE 1897

BANCHETTO UFFICIALE

DATO IN OCCASIONE

DELLA INAUGURAZIONE

DELLA

LUCE ELETTRICA

IN PISTOIA

Ill.mo Sig. _____

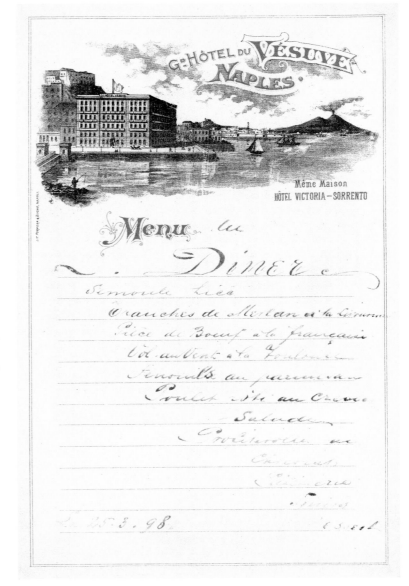

G. HÔTEL DU VÉSUVE NAPLES.

Même Maison
HÔTEL VICTORIA – SORRENTO

Menu du

DÎNER

OPPOSITE Grand Hôtel, 1897, Rome, Italy

ABOVE Banchetto Ufficiale, 1897, Pistoia, Italy

When electric streetlights were first illuminated in this Tuscan town, the city fathers threw a grand civic celebration. The main public event was the *Distribuzione di Buoni di Pane e Carne ai Poveri della Città* ("Distribution of Vouchers for Bread and Meat to the City's Poor"). Later the city's rich sat down to a private banquet, which was not listed in the souvenir. *That* menu was placed inside separately.

Als in dieser toskanischen Stadt die elektrische Straßenbeleuchtung in Betrieb genommen wurde, veranstalteten die Stadtväter ein großes Bürgerfest. Die wichtigste öffentliche Veranstaltung war

die Verteilung von Gutscheinen für Brot und Fleisch an die Armen der Stadt. Später nahmen die Reichen der Stadt an einem privaten Bankett teil, von dem auf der Ankündigung nichts zu lesen war. Die Speisekarte für dieses Ereignis wurde separat gereicht.

Pour l'inauguration de l'éclairage électrique de cette ville de Toscane, les édiles organisent une grande fête. Le principal événement public est la *Distribuzione di buoni di pane e carne ai poveri della città* («Distribution de bon pain et de viande aux pauvres de la ville»). Plus tard, les riches citoyens de la ville participeront à un banquet privé qui n'apparaît pas dans ce souvenir. Le menu de ce dîner y était inséré séparément.

RIGHT Grand Hôtel du Vésuve, 1898, Naples, Italy

HÔTEL SUISSE

POMPEI

PAGE 82 Marsala, c. 1897, Italy

PAGE 83 Hôtel Suisse, c. 1898,
Pompei, Italy

THIS PAGE & OPPOSITE *SS Australien,*
Messageries Maritimes, 1899

Auguste Vimar applied his expertise as a
children's book illustrator to a series of
zoologically anthropomorphic menu
cards. Each card showed two animals in
the act of food preparation or service. In
1895 Paul Gauguin traveled on this ship
for his last voyage to Tahiti. Vimar's
playfulness would have been a contrast
to Gauguin's stormy temperament.

Auguste Vimar ließ seine Erfahrung
als Kinderbuchillustrator in eine Reihe
zoologisch-anthropomorpher Speisekarten einfließen. Auf jeder waren zwei

Tiere beim Zubereiten oder Servieren
von Speisen abgebildet. 1895 trat Paul
Gauguin auf dem Schiff seine letzte
Reise nach Tahiti an. Vimars Verspieltheit
stand in starkem Kontrast zu Gauguins
stürmischem Temperament.

Auguste Vimar met son savoir-faire d'illustrateur de livres pour enfants au service
d'une série de menus ornés d'animaux
anthropomorphes. Chaque menu montre
deux animaux préparant ou servant les
mets. En 1895, Paul Gauguin effectua
son dernier voyage à Tahiti à bord de
ce paquebot. L'esprit enjoué de Vimar
est à l'opposé du caractère tourmenté
de Gauguin.

PREMIÈRE CLASSE

le 8 Juin 1899

PAQUEBOT
"Australien"

DINER

POTAGE

Pâte fine

RELEVÉ

Ramequins au Parmesan

ENTRÉES

Boeuf braisé Flamande
Poisson à la Orly
Poulet s/ truffes et Champignon

ROTIS

Oie
Longe de veau

SALADE

de Saison

LÉGUMES

Salsifis à la Poulette

ENTREMETS

Glace citron — Gâteau chocolat

DESSERT

Assorti

CAFÉ

IMP. MARSEILLAISE, R. SAINTE, 39.   MOD Nº 70

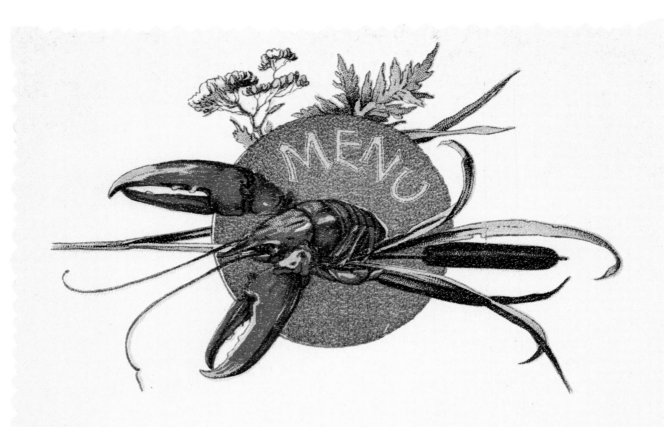

Huitres de l'est sur Coquille

Sauterne   *POTAGE*

Consomme' en tasse

∼ഺ∼

HORS D'OEUVRE

Salade   Crevette   Mayonnaise

Ce'leri   Olives   Amandes   Salees

∼ഺ∼

Bordeaux   *ENTREES*

Poulet Saute aux Champignom

Ris de veau en caisse

∼ഺ∼

ROTIS

Dinde sauce Canneberge

Champagne   Petits pois Francais

Salade Escarolle

∼ഺ∼

DESSERT

Glace Napolitaine

Fromage   Fruits   Gateaux

Cafe'

OPPOSITE **Stock menu, c. 1899, France**

RIGHT & BELOW **Bretel Frères, 1900, Paris, France**

Proud of their prize-winning butter, the Bretel brothers offered sets of menu cards for family dinners. Many such manufacturers of products consumed at the domestic dinner table offered packets of cards that were blank with the exception of the advertisement.

Die Bretel-Brüder waren stolz auf ihre preisgekrönte Butter und boten Speisekartensets für Familienessen an. Auch viele andere Hersteller, deren Lebensmittel am heimischen Esstisch verzehrt wurden, hatten Speisekarten im Angebot, die bis auf die Werbung leer waren.

Fiers de leur beurre primé, les frères Bretel offrent des jeux de menus pour dîners de famille. Il est courant que les producteurs d'aliments consommés à la table familiale offrent des séries de menus vierges, à l'exception du message publicitaire.

Ch. MOREUX, Propriétaire

ABOVE LEFT **Grand Restaurant de l'Hippo-Palace, 1901, Paris, France**

ABOVE RIGHT **Restaurant de Tabarin, 1905, Paris, France**

Adolphe Willette created a bizarre tableaux of cannibalistic putti, perhaps catering to the spirit of the restaurant associated with Bal Tabarin, one of the most famous of Montmartre's dance halls. In addition to designing the Moulin Rouge cabaret, the multifaceted Willette designed elements of the cabaret Le Chat Noir, the café La Palette d'Or, and the ceiling of La Cigale music hall.

Mit seinem bizarren Bild kannibalischer Putten wollte Adolphe Willette vielleicht auf die Stimmung in dem Restaurant anspielen, das an das Bal Tabarin, eines der berühmtesten Tanzlokale des Montmartre, angeschlossen war. Das Multitalent

Willette dekorierte nicht nur das Kabarett Moulin Rouge, sondern entwarf auch Elemente des Kabaretts Le Chat Noir und des Cafés La Palette d'Or sowie die Decke des Konzertsaals La Cigale.

Adolphe Willette est l'auteur de cette étrange scène où sont attablés des angelots cannibales, peut-être pour répondre à l'esprit du restaurant du Bal Tabarin, l'un des plus célèbres de Montmartre. Le très talentueux Willette est aussi le décorateur du Moulin-Rouge, d'une partie du cabaret du Chat noir, du café La Palette d'Or et du plafond du music-hall La Cigale.

RIGHT **Hubertusstock, 1902, Groß Schönebeck, Brandenburg, Germany**

OPPOSITE **Banquet des Maires de France, Exposition Universelle, 1900, Paris, France**

PAIX

LIBERTÉ FRATERNITÉ

22 SEPTEMBRE 1900

SITA

Le Maître Brahma
Dieu de l'Inde rose
A nos cœurs t'impose.

Femme de Rama,
Sitâ, belle épouse
Hautaine et jalouse,

Quel autre t'aima ?

On dit dans l'Histoire
Qu'après sa victoire
Ravana te prit ;

Mais que ton esprit
Et ton corps fidèles
Trouvèrent des ailes.

MAURICE VAUCAIRE

ÉDITÉ
PAR LA
PHOSPHATINE FALIÈRES

Typ. Goupil & Cie.

Paris. — Déposé.

SIAM ET CAMBODGE — SITA APPORTANT L'ORANGE A SES PEUPLES.

For a series of advertising menu sheets,
the company employed painter Louis
Chalon and lyricist Maurice Vaucaire
to collaborate on a dozen designs for a
visual and poetic tour of countries with
a connection to oranges. The reverse side
has space for the bill of fare.

Für eine Reihe von Werbespeisekarten
beauftragte das Unternehmen den Maler
Louis Chalon und den Lyriker Maurice
Vaucaire damit, gemeinsam Dutzende
Entwürfe für eine visuelle und poetische
Reise durch Länder zu entwerfen, die
einen Bezug zu Orangen hatten. Auf der
Rückseite wurde Platz für die Speisekarte
gelassen.

Pour une série de menus publicitaires,
cette entreprise fait appel à Louis Chalon
et au parolier Maurice Vaucaire, auteurs
d'une douzaine de menus qui sont
autant d'invitations à un voyage visuel et
poétique à travers des pays où poussent
les oranges. La liste des plats peut être
inscrite au verso.

RIGHT & BELOW **Luncheon for King
Edward VII and Queen Alexandra,
Guildhall, 1902, London, England**

Fête Coloniale du 2 Août 1900

MENU

Consommé aux Nids de Salanganes
Crème d' Ygnames
Cantaloups Frappés
Truite Saumonée au Currie
Filet de Bœuf Fermière
Poulardes Farcies à la Néva
Sorbets à l' Armagnac
Punch au Rhum Saint-James
Cochons de Lait laqués sur Champ de Truffes
Pains de Canetons de Rouen
Salade Exotique
Fruits frappés au Cherry-Brandy
Glace au Moka
Dessert
＊

VINS

Madère Soleras
St-Émilion en carafes — Graves en carafes
Champagne frappé
Château-Yquem 1893
Château Cos d'Estournel 1887
Chambertin 1881
Pommery Greno Sec
Café de la Nouvelle-Calédonie

PROGRAMME

PREMIÈRE PARTIE

1. **La Tzigane,** par l'Orchestre (Chef M. PIRARD).
2. **La Marche de Fodé-Kaba,** par les Joueurs de CORA Sénégalais.
3. A **Si Manman mouin mort ..** ⎫ Airs chantés par Mme Marie DRIVOS,
   B **Adié Madras, Adié Foulard** ⎭ Créole de la Martinique.
4. **Airs variés Malgaches,** par les Joueurs de VALHIA Malgaches.
5. **Morceau d'Ensemble,** par l'Harmonie Malgache.

ENTR'ACTE

CINÉMATOGRAPHE — Musique d'Orchestre.

DEUXIÈME PARTIE

1. **Airs Créoles,** par l'Orchestre......................... BARRÈS
2. A **Danse des Femmes aux Vases** . ⎫
   B **Danse des Guerriers**.......... ⎬ par la troupe des Danseurs
   c **Danse des Baguettes**.......... ⎭ et Chanteurs Cinghalais.
3. **Orchestre Annamite**
4. **Mademoiselle Cléo de Mérode**
   dans ses Danses Cambodgiennes.
5. **"La Marseillaise"**
   Chantée par un groupe d'Indigènes Coloniaux.
   (Algériens — Tunisiens — Sénégalais —
   Martiniquais — Malgaches — Annamites
   — Dahoméens.)
   Avec accompagnement d'Orchestre et de l'Harmonie Malgache.

ABOVE & OPPOSITE **Fête Coloniale,
Exposition Universelle, 1900, Paris,
France**

In 1900 poet and illustrator Eugène Le
Mouël sketched one of the more unusual
summer evening parades in Paris.
Beginning at the "miniature colonial
empire" constructed at the Trocadero, a
procession of Africans and Indochinese
with banners and musical instruments
circled the Champs de Mars. An after-
dinner fête included a fully catered feast.

Im Jahr 1900 skizzierte der Dichter und
Illustrator Eugène Le Mouël einen eher
ungewöhnlichen Umzug, der an einem
Sommerabend in Paris stattfand. Von
dem „Miniatur-Kolonialreich", das am
Trocadero aufgebaut war, zog eine Prozes-
sion von Afrikanern und Südostasiaten
mit Fahnen und Musikinstrumenten
über das Champ de Mars. Danach gab es
ein Fest inklusive Speisen und Getränken.

En 1900, Eugène Le Mouël, poète et
illustrateur, dessine l'un des défilés
parisiens les plus insolites, donné par une
soirée d'été. Partie de l'«empire colonial
en miniature» bâti au Trocadéro, une
parade d'Africains et d'Indochinois fait le
tour du Champ-de-Mars, avec bannières
et instruments de musique. Un dîner
complet a lieu ensuite.

EXPOSITION DE 1900

COLONIES FRANÇAISES
PAYS DE
PROTECTORAT

EUGÈNE LE MOUËL

COMMISSAIRE ADJT DE ST PIERRE ET MIQUELON.

STERN, GR.

Francisco Nicolas Tamagno, an Italian-born, Paris-based artist best known for his advertising posters, created the image of *Delna, La Vivandiére*, a woman who sold food and drink to soldiers—or, in this case, endorsed an alcohol-laced stomach tonic and digestive.

Francisco Nicolas Tamagno, ein in Italien geborener und in Paris lebender Künstler, der vor allem für seine Werbeplakate bekannt war, kreierte das Bild *Delna, La Vivandière*, das eine Frau zeigt, die Speisen und Getränke an Soldaten verkauft oder – wie in diesem Fall – einen Magen- und Verdauungsschnaps anpreist.

Peintre parisien d'origine italienne connu pour ses affiches publicitaires, Francisco Nicolas Tamagno est l'auteur de l'affiche *Delna, la vivandière*, qui vend vivres et boissons aux soldats. Ici, elle vante une boisson alcoolisée, tonique et digestive.

BELOW RIGHT **Hôtel Continental, c. 1900, Paris, France**

OPPOSITE **Folies-Bergère, c. 1900, Paris, France**

OPPOSITE *SS Hohenzollern*, Norddeutscher Lloyd Bremen, 1901

LEFT **Private dinner menus, 1902, Paris, France**

Twice in 1902, a group of chemists sat down to a private dinner with a primitively drawn menu by a Sunday painter placed before them. One of the diners was Gaston Charlot, a pharmacist from Paris' Laennec Hospital. His son, also named Gaston, became a noted scientist and the founder of analytic chemistry in France. Perhaps these menus served as an inspiration (or a warning) to always wear clothing in the lab.

Im Jahr 1902 nahm eine Gruppe von Chemikern zweimal an einem privaten Abendessen teil, bei dem ihnen eine primitiv gezeichnete Speisekarte eines Sonntagsmalers vorgelegt wurde. Unter den Gästen war auch Gaston Charlot, ein Apotheker aus dem Pariser Hôpital Laennec. Sein Sohn, der ebenfalls Gaston hieß, wurde ein bekannter Wissenschaftler und der Begründer der analytischen Chemie in Frankreich. Vielleicht waren diese Speisekarten eine Inspiration (oder Warnung), im Labor stets Kleidung zu tragen.

En 1902, un groupe de chimistes se retrouve à deux reprises pour un dîner dont le menu a été dessiné par un peintre du dimanche. L'un des convives est Gaston Charlot, pharmacien de l'hôpital Laennec à Paris. Son fils, aussi prénommé Gaston, deviendra un grand scientifique, fondateur de la chimie analytique française. Peut-être ces menus ont-ils servi d'inspiration, ou d'avertissement, pour toujours rester habillé au laboratoire.

BELOW **Champagne Montebello, c. 1900, France**

Fest-Mahl

zur Feier

des Allerhöchsten Geburtstages

Sr. Majestät des Kaisers & Königs.

Wiesbaden, den 27. Januar 1902.
Victoria-Hotel.

RED STAR LINE.
DINNER MENU.

S. S. ZEELAND. 18th June 1903

Little Neck Clams

Celery   Caviar on Toast   Olives

Cream of Asparagus   Consommé Dubourg

Halibut au Gratin Italienne
Pommes Pont-Neuf

Petits Bouchées à la Reine

Sirloin of Beef, Jardinière

Haunch of Mutton, Flageolette
Fried Egg Plant   Roast Potatoes

Roast Duckling, Apple Sauce
Escarole Salad

Philadelphia Pudding
Strawberry Ice Cream
Assorted Turkish Bonnets

CHEESE
Gorgonzola   Cream

Dessert   Café Noir

Champagne.

FRITZ SCHMELLER & Cº NÜRNBERG.

Norddeutscher Lloyd
Bremen,

AMERIKA.
Asien - Australien.

Dep. 1455

CHAMPAGNE MONTEBELLO

CHROMO·LITH.E.PLANTET.AY

MENU

Au Dessert : SABLÉ DES FLANDRES

„GALA PETER"

MENU

„GALA PETER" le *premier* des Chocolats au lait.

OPPOSITE **Champagne Montebello, c. 1900, France**

ABOVE LEFT **Sable des Flandres, c. 1900, France**

ABOVE RIGHT **Gala Peter, c. 1900, France**

PROGRAMA

CASINO SAN-SÉBASTIAN

CH. GRABBE IMP. 36, Rue de LANCRY, PARIS

MENU

Para el día 21 de Septiembre

ALMUERZO

Hors d'œuvre
Œufs pochés à l'Estragon
ou œufs au choix

Poisson
Truites de rivière Meunière
Soles dorées Citron

Entrée
Rognons sautés au
Champignons

Grillade
Côtes de mouton
aux pommes souflées
Entrecôtes au bœurre
d'anchois

Plat froid
Panaché de viande à la gelé

Patisserie
Sacristain
Fruits et fromages

COMIDA

Potage
Condé aux croutons
Consommé Riche

Poisson
Filets de Soles à la Orly

Entrée
Tournedos à la d'Orléans

Légume
Choux-fleurs sautés
au bœurre

Rôti
Poulet de grains au cresson
Salade

Entremet
Crème renversée au Moka
Desserts

HELADOS DEL DIA

Vanille.—Fraises.—Limón helado.

Five ó Clock tea   Soupers Froids

CASINO
San-Sebastian
PROGRAMA

CH. CRABBE IMP. 36, Rue de LANCRY, PARIS

MENU

PARA EL DÍA 15 DE AGOSTO

ALMUERZO

Hors d'œuvre

Poisson

Petites fritures au citron

Plat du jour

Escalopes de veau chasseur

Grillade

Gigot de prés-salé bretonne

Patisserie

Brioche mousseline

Fruits et fromage

COMIDA

Potage

Perles du Japon

Poisson

Merlus pochée sauce Riche

Entrée

Poulet braisé masseine

Légume

Choux fleurs sautés au beurre

Rôti

Aloyeau au cresson

Salade

Entremets

Glace arlequin.—Limón helado.

Desserts

Five O'Clock tea—Soupers froids

OPPOSITE & ABOVE **Casino San-Sebastian, 1903, San Sebastian, Spain**

ABOVE LEFT Champagne Montebello, c. 1900, France

ABOVE RIGHT Biscuits Lefèvre-Utile, c. 1900, France

A commercial baker hired Breton artist Marie de Bannalec to create menus focused on the region of Brittany where these famous cookies were made. The printing techniques of gilt embossing and chromolithography further enhanced these fine pieces.

Eine Bäckerei beauftragte die bretonische Künstlerin Marie de Bannalec mit der Gestaltung von Speisekarten mit Bezug zur Bretagne, wo diese berühmten Kekse hergestellt wurden. Durch die Drucktechniken der Goldprägung und Chromolithografie wurden die Kunstwerke zusätzlich veredelt.

La célèbre biscuiterie fait appel à l'artiste bretonne Marie de Bannalec pour réaliser des menus dont le thème est la Bretagne, région d'origine des biscuits. Ces très belles illustrations sont mises en valeur par le gaufrage à dorure et la chromolithographie.

OPPOSITE Abbaye-Albert, 1909, Paris, France

Artist Georges Redon perfectly captured the alcoholic abandonment of an evening at a Montmartre restaurant. One visitor commented, "Many of the women who regularly go to the Abbaye are startling in appearance, and there is no doubt as to the business they are bent on."

Der Künstler Georges Redon hat den abendlichen Alkoholrausch in einem Restaurant am Montmartre perfekt eingefangen. Ein Besucher kommentierte: „Viele der Frauen, die regelmäßig ins Abbaye gehen, sehen blendend aus, und es besteht kein Zweifel an ihren Absichten."

L'illustrateur Georges Redon rend à la perfection l'abandon suscité par l'alcool lors d'une soirée dans un restaurant de Montmartre. « Bien des femmes qui fréquentent l'Abbaye frappent par leur tenue et l'on ne peut douter de l'activité à laquelle elles se consacrent », souligne un visiteur.

Carte des Vins

ABBAYE - ALBERT

ABOVE Savoy, 1905, London, England

OPPOSITE *SS Grosser Kurfürst*, Norddeutscher Lloyd Bremen, c. 1909

Norddeutscher Lloyd
Bremen.

Algier, Moschee Abder-Rahman.

Mme Larue

Renowned Art Nouveau artist Alphonse Mucha, known for his paintings and poster designs, created a rare menu for a private dinner held by the wife of the famous Paris art dealer Siegfried Bing.

Der berühmte Jugendstilkünstler Alphonse Mucha, bekannt für seine Gemälde und Plakatentwürfe, entwarf eine ungewöhnliche Speisekarte für ein privates Abendessen, das die Frau des berühmten Pariser Kunsthändlers Siegfried Bing ausrichtete.

Adepte de l'Art nouveau, renommé pour ses peintures et ses affiches, Alphonse Mucha a réalisé ce menu singulier d'un dîner privé, organisé par l'épouse de Siegfried Bing, célèbre marchand d'art parisien.

OPPOSITE **Grand Hotel National, 1904, Lucerne, Switzerland**

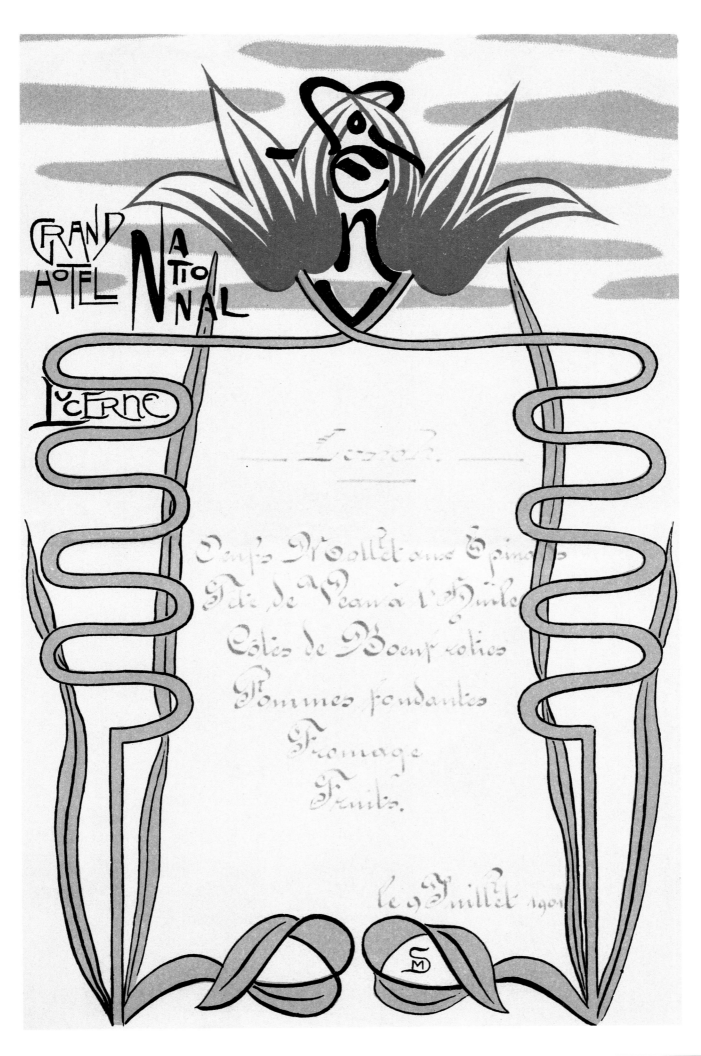

ABOVE & OPPOSITE **Désiline, c. 1904, France**

Désiline, an end-of-meal liqueur, was marketed through a series of advertising menu cards as a digestive tonic, perfect for settling the stomach after a heavy meal.

Der Digestif Désiline wurde auf verschiedenen Werbespeisekarten als verdauungsförderndes Tonikum beworben, das den Magen nach einer schweren Mahlzeit beruhigen sollte.

Un ensemble de menus publicitaires vante les mérites de la Désiline, tonique digestif idéal pour alléger l'estomac après un repas lourd.

LVNCH	DINER	SOVPER
Mk. 3.—	*Mk. 4.50*	*Mk. 3.—*
Eier à l'Estragon oder Turbot à la meunière Kartoffeln Frische Rinderzunge à la Chipolata Kartoffelpurée Käse und Butter oder Süsse Speise.	Sardinen in Oel Sellerie-Suppe Rhein-Salm mit holl. Sauce Kartoffeln Kalbsrücken m. jungen Gemüsen Junge Ente gebraten Salat — Compot Savarin mit Kirschwasser Käse und Butter Früchte.	Stangenspargel mit rohem Schinken Sauce hollandaise Rehkeule mit Rahmsauce Petersilien-Kartoffelu.Salat Käse und Butter oder Süsse Speise.

TAGESKARTE

den 21. Mai 1906.

Sellerie-Suppe	—.50	Frische Rinderzunge à la Chipolata	2.—
Kraftbrühe mit Mark	—.75	Kalbsmilcher geb. Sce. Tomates .	2.—
Schildkröten-Suppe	—.75	Kalbsfilet à la Zingara	1.50
Beluga-Caviar unges., Toast, Butter	3.—	Kalbsrücken mit jungen Gemüsen	2.50
Astrachan-Caviar ges. „. „.	2.50	Mutton Chops mit Pommes frites .	1.75
Schwedische Platte (1 bis 2 Pers.)	3.—	Hammelcôtelette Sauce Soubise .	2.50
3 Stück Oel-Sardinen mit Butter .	1.—	Frischer Rehrücken mit Apfelmuss	3.—
Eier à la Meyerbeer	1.75	Rehkeule mit Rahmsauce . . .	2.50
Westf. Schinken	1.50	1 Fasan gebraten	7.—
Carlton-Delicatess-Aufschnitt . . .	2.—	1 Haselhuhn	3.50
½ Helgol. Hummer je nach Grösse M. 2.50 bis	3.—	1 Poularde en Casserole 10.— bis	12.-
Kalter Rheinsalm Sce. Mayonnaise	2.50	Wiener Backhuhn mit Salat . . .	4.—
Mayonnaise von Lachs	1.50	Junge Hamburger Ente	7.50
Rheinsalm am Rost Sce. Béarnaise	3.—	1 Port. junge Hamburger Gans mit frischem Gurken-Salat	3.—
Seezunge au gratin	2.50	Frischer Stangenspargel m. geräucherten Lachs	2.25
Steinbutte nach Müllerin-Art . .	2.50	Engl. Sellerie mit Ochsenmark . .	1.50
Forelle blau mit fr. Butter . . .	3.50	Frische Artischoken Sce. Mousseline	1.50
Warmer Schinken mit Spinat . .	2.50	Sellerie-Salat, frischer Gurken-Salat	—.75
Karpfen blau mit Meerrettig. . .	2.—	Stangenspargel Sauce hollandaise	1.50
Zander mit Buttersauce . . .	1.50	Savarin mit Kirsch	1.—
Porterhousesteak à la Jardinière .	8.—	Frische Ananas 1.—, Aepfel, Orangen	—.50
Roastbeef à la Jardinière	2.—	Frische Erdbeeren	2.—
Tournedos à la Metropole . . .	2.50	Coupes aux Fraises	2.—
Entrecote à la moëlle	2.50	Diverse Käse und Compots . . .	....

COMPAGNIE GÉNÉRALE T

C.G.T.

SERVICES MARITI

NSATLANTIQUE

C.G.T.

POSTAUX

Featuring various national flags and an
image of a CGT Line steamer, this
souvenir menu could be posted by a
passenger directly from the ship.

Diese Souvenirkarte mit verschiedenen
Nationalflaggen und dem Bild eines
Liniendampfers der Compagnie Générale
Transatlantique (CGT) konnten die Passa-
giere direkt auf dem Schiff aufgeben.

Depuis ce paquebot français, les passagers
pouvaient poster ce menu-souvenir,
orné de pavillons nationaux et d'une
illustration du navire.

COMPAGNIE GÉNÉRALE TRANSATLANTIQUE

MENU

PAQUEBOT " LA TOURAINE "

8 Septembre 1906

DÉJEUNER

Beurre   Radis

Hure

Poissons frits

Blanquette de Veau

Entrecotes Maître d'Hotel

Pommes Pont-Neuf

PETITS GATEAUX

FROMAGE & FRUITS

BOUQUET PARTHENIS

ED. PINAUD, 18, PLACE VENDÔME, PARIS

Red Star Line
Antwerp-Dover-New York

Dinner Menu

Kartoffelpuerree Suppe	Purée Parmentier
Sauerkraut, Frankfurter Wuerstchen und Speck	Frankfurter Sausage, Sauerkraut Boiled Potatoes
Kartoffel	
Schmorbraten, Buerger Art	Beef Braisé, Bourgeoise
Kartoffel Gebaeckchen a la Duchesse	Pommes Duchesse
Gebratenes Huhn mit Apfelmus	Roast Chicken, Apple Sauce
Salat	Salad
---	--
Gefrornes	Ice Cream
Fein Gebaeck	Assorted Pastry
Fruechte	Fruit
Kaffee	Coffee

OPPOSITE **Hôtel de Ville, 1906, Paris, France**

When the mayor of Paris hosted an elaborate public banquet for the Lord Mayor of London and his entourage, painter Georges Picard created the elaborate mural-like cover. Paris's finest society printer, Stern, engraved it. That same year, Picard painted the ceilings of the Petit Palais's south pavilion.

Als der Bürgermeister von Paris ein üppiges, öffentliches Bankett für seinen Amtskollegen, den Lord Mayor of London, und dessen Begleiter ausrichtete, schuf der

Maler Georges Picard dieses kunstvolle, wandbildartige Titelbild. Gestochen wurde es bei Stern, der Druckerei der feinen Pariser Gesellschaft. Im selben Jahr bemalte Picard die Decken im Süd-pavillon des Petit Palais.

À l'occasion d'un grand banquet public donné par le maire de Paris en l'honneur du maire de Londres et de sa suite, le peintre Georges Picard signe cette couver-ture digne d'une fresque, gravée par Stern, le meilleur graveur de la haute société parisienne. La même année, Picard réalise les peintures du plafond du pavillon sud du Petit Palais.

The American Society in London
Thanksgiving Day Banquet
Thursday November 28th 1907

Hotel Cecil
London

Millard Hunsiker
Chairman

Thomas E. Feild
Vice-Chairman

15 OCTOBRE 1906

G. PICARD

STERN Graveur.

FAR LEFT *SS Kaiser Wilhelm der Grosse*, Norddeutscher Lloyd Bremen, 1904

LEFT Café de Paris, 1907, Paris, France

RIGHT 314ᵉ Diner du Bon-Bock, 1907, Paris, France

Laurent Bell illustrated an invitation to the private eating club's New Year's fête held on January 4, 1907.

Laurent Bell illustrierte die Einladung zum Neujahrsfest eines privaten Dinnerklubs, das am 4. Januar 1907 stattfand.

Laurent Bell a illustré ce carton d'invitation pour la fête du Nouvel An organisée par le club du Bon-Bock le 4 janvier 1907.

315ᵉ Dîner du Bon-Bock

JOIE ET MOUSSE
—
Ainsi qu'une mousse légère,
La joie, aux festins du Bon-Bock,
Jaillit toujours au même choc
D'un verre qui rencontre un verre.

Donc, ô Reine des échansons,
Sur l'an nouveau qui vient d'éclore,
O Muse, incline ton amphore,
Source du rire, des chansons.

Et verse-nous, Muse jolie,
Verse-nous un flot débordant,
Tandis que notre Président
Brandit un grelot de Folie !

Abel LEGER.

LEFT **Cailler's Schweizer Milch-Chocolade, 1907, Switzerland**

The Swiss chocolatier Cailler published menu cards on various themes: folk costumes, castles, landscapes, and sultry maidens. Milk chocolate never seemed so exotic and erotic. In true business form, the company also expounded facts about its operation on the backside.

Der Schweizer Chocolatier Cailler gab Speisekarten zu verschiedenen Themen heraus: Trachten, Schlösser, Landschaften und sinnliche Jungfrauen. Noch nie hatte Milchschokolade so exotisch und erotisch gewirkt. In bester Geschäftsmanier veröffentlichte das Unternehmen auf der Rückseite auch Informationen über seinen Betrieb.

Le chocolatier suisse Cailler édite des menus thématiques : costumes folkloriques, châteaux, paysages et jeunes femmes sensuelles. Jamais le chocolat au lait n'a paru aussi exotique qu'érotique. Très professionnel, le fabricant détaille au dos ses activités.

Fêtes du Jubilé du Club Nautique Nice
1883
1908

IMP GANDINI NICE

M. Debenedetti

The Fourth of July 1906.

MENU

Hors d'Oeuvres
Casserole de Langouste
Riz Pilaw
Mignon de Poulet Maryland
Cream Corn
Chops de Pré Salé Grillés
Pommes chips
Cailles glacées Roosevelt
Coeur de Romaine
Fraises Melba
Gateau Alice
Fruits
Desserts

VINS

Sherry (very old)
1900 Caseler
1893 Pontet Canet
1898 Giesler & Co. (extra sup. dry)
1898 Avize (Special cuvée National)

GRAND HOTEL NATIONAL LUCERNE

LEFT Grand Hotel National, 1906, Lucerne, Switzerland

BELOW LEFT Aeroplane Club of Great Britain and Ireland, 1909, London, England

The Wright brothers' successful flights in 1908 in France and a disagreement with the Aero Club of Great Britain inspired some English aerial enthusiasts to start their own group. Gathered at the Savoy Hotel on a January night, 160 men declared their devotion to the development of aerial navigation. However, the club crashed in 1910.

Infolge der erfolgreichen Flüge der Wright-Brüder im Jahr 1908 in Frankreich und einer Meinungsverschiedenheit mit dem Aero Club of Great Britain kamen einige englische Flugbegeisterte auf die Idee, einen eigenen Verein zu

gründen. An einem Januarabend versammelten sich 160 Männer im Savoy Hotel und verkündeten, sich der Entwicklung der Luftnavigation verschreiben zu wollen. Der Klub löste sich jedoch 1910 wieder auf.

Les vols réussis des frères Wright en France en 1908, ainsi qu'un différend avec l'Aéroclub de Grande-Bretagne, incitent des Anglais passionnés d'aviation à fonder leur propre groupe. Réunis à l'hôtel Savoy de Londres par un soir de janvier, 160 hommes déclarent s'engager dans le développement de la navigation aérienne. Mais leur club périclitera en 1910.

BELOW RIGHT Unknown restaurant, 1907, Paris, France

OPPOSITE Reggiori Bros. Restaurant, 1908, London, England

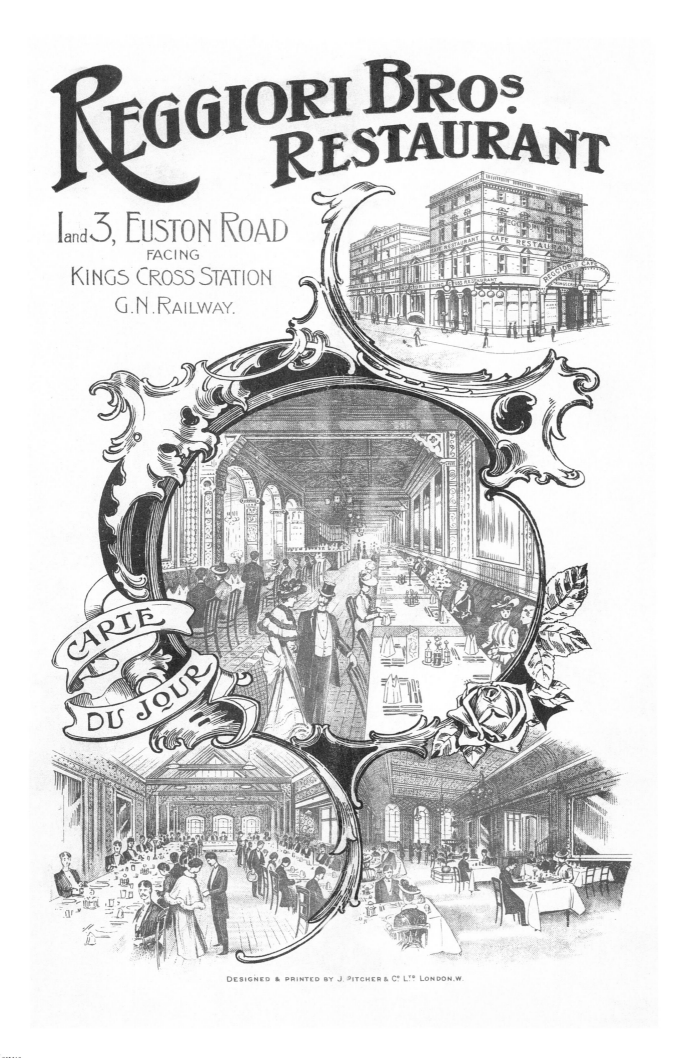

REGGIORI BROS. RESTAURANT

1 and 3, EUSTON ROAD
FACING
KINGS CROSS STATION
G.N. RAILWAY.

CARTE DU JOUR

DESIGNED & PRINTED BY J. PITCHER & Cº Lᵀᴰ LONDON. W.

MAXIM'S

Réveillon 1910

Menu
1910–1919

GRÉGOIRE, 25, rue Marbeuf

« Je n'abandonne ma Grégoire que pour aller dîner au Grand Vatel!»

ABOVE **Château de Madrid, 1910, Paris, France**

RIGHT **Banquet for King George V and Queen Mary, Guildhall, 1911, London, England**

As part of the coronation ceremonies for King George V and Queen Mary, the Lord Mayor hosted a sumptuous luncheon catered by the reliable firm Ring & Brymer.

Im Rahmen der Krönungszeremonien von König Georg V. und Königin Mary veranstaltete der Bürgermeister von London ein üppiges Mittagessen, das von der zuverlässigen Firma Ring & Brymer geliefert wurde.

Au cours des cérémonies du couronnement du roi George V et de la reine Mary, le maire de Londres donne un somptueux déjeuner, sous la houlette de Ring & Brymer, traiteur de confiance.

Ministère
des
Affaires Étrangères

Jules Chéret's poster designs were not so much representative of a graphic style but an emotional state. His dramatic cover for a dinner honoring foreign ministers suggests an evening *not* devoted to politics.

Die Plakatentwürfe von Jules Chéret waren weniger Ausdruck eines grafischen Stils als vielmehr eines Gefühlszustands. Sein dramatisches Titelbild für ein Diner für Außenminister deutet auf einen Abend hin, der nicht der Politik gewidmet war.

Dans les affiches de Jules Chéret, le graphisme compte moins que les sentiments qu'elles expriment. La couverture spectaculaire de cette carte d'un dîner en l'honneur de ministres étrangers atteste que la politique était au menu.

OPPOSITE **Les Ambassadeurs, 1912, Paris, France**

Though he also designed posters, painter Noël Dorville was best known for his caricatures. The cover for one of Paris's more famous cafés conveys a subtle satiric tone. An overdressed gent with a plume-encased date is observed by a man straight out of an Edvard Munch painting.

Der Maler Noël Dorville entwarf zwar auch Plakate, war jedoch vor allem für seine Karikaturen bekannt. Das Titelbild für eines der berühmtesten Pariser Cafés hat eine subtile satirische Note. Ein übertrieben gekleideter Herr wird von einer Dame im Federmantel begleitet und von einem Mann beobachtet, der direkt aus einem Edvard-Munch-Gemälde stammen könnte.

Également affichiste, le peintre Noël Dorville est surtout connu pour ses caricatures. La couverture du menu d'un des cafés parisiens les plus célèbres se teinte d'une subtile satire. Un homme tout droit sorti d'un tableau d'Edvard Munch observe un monsieur très élégant, accompagnant une femme bien emplumée.

LES AMBASSADEURS

CONSERVES SAXON

ABOVE **Conserves Saxon, 1910, Switzerland**

OPPOSITE **Private dinner menu, 1910, France**

BELOW *SS Berlin*, **Norddeutscher Lloyd Bremen, 1911**

Passengers traveling from America would instantly recognize the racial stereotypes of the jolly plantation and Stephen Foster's 1851 minstrel song, "The Swanee River (Old Folks at Home)."

Passagiere aus Amerika hatten keine Probleme, die ethnischen Stereotype von der fröhlichen Plantage und Stephen Fosters Minstrel-Song *The Swanee River (Old Folks at Home)* von 1851 wiederzuerkennen.

Les passagers en provenance d'Amérique déchiffraient sans faillir les clichés raciaux de cette plantation joyeuse et de la chanson de music-hall « The Swanee River (Old Folks at Home) », écrite en 1851 par Stephen Foster.

MENU

MAI
21
1916

Menu

	CHAUFROIX DE PERDREAUX FARCIS AU FOI D'OIE
Madère 1865	
	TORTUE VERTE · · · VIEILLE FINE CHAMPAGNE 1825
Château Latour Blanche 1880	
	GRENOUILLES SAUTEES A SEC VERCINGETORIX
Grand Vin Château Margaux 1er Vin 1890	
	FILET DE FAISAN ROTI PIQUE AUX TRUFFES
Romanée Conti 1896	
	PALMIER DES INDES SAUCE MOUSSELINE
Perrier Jouet Cuvée Reservée	
	SALADE DE COEURS DE LAITUE A LA FRANÇAISE
Vieille Chartreuse	
	GELEE DE FRAISES ET FRAMBOISES AU CHAMPAGNE
Pousse-Café Arc-en-ciel	
	FRIANDISES · · · CAFE EUGENIE

Guillaume

DEVAMBEZ, GR..

OPPOSITE **Private dinner menu, c. 1906, France**

Posed like Enrico Caruso ready to sing "Vesti la giubba," a handcrafted *pagliaccio* made a novel seating card.

Als originelle Speisekarte diente der handgefertigte *pagliaccio* in der Pose von Enrico Caruso, der sich bereit macht, *Vesti la giubba* zu singen.

Tel un Enrico Caruso s'apprêtant à chanter «Vesti la giubba», ce Paillasse fabriqué à la main tient lieu de marque-place fantaisie.

RIGHT **Unknown restaurant, 1916, Paris, France**

Menu

Huîtres de Marennes
Consommé aux diablotins
Crème de laitue
Bar Dronant
Poulet cocotte paysanne
Terrine de Gibier
Salade
Fromage
fruits
Café, liqueurs
Vins:
Chablis
St Emilion Jeu carafe
Pommard
Champagne

Mr Thierry

Le 7 Janvier 1918

La Distribution

OPPOSITE **Private dinner menu, 1918, France**

The playful cartoon gendarmes are reminiscent of André Hellé's famous wooden toy figures. As in his popular children's books, the characters were usually printed in bright, solid colors.

Die verspielten gezeichneten Gendarmen erinnern an die berühmten Holzspielzeugfiguren von André Hellé. Wie in seinen beliebten Kinderbüchern wurden die Figuren in kräftigen Volltönen dargestellt.

Ces amusants gendarmes rappellent les célèbres personnages en bois d'André Hellé. Ils ont les couleurs vives de ses livres pour enfants tant appréciés.

Le Réveil

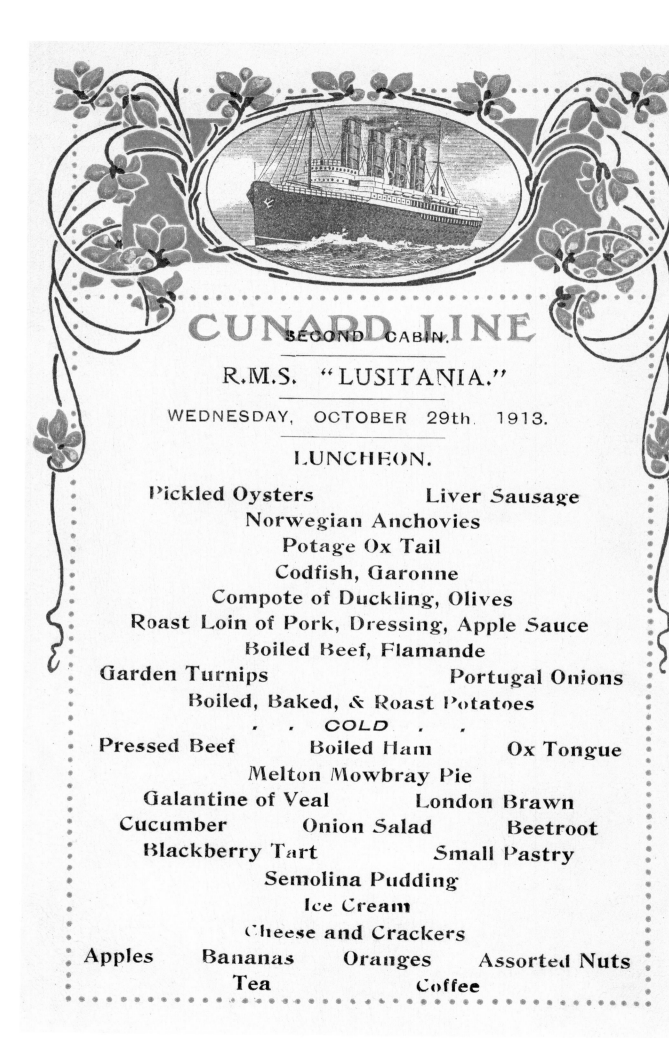

CUNARD LINE

SECOND CABIN.

R.M.S. "LUSITANIA."

WEDNESDAY, OCTOBER 29th. 1913.

LUNCHEON.

Pickled Oysters   Liver Sausage

Norwegian Anchovies

Potage Ox Tail

Codfish, Garonne

Compote of Duckling, Olives

Roast Loin of Pork, Dressing, Apple Sauce

Boiled Beef, Flamande

Garden Turnips   Portugal Onions

Boiled, Baked, & Roast Potatoes

. . COLD . .

Pressed Beef   Boiled Ham   Ox Tongue

Melton Mowbray Pie

Galantine of Veal   London Brawn

Cucumber   Onion Salad   Beetroot

Blackberry Tart   Small Pastry

Semolina Pudding

Ice Cream

Cheese and Crackers

Apples   Bananas   Oranges   Assorted Nuts

Tea   Coffee

COMPAGNIE INTERNATIONALE
DES
WAGONS-LITS
ET DES
Grands Express Européens

PARIS-NEVERS (Train 927)

AVIGNON-VINTIMILLE (Trains 7 et 10)

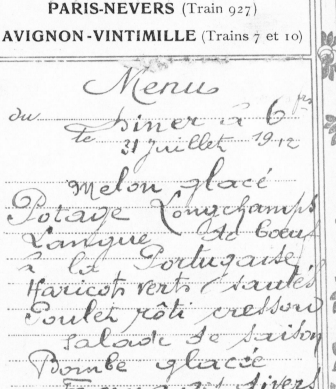

Menu
du Dîner à 6 fr.
le 31 Juillet 1912

Melon glacé
Potage Longchamps
Langue de Boeuf
à la Portugaise
Haricots verts sautés
Poulet rôti cresson
Salade de saison
Bombe glacée
Fromages divers
Corbeille de fruits

Liqvor Grand Marnier le verre 1 fr.

TARIF DES REPAS

1er Déjeuner : café, thé, cacao ou chocolat Van Houten avec lait,
pain et beurre 1 50
Déjeuner à la fourchette (vin non compris) . . . 4 »
Dîner (vin non compris) . . . . 6 »
Collation composée de thé ou café avec pain, beurre, fruits ou
Inconfitures (service Avignon-Vintimille : train 10, de 2 h. à 5 h.). 2 »

« Velma » et « Milka » Suchard, chocolats pour croquer.
La grande boîte . . . . . 1 »
La petite boîte . . . . . . » 50

Modèle 11   Août 1912

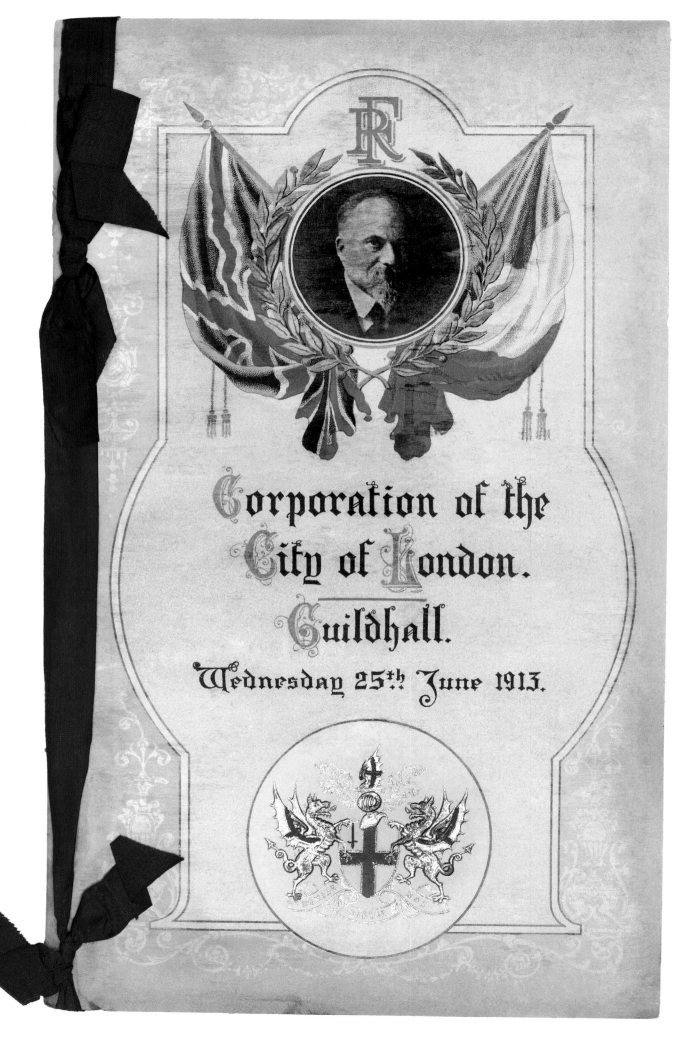

Corporation of the
City of London.

Guildhall.

Wednesday 25th June 1913.

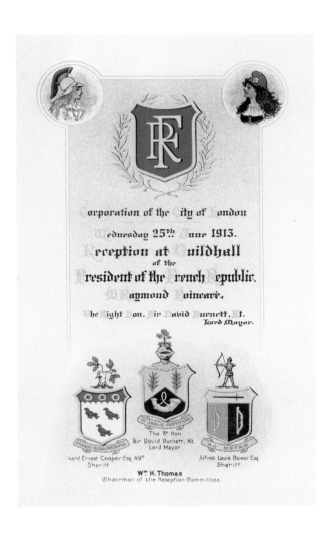

OPPOSITE, LEFT, & BELOW **Banquet for the president of France, Guildhall, 1913, London, England**

The state banquet for Raymond Poincaré was a very French affair, except for the very British baron of beef. As *New Larousse Gastronomique* noted, "In England the dish is much esteemed."

Das Staatsbankett für Raymond Poincaré war eine sehr französische Angelegenheit, abgesehen von dem durch und durch britischen *Baron of Beef* (ungeteilten Lendenstücken). Im *New Larousse Gastronomique* hieß es: „In England wird das Gericht sehr geschätzt."

Le banquet d'État donné en l'honneur du président Raymond Poincaré est tout ce qu'il y a plus français, à l'exception d'un double aloyau bien britannique. « En Angleterre, c'est un plat très estimé », précise le *Nouveau Larousse gastronomique*.

PAGE 140 *RMS Lusitania*, Cunard Line, 1913

PAGE 141 Compagnie Internationale des Wagons-Lits et des Grands Express Européens, 1912, France

THE CRYPT.
Under Guildhall.—(XV. Century).

Déjeûner.

Menu.

Punch.

Sherry.
Amontillado.

Hock.
Rudesheimer.

Champagne.
Pommery, 1900.
Clicquot, 1904.

Claret.
Leoville Barton, 1899.

Port.
Gonzalez's
Old Portugal.

Grand Chartreuse.

Perrier.
Schweppes' Malvern
Waters.

TORTUE.   TORTUE CLAIRE.

SAUMON MAYONNAISE.
SALADE DE HOMARD.

CAILLES À LA BORDEAUX.

CÔTELETTES D'AGNEAU À LA TOMATE.

BARON OF BEEF.

POULETS BECHAMELLE.

LANGUE DE BŒUF FUMÉE.

GELÉE À L'ORANGE.
MÉRINGUES À LA FRANÇAIS.
CRÈME D'ANANAS   BAVAROIS AUX FRUITS.
MAIDS OF HONOUR.
PATISSERIE PRINCESSE.

GLÀCÉ.   DESSERT.

The very large *enseigne* on the roof visually proclaims the name and specialty of the restaurant founded in 1832. Naturally, *l'Escargot de Bourgogne* starts the meal. In 1925 food writer Robert Burnand commented that after dining here no one could "deny the beauty of life." Located in the 1st arrondissement, the restaurant is now known as L'Escargot Montorgueil.

Das übergroße Aushängeschild auf dem Dach bezieht sich sowohl auf den Namen als auch die Spezialität des 1832 gegründeten Restaurants. Natürlich beginnt das Essen mit *L'Escargot de Bourgogne*. Der Kochbuchautor Robert Burnand schrieb 1925, dass niemand „die Schönheit des Lebens leugnen" könne, der einmal in diesem Lokal gegessen habe. Das im 1. Arrondissement gelegene Restaurant heißt heute L'Escargot Montorgueil.

La très grande enseigne qui surplombe l'entrée annonce le nom et la spécialité de ce restaurant fondé en 1832. Le menu s'ouvre évidemment par des *escargots de Bourgogne*. En 1925, le critique gastronomique Robert Burnand déclare qu'après y avoir mangé, on ne peut plus « nier la beauté de la vie ». Situé dans le 1er arrondissement de Paris, l'établissement s'appelle aujourd'hui L'Escargot Montorgueil.

Après le Repas prenez un "KERMANN"

OPPOSITE Père Kermann, 1915, France

BELOW Restaurant des Ambassadeurs,
1914, Paris, France

„Ambassadeurs"
Champs-Elysées

Café de la Rotonde

PAGE 148 Restaurant des Ambassadeurs, 1917, Paris, France

PAGE 149 Café de la Rotonde, c. 1913, Paris, France

RIGHT Dinner for General John Pershing, House of Commons, 1919, London, England

FAR RIGHT Undertakers' Victory Dinner, 1919, Leeds, England

A few weeks after the armistice, a trade association held a bittersweet and unintentionally macabre celebration. The food was heavy and unimaginative, the toasts obligatory.

Wenige Wochen nach dem Waffenstillstand veranstaltete ein Handelsverband eine bittersüße, ungewollt makabre Feier mit schweren, einfallslosen Speisen und den obligatorischen Trinksprüchen.

Quelques semaines après l'armistice, une association britannique d'entrepreneurs de pompes funèbres donne un dîner aigre-doux et involontairement macabre. Les plats sont lourds et sans inventivité, les toasts de rigueur.

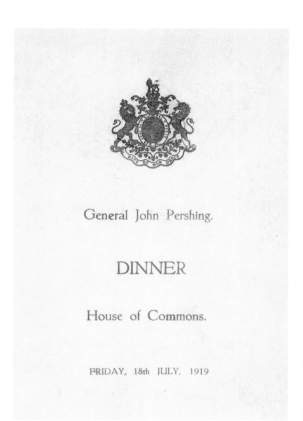

General John Pershing.

DINNER

House of Commons.

FRIDAY, 18th JULY, 1919

... BRITISH ...
UNDERTAKERS' ASSOCIATION.

LEEDS CENTRE.

VICTORY
DINNER.

FRIDAY, DECEMBER 5th, 1919.

VICTORY HOTEL
and RESTAURANT.
LEEDS.

107TH ANNIVERSARY
- OF THE -
NELSON·CLUB.
R.A.O.W.C.

1805   1913

19   13.

·Gentlemen·
the·toast·to-night
·is·
·NELSON·

LEFT Nelson Club at Romano's Restaurant, 1913, London, England

OPPOSITE Restaurant des Ambassadeurs, 1917, Paris, France

A month after the first American soldiers entered combat, the Comité France-Amerique was treated to simple fare at this elegant 16th arrondissement restaurant. Mary Bremer's depiction of a French girl holding a *tri-coloré* ribbon against the American flag communicates the delicate sentiment of national friendships.

Einen Monat, nachdem die ersten amerikanischen Soldaten in den Krieg zogen, wurden dem Comité France-Amerique in diesem eleganten Restaurant im 16. Arrondissement einfache Speisen serviert. Mary Bremers Darstellung eines französischen Mädchens mit einem Band der Trikolore vor der amerikanischen Flagge spiegelt die zarten freundschaftlichen Bande zwischen den Nationen wider.

Un mois après l'entrée des soldats américains dans la Première Guerre mondiale, le Comité France-Amérique a droit à un repas simple dans ce restaurant élégant du 16e arrondissement. L'amitié qui unit les deux nations s'exprime dans ce dessin de Mary Bremer, où une jeune Alsacienne tient un ruban tricolore devant un drapeau américain.

Larue est là, rue Royale.

RESTAURANT LARUE

27, RUE ROYALE

NIGNON, Directeur

⸺⸺

MENU

⸺⸺

Novembre 1913

Menu

PIERROT A LA LUNE
Tu goûteras, ma mie, un peu de ce COINTREAU!
. . . .
Obéissante à son poète,
La Lune boit et ne s'arrête,
Car de ce nectar on n'en boit jamais trop!

CRÉATIONS COINTREAU

Triple-Sec

Guignolet Cointreau

Gt(berry Lacet d'Or

Menthe Anglaise

J.K.B Vin Cointreau

Au DESSERT : Un Verre Liqueur COINTREAU (Triple Sec)

LEFT **Cointreau, c. 1910, France**

As Pierrot tells the Moon, one cannot drink too much of this nectar at the end of a meal. The restaurant owner doubtlessly wished the diner to feel the same.

Wie Pierrot dem Mond erzählt, kann man nach dem Essen gar nicht genug von diesem Nektar trinken. Der Restaurantbesitzer wünschte sich zweifellos, dass es seinen Gästen genauso ging.

Comme le dit Pierrot à la lune, « de ce nectar on n'en boit jamais trop », ce que le restaurateur espère aussi sûrement de la part de ses clients.

BELOW **Maxim's, 1918, Paris, France**

OPPOSITE **La Tour d'Argent, c. 1917, Paris, France**

ABOVE LEFT **Restaurant Larue, 1913, Paris, France**

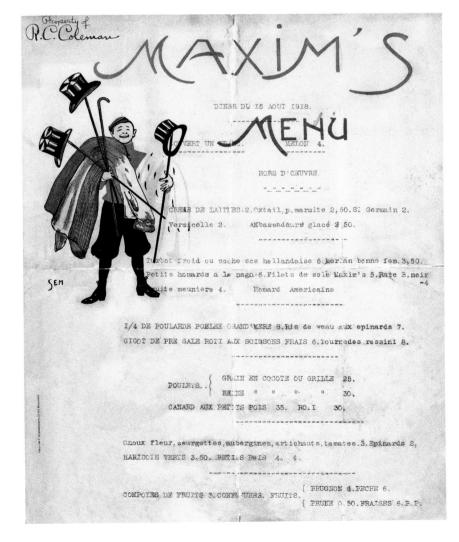

OPPOSITE **Café de la Rotonde, 1925, Paris, France**

BELOW **Amer Picon, c. 1920, France**

MENU
1920–1929

BELOW LEFT & RIGHT *SS Zeeland*,
Red Star Line, 1921

OPPOSITE *SS La Lorraine*, **Compagnie
Générale Transatlantique, 1920**

The quality of the food and wine was an
attraction to sailing aboard ships of the
France-based CGT line. The wines were
especially appreciated by Americans
escaping Prohibition, which had begun
on January 17, 1920.

Die Qualität des Essens und des Weins war
ein Anreiz, auf den Schiffen der französischen Compagnie Générale Transatlantique (CGT) zu reisen. Die Weine wurden
besonders von den Amerikanern geschätzt,
die der am 17. Januar 1920 eingeführten
Prohibition entfliehen wollten.

La qualité des repas et des vins servis
à bord de ces paquebots français est
attrayante. Les Américains, qui subissent
la prohibition depuis le 17 janvier 1920,
sont particulièrement sensibles à la carte
des vins.

·LUNCHEON·MENU·"FIRST CLASS"

Smoked Eels   Radishes   Rollmops
Spring Onions

Consommé Carmen   Potage Albion

Fillets of Gurnet
Corned Brisket of Beef with Vegetables
Welsh Rarebit to Order
Broiled Sqaub on Toast

Baked Jacket, Boiled & Straw Potatoes

COLD

Ribs of Beef   Ox Tongue   York Ham
Liver Sausage

Salad : Victoria   Lettuce and Sliced Tomatoes

Devonshire Dumplings, Hard Sauce   Custard Tartlets

Cheese : Gruyère   Brie   Roquefort

Crackers   Coffee

S.S. ZEELAND   June, 22, 1921

Band Programme on other side

·LUNCHEON·MENU·"FIRST CLASS"

Eggs Anchois   Queen Olives   Smoked Sardines

Consommé Nouilles   Potage Danoise

Fillets of Plaice
Corned Shoulders of Pork with Lima Beans
Fricassee of Veal
Broiled Mutton Chops
From the Grill **(to Order)** Pork Cutlets

Baked Jacket, Mashed & Lyonnaise Potatoes

COLD

Pressed Beef   Ox Tongue   York Ham
Roast Gosling

Salad : Flamande   Lettuce & Sliced Tomatoes

Apple Pudding   Scotch Shortcake

Cheese : Edam   Brie   Stilton

Crackers   Coffee

S.S. ZEELAND   December, 19, 1921

COMPAGNIE GÉNÉRALE
TRANSATLANTIQUE

OPPOSITE **Rathaus Keller, 1928, Nuremberg, Germany**

BELOW **Bourgogne J. Mommessin, c. 1920, France**

ABOVE **Chez Hansi, c. 1927, Paris, France**

A menu for this Montparnasse restaurant is an early example of the branding of Jean-Jacques Waltz, aka Hansi. Though his Alsatian-themed illustrations are now seen as clichés, much of his work was satiric and considered politically subversive.

Die Speisekarte dieses Restaurants in Montparnasse ist ein frühes Beispiel für die Markenführung von Jean-Jacques Waltz alias Hansi. Auch wenn seine elsässischen Themenillustrationen heute als klischeehaft gelten, waren viele seiner Arbeiten satirisch und politisch subversiv.

Ce menu d'un restaurant parisien de Montparnasse est l'un des premiers exemples de cartes illustrées par Jean-Jacques Waltz, dit Hansi. Ces images d'Alsace paraissent aujourd'hui stéréotypées, mais la plupart étaient considérées comme satiriques et subversives.

Au Père Tranquille

Aux Halles

16, Rue Pierre-Lescot

Tél. : LOUVRE 20-34
R. C. Seine 177.198

Couvert : 5

Huitres de Claires :
La douzaine :

Escargots de Bourgogne :
La douzaine :

Beurre : 4

Taxe : **10 %**

Les Repas sans VINS
5 francs en plus par personne.

CARTE DE SOUPER

POTAGES
Soupe à l'Oignon 7 - Soupe Gratinée 8
Consommé en Tasse 6. - Consommé Œuf Poché 10
Râpé

HORS-D'ŒUVRE DIVERS

POISSONS
Langouste Mayonnaise
Moules Marinières
Ecrevisses à la Nage 5 f la pièce

ENTRÉES
Œufs au Jambon 15 - Omelette Parmesan 15
Œufs Plat 12 - Œufs Brouillés aux Truffes 15
Entrecôte Grillée Pommes 18 - Choucroute Garnie 16
Tripes à la Mode de Caen 16
Poulet Rôti à la Broche

VIANDES FROIDES
Jambon 15 - Veau 15
Rosbif 15 - Poulet, Aile 25 - Cuisse 22
Assiette Anglaise 18
Salade 8

LÉGUMES
Petits Pois au Beurre 10 - Cèpes Bordelaise 12
Pommes Sautées 8 - Haricots Beurre 10

FROMAGES 6

ENTREMETS & FRUITS
Compote 15 - Poires Flambées 15
Omelette au Rhum 18 - Biscuits 15 - Ananas au Kirsch 15
Banane 6 - Poire 18 - Pomme 18 - Orange 10
Fraises 15 f Mandarine - Raisin - Amandes 12 Cerises 15

COMP. ARFEUILLE - EDITION.

cigarettes naja

menu

Après un bon repas fumez une cigarette Naja, la moins chère des cigarettes en tabac d'Orient.

OPPOSITE **Au Père Tranquille, c. 1921, Paris, France**

The *carte de souper*, with its famous *soupe à l'oignon*, was available from midnight to seven in the morning. A bowl at 4 a.m. was a ritual for some tourists. The exploration of this neighborhood was a must for anyone who wished "to take away a complete idea of the pleasures of the French capital."

Die *Carte de Souper* mit der berühmten *Soupe à l'oignon* (Zwiebelsuppe) war von Mitternacht bis 7 Uhr morgens erhältlich. Für manche Touristen kam es einem Ritual gleich, um 4 Uhr morgens eine Schale davon zu essen. Die Erkundung des umliegenden Viertels war ein Muss für jeden, der "sich ein vollständiges Bild von den Vergnügungen der französischen Hauptstadt machen wollte".

Cette «carte de souper» et sa fameuse *soupe à l'oignon* sont disponibles de minuit à 7 heures du matin. Certains touristes font un rituel du bol de soupe consommé à 4 heures du matin. La visite du quartier des Halles s'impose à tous ceux qui veulent «se faire une idée précise des plaisirs de la capitale».

LEFT Cigarettes Naja, c. 1925, France

BELOW LEFT Champagne Henri Abelé, 1920, France

BELOW RIGHT Unknown restaurant, 1927, France

EPOQUE 1900

CHAMPAGNE HENRI ABELÉ

RESTAURANT DU GRAND HOTEL

MENU du _____ 192

DÉJEUNER

DINER

Carte des Vins

CARTE DU JOUR

	La bout.	La ½ bout.
Grand ordinaire: rouge et blanc	3.ᶠ	1.ᶠ75
Table d'Hôte	2.ᶠ	1.ᶠ

Vins rouges:

	La bout.	La ½ bout.
Médoc;	5.ᶠ	2.ᶠ75
Saint-Estèphe;	7.ᶠ	4.ᶠ
Saint-Julien;	9.ᶠ	5.ᶠ
Saint-Émilion;	9.ᶠ	5.ᶠ
Pauillac;	9.ᶠ	5.ᶠ
Château Latour 1907. (Cachet du château)	35.ᶠ	"
d°. Pontet-Canet;	14.ᶠ	7.ᶠ50
d°. Fieuzal 1908 (Cachet du château)	15.ᶠ	"
d°. Léoville Lascaze 1914 (cachet du château)	26.ᶠ	"
d°. Haut-Brion 1912; (cachet du château)	20.ᶠ	"
d°. Cos d'Estournel; 1914 (—d°.)	25.ᶠ	"
d°. Carbonnieux 1914 (—d°.)	27.ᶠ	"
d°. Margaux 1912 (—d°.—)	30.ᶠ	"

Vins blancs

	La bout.	La ½ bout.
Graves;	6.ᶠ	3.ᶠ50
Cérons;	10.ᶠ	5.ᶠ50
Graves: (Rosechâtel dry	12.ᶠ	6.ᶠ50
Château La Montagne	18.ᶠ	9.ᶠ50
Sauternes;	12.ᶠ	6.ᶠ50
Barsac;	12.ᶠ	6.ᶠ50
Graves Dry (Monopole) "olivier"	12.ᶠ	6.ᶠ50
Sauternes; (Château La-Tourte	15.ᶠ	8.ᶠ
Château Guiraud 1914 (Cachet du château)	30.ᶠ	"
d°. Filhot 1914 (— d°.)	30.ᶠ	"
d°. Carbonnieux	20.ᶠ	11.ᶠ

Bourgognes: Vins rouges.

	La bout.	La ½ bout.
Macon;	10.ᶠ	5.ᶠ50
Beaujolais;	11.ᶠ	6.ᶠ
Beaune;	14.ᶠ	7.ᶠ50
Pommard;	14.ᶠ	7.ᶠ50
Corton;	20.ᶠ	11.ᶠ
Chambertin; (1911)	35.ᶠ	"

Vins blancs

	La bout.	La ½ bout.
Chablis;	10.ᶠ	5.ᶠ50
d°. Premières;	20.ᶠ	"
Montrachet; (1908)	35.ᶠ	18.ᶠ

	La bout.	La ½ bout.
Cidre mousseux; "Bol"	8.ᶠ	"

Vins mousseux:

	La bout.	La ½ bout.
Royal Seyssel; Carte blanche dry	18.ᶠ	10.ᶠ
d°. d°. (demi sec)	18.ᶠ	10.ᶠ

Champagnes

	La bout.	La ½ bout.
Moët & Chandon Carte Bleue;	32.ᶠ	17.ᶠ
d°. Carte blanche;	32.ᶠ	"
d°. White Star (vin sec)	40.ᶠ	21.ᶠ
d°. Brut Impérial (vin très sec)	40.ᶠ	21.ᶠ
Louis Roederer (grand vin sec)	40.ᶠ	"
Pommery & Greno, Drapeau américain	40.ᶠ	"
d°. cachet Nature (vin très sec)	40.ᶠ	"
Piper Heidsieck; Brut extra sec 1906 (vin très sec)	45.ᶠ	"
Charles Heidsieck; (Royal demi sec)	36.ᶠ	"
d°. (Goût Américain)	40.ᶠ	"

Vins divers et Etrangers

	La bout.	La ½ bout.
Valdepeñas;	6.ᶠ	"
Rioja vieux; (Blanc & rouge)	10.ᶠ	"
Jurançon; (Blanc)	10.ᶠ	5.ᶠ50

	La bout.	Le verre
Porto;	18.ᶠ	2.ᶠ50
Xérès;	18.ᶠ	2.ᶠ50
Madére;	18.ᶠ	2.ᶠ50
Malaga;	18.ᶠ	2.ᶠ50
Oberena Soda basque (au citron et grenadine)		0.ᶠ75

Bière — Limonade

	La bout.	La ½ bout.
Bière;	2.ᶠ	
Simonade;	1.ᶠ25	0.ᶠ75
Siphon;	0.ᶠ75	

Eaux minérales

	La bout.	La ½ bout.
Eau de la table de Cambo;	1.ᶠ75	"
Saint-Galmier;	2.ᶠ	1.ᶠ50
Vichy;	2.ᶠ50	2.ᶠ
Vals;	2.ᶠ50	2.ᶠ
Vittel;	2.ᶠ50	2.ᶠ
Perrier;	3.ᶠ	2.ᶠ25
Evian;	2.ᶠ50	2.ᶠ
Pougues;	2.ᶠ50	

Apéritifs et liqueurs

Apéritifs; (depuis)	1.ᶠ50	
Liqueurs; de marque; d°.	"	
Café filtre	1.ᶠ	"

RESTAURANT DE L'ANE ROUGE

TÉLÉPHONE
CENTRAL 41-41

L'ANE ROUGE

A. CHOULOT
Propriétaire
28, A^e TRUDAINE

CAREL FRÈRES, GRAVEURS, PARIS.

ÉVIAN CACHAT

HUITRES

COQUILLAGES

POISSONS DE MER

CRUSTACÉS

BOUILLABAISSE
ET
PLATS SPÉCIAUX

LIVRAISONS DANS TOUT PARIS

TÉLÉPHONE: Central 40-53

IMP. J. ACKER & CIE, PARIS

PAGE 162 **Restaurant du Grand Hôtel,**
c. 1921, Paris, France

PAGE 163 **Restaurant de l'Âne Rouge,**
c. 1925, Paris, France

ABOVE **Maison Prunier, 1920, Paris,**
France

Though he was practically the house
artist for Maxim's, Georges Goursat
(known as Sem) applied his talents to a
menu card for another well-known
restaurant. Prunier promised the delivery
of fresh seafood as well as bouillabaisse
and special dishes anywhere in Paris.

Obwohl er mehr oder weniger der Haus-
künstler des Maxim's war, ließ Georges
Goursat (auch bekannt als Sem) sein
Talent in die Speisekarte eines anderen
bekannten Restaurants einfließen.
Prunier bewirbt darauf die Lieferung von
frischen Meeresfrüchten, Bouillabaisse
und speziellen Gerichten in ganz Paris.

Illustrateur quasiment attitré du Maxim's,
Georges Goursat (*alias* Sem) a consacré
son talent au menu d'un autre restaurant
célèbre. Prunier promet de livrer fruits
de mer frais, bouillabaisse et autres mets
dans tout Paris.

OPPOSITE **Brasserie des Moulins,**
1922, Paris, France

Brasserie des Moulins offered typical fare
and plenty of fresh beer to visitors of the
intoxicating Pigalle quarter.

Die Brasserie des Moulins bot den Besu-
chern des berauschenden Pigalle-Viertels
typische Gerichte und viel frisches Bier.

La Brasserie des Moulins propose un
menu classique et de la bière à flots aux
visiteurs du quartier enivrant de Pigalle.

COUVERT : 1 fr.   TÉLÉPHONE : NORD 08-06

BRASSERIE des MOULINS
112, Boulevard Rochechouart, PARIS XVIII

Gaston Bellanger
Propriétaire

Menu 31 Juillet 1922

SPÉCIALITÉS

Pied de Mouton,
Poulette 3.00

Melon à la Tranche 2.00

Potages

Consommé Cheveux d'ange 1.00
Soupe à l'oignon 1.50, Gratinée 1.75
Hors d'œuvre assortis 2.00
Beurre 0.50 p.b.

Œufs

Œufs pochés vert pré 3.00
Omelette parmentier 3.50

Poissons

Filets de Sole Orly 3.75
Turbot Hollandaise 4.50
Écrevisses à la nage 1.00 pièce
Matelotte d'anguille 5.00
Demi langouste mayo 5.00

Entrées

Contre filet rôti au Céleri 4.50
Côte de mouton grillé pdt pois 4.00
Ris de Veau Zingara 4.50
Demi Pigeon egamont 6.00
Choucroute Francfort 3.50
Terrine Maison 3.50

Repas dans vissoy 0.50 sup.

Grillades

Chateau 6.00   Steack 5.00

Rôtis

Poulet 25.00   Pigeon 10.00

Froids

Jambon 4.00, Veau 3.50, Roastbeef 4.00
Quart de poulet 6.00
Piccalilly 0.50

Légumes

Haricots verts 2.00, Petits pois 2.50,
Artichaut 1.75, Chou fleurs 2.00,
Céleri demi glace 2.50,
Salades 1.50, œufs dur 0.75
Fromages 1.50, Suisse 1.25

Desserts

Tarte maison 2.00, amandes, Pêches 1.75
Raisins 2.00, Cœur à la crème 2.00,
Fraises 2.00, Crème d'Isigny 2.00,
Biscuits 2.00, Gateaux secs 1.00
Glaces : Napolitaine 1.75

BIÈRES : Blonde & Brune

BOCK......	**0.50**
DEMI.......	**0.75**
CAFÉ..........	**0.60**
CAFÉ-FILTRE.	**0.90**
Porto-Salvicente....	**1.75**
Muscat Impérial	**1.75**

Prunelle Extra-Dry "L'Héritier Guyot"
Véritable Quetsch d'Alsace

Si vous voulez que la bonne bouteille
soit meilleure, commandez-la à temps.

Voir au dos la Carte des Vins.

Suzanne et les deux vieillards.

MENU

MENU

MENU

MENU

MENU

OPPOSITE & THIS PAGE **Mictasol,
c. 1935, France**

Advertising menu cards featuring cartoons
by the artists Roger Cartier and Félix
Lorioux promote Mictasol, a tonic for
urinary issues. Issued in packets of six,
they were used at private events such as a
dinner party for medical students.

Die Speisekarten mit den Karikaturen der
Künstler Roger Cartier und Félix Lorioux
werben für Mictasol, ein Tonikum gegen
Harnwegserkrankungen. Sie wurden
in Sechserpackungen herausgegeben und
waren für private Veranstaltungen wie
Dinnerpartys von Medizinstudenten
gedacht.

Le Mictasol, tonique contre les problèmes
urinaires, est vanté sur ces menus illustrés
par Roger Cartier et Félix Lorioux. Vendus
par six, ils sont destinés à des dîners privés,
comme celui des étudiants en médecine.

Eden-Roc

CAP D'ANTIBES

ALBESSARD. EDIT. IMP. PARIS

TOUS DROITS RESERVES

OPPOSITE Eden-Roc Restaurant, 1923, Antibes, France

RIGHT Ciro's, 1922, Paris, France

BELOW Ledoyen, 1929, Paris, France

An Art Deco design of a scene from ancient Greece was Ledoyen's way of hinting at its own pedigree (established 1792) and its current popularity. Small tables under the trees made it a fine place for an elegant soiree.

Mit der Darstellung einer antiken griechischen Szene im Art-déco-Stil wollte das Ledoyen auf seine langjährige Erfahrung (1792 eröffnet) und seine Popularität im Jahr 1929 hinweisen. Mit seinen kleinen Tischen unter Bäumen eignete es sich hervorragend für eine elegante Soiree.

Avec cette scène de la Grèce antique revue par l'Art déco, le restaurant Ledoyen (fondé en 1792) met en avant son pedigree ainsi que sa renommée du moment. Ses petites tables sous les arbres en font un lieu exquis pour une soirée élégante.

LEDOYEN   CHAMPS-ÉLYSÉES

The Berkeley
London

PAGE 170 **Hôtel du Rhin, c. 1928,** **Loechle-Kembs, France**

PAGE 171 **New Year's Eve dinner,** **The Berkeley, 1924, London, England**

LEFT & OPPOSITE **Champagne Lucien** **Remy, c. 1925, France**

Two fine examples from Lucien Remy's series of attractive Art Deco menu cards made drinking champagne *très chic*.

Zwei schöne Beispiele aus Lucien Remys Reihe hübscher Art-déco-Speisekarten, durch die das Trinken von Champagner *très chic* wurde.

Ces deux très beaux exemplaires de menus Art déco réalisés pour Lucien Remy font du champagne un vin décidément très chic.

Champagne Lucien REMY
EPERNAY

IMP. V. IDOUX & C⁹ NANCY

menu

Champagne Lucien REMY
EPERNAY

Zum Löwenbräu

Haus Vaterland

GASTSTÄTTEN · G·M·B·H   BETRIEB KEMPINSKI BERLIN
BERLIN · W·9   KÖTHENER-STR. 1-5

SCHULPIG

OPPOSITE & THIS PAGE Haus Vaterland, c. 1928, Berlin, Germany

Designer Karl Schulpig created the menu for Berlin's theme park and Bavarian beer hall, Haus Vaterland (Fatherland House). At the time, it included the largest café in the world with attractions imitating Viennese, Hungarian, and Turkish cafés. It was described as "a beacon of commercial kitsch." Surviving menus are a fine record of Schulpig's contribution to commercial graphic design.

Der Designer Karl Schulpig schuf die Speisekarte für das Brauhaus im Berliner Vergnügungspalast Haus Vaterland. Damals gab es dort die größte Gaststätte der Welt mit Themenrestaurants, die Attraktionen aus Wien, Ungarn oder der Türkei anboten. Dies wurde als „Leuchtturm des kommerziellen Kitsches" bezeichnet. Die erhaltenen Speisekarten sind ein Beleg für Schulpigs Beitrag zum kommerziellen Grafikdesign.

L'illustrateur Karl Schulpig est l'auteur des menus de Haus Vaterland (« la maison de la patrie »), parc à thème berlinois et halle aux bières bavaroise. On y trouve le plus grand café du monde, avec des reconstitutions de cafés viennois, hongrois et turcs. L'endroit est qualifié de « phare du kitsch commercial ». Les menus parvenus jusqu'à nous témoignent de la qualité de l'apport de Schulpig au dessin commercial.

BELOW Restaurant Lucas-Madeleine, c. 1925, Paris, France

A clever design by A. Bertrand creates the illusion of a waiter about to reveal either the menu or the restaurant. The simple *Grands et Petits Salons* hints at one possible reason for its popularity with ambassadors and cabinet ministers. A private room was just the place to enjoy, among other pleasures, the superb cuisine and wine cellar.

Das raffinierte Design von A. Bertrand zeigt einen Kellner, der so aussieht, als wollte er etwas über die Speisekarte oder das Restaurant verraten. Die schlichten *grands et petits salons* könnten einer der Gründe gewesen sein, warum das Lokal bei Botschaftern und Kabinettsmitgliedern so beliebt war. In einem privaten Raum konnte man hervorragend exquisite Küche und edle Tropfen genießen und anderen Vergnügungen nachgehen.

Cet habile dessin d'A. Bertrand donne l'illusion que le serveur s'apprête à dévoiler le menu ou le restaurant. La mention «Grands et petits salons» est peut-être un indice de sa popularité auprès des ambassadeurs et des ministres. Un petit salon est, en effet, le lieu idéal pour apprécier, entre autres plaisirs, la cuisine et la cave raffinées.

OPPOSITE Restaurant des Gaufres, c. 1925, Paris, France

Waffles were a popular snack often prepared by street vendors, not by chefs at high-class outdoor cafés, but the crowd at a Right Bank restaurant suggests a clientele eager for the best-quality waffles known as *métiers*.

Waffeln waren ein beliebtes Feingebäck, das in der Regel nicht von den Köchen eleganter Straßencafés, sondern von Straßenverkäufern zubereitet wurde. Der Andrang in diesem Restaurant am Rive Droite deutet jedoch darauf hin, dass es die Kundschaft nach den besten Waffeln der Stadt – den sogenannten *métiers* – verlangt.

Souvent préparées à la devanture des grands cafés par des vendeurs plutôt que par les chefs, les gaufres sont très prisées. Mais la clientèle qui se presse devant ce restaurant de la rive droite exige des «métiers», gaufres de la meilleure qualité.

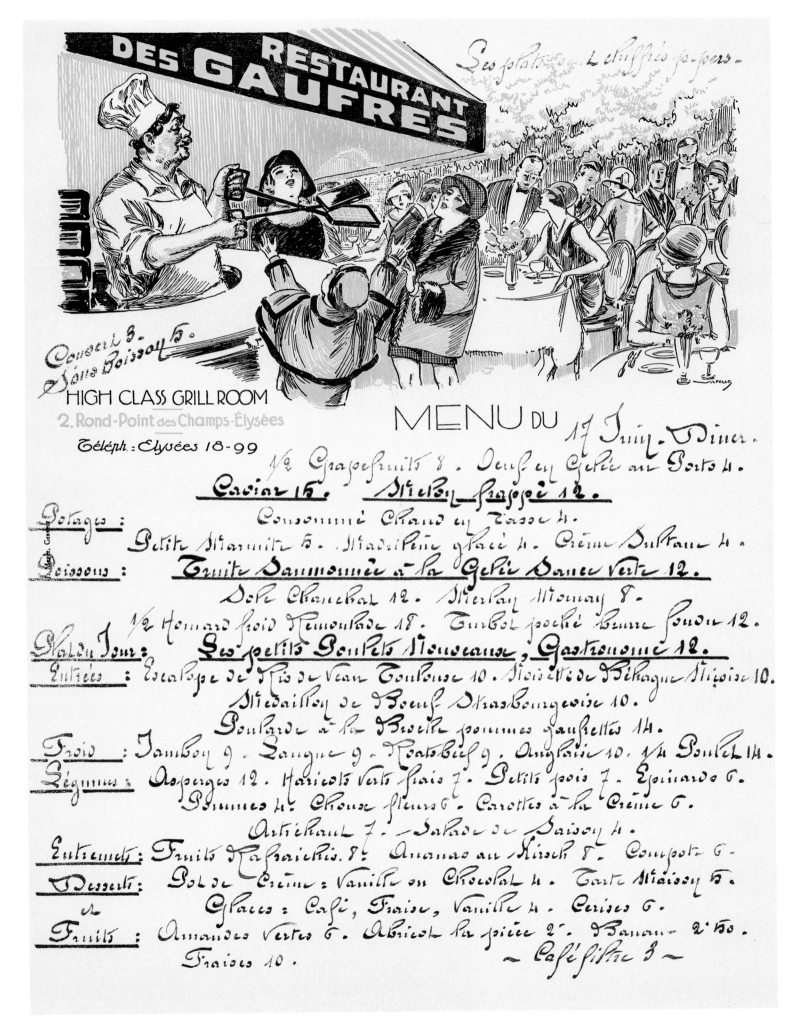

5 MAI 1923

LA TOUR d'ARGENT

15, Quai de la Tournelle
PARIS

1582

Chanfroud-Chabas.

HOTEL ROBLIN
6, Rue Chauveau-Lagarde (Madeleine)

HOTEL SAN RÉGIS
12, Rue Jean-Goujon (Ch.-Élysées)
André **TERRAIL**, Propriétaire

L'ESCARGOT
38, Rue Montorgueil (Halles)

OPPOSITE **Société des Médecins**
Bibliophiles, 1923, Paris, France

ABOVE **La Tour d'Argent, 1927,**
Paris, France

La seule utilité de l'eau

OPPOSITE Ciro's, 1929, Paris, France

ABOVE Ciro's, 1926, Paris, France

LES CHEFS~D'ŒUVRE
ÉPHÉMÈRES

IMP. GASTAUD NICE

PAGE 182 **Café de la Paix, 1927, Paris, France**

The restaurant's daily masterpieces included complicated mousses and lobsters with caviar piled on the carapace. Artist Maurice Berty made a specialty of capturing various eras through his illustrations.

Zu den täglichen Meisterwerken des Restaurants gehörten komplizierte Mousses und Hummer mit Kaviar, der auf dem Panzer aufgetürmt wurde. Der Künstler Maurice Berty war darauf spezialisiert, verschiedene Epochen in seinen Illustrationen festzuhalten.

Parmi les chefs-d'œuvre quotidiens de ce restaurant, on peut déguster des mousses élaborées et des homards surmontés de caviar. Dans ses illustrations, l'artiste Maurice Berty a pour habitude de mélanger les époques.

PAGE 183 **Restaurant du Grand Cercle, 1927, Nice, France**

ABOVE **Dinner for Les Cent Bibliophiles, 1921, Paris, France**

André Deslignères connects with this club's various interests. Some of those interests were, of course, picnics and book collecting. The private group was one of numerous bibliophilic dining clubs active between the wars.

André Deslignères konnte an die verschiedenen Interessen dieses Klubs anknüpfen, zu denen natürlich auch Picknicks und das Sammeln von Büchern gehörten. Die private Gruppe bildete einen von vielen bibliophilen Dinnerklubs, die in der Zwischenkriegszeit aktiv waren.

André Deslignères s'intéresse aux goûts variés de ce club, qui, bien entendu, comprennent les pique-niques et la bibliophilie. Ce cercle est l'un des nombreux clubs de bibliophiles gastronomes de l'entre-deux-guerres.

RIGHT **Grill Room du Café de Paris, 1926, Monte Carlo, Monaco**

OPPOSITE *SS Lapland*, **Red Star Line, 1927**

O.6

S S. "LAPLAND"   June 3rd, 1927.

Luncheon Menu

HORS D'ŒUVRES

Cods Roe in Tomato   Croûte d'Ecrevisse Tartare   French Sardines

Saumon Fumé   Slaw Relish   Salade Macedoine

Saucisson Bologna   Langue de Bœuf sur Canapé

HOT

Consommé Clair   Clam Chowder

Broiled Mackerel, Anchovy Butter

Eggs Zingara   Macaroni Italienne

Ox Tail, Bourgeoise

Boiled Chicken & Bacon, Bechamel

Dressed Cabbage   Carolina Rice

Baked Jacket, Sweet, Boiled, Mashed & Straw Potatoes

GRILL TO ORDER (10 to 20 minutes)

Squab on Toast   Minute Steak

COLD BUFFET

Roast Beef   Lunch & Liver Sausages   Ox-Tongue

York Ham   Brawn   Galantine of Turkey   Virginia Ham

SALADS

Potato   Lettuce & Tomato   Ringed Onions

SWEETS

Rice Custard   Cranberry Apple Pie   Coventry Puffs

CHEESE

Cheshire   Gruyere   Brie   Gorgonzola

Ice Cream & Wafers   Dessert   Coffee

Cette carte vous apparaîtra lumineuse dans l'obscurité
après avoir été préalablement exposée à la lumière.

OPPOSITE **Poccardi, 1927, Paris, France**

A chic group out on a Saturday night
romp review the menu of this well-
known Italian restaurant. Instructions
on the bottom of the card explain how
to make the piece glow. If Paris is *La Ville
Lumière*, then why not an advertisement
that glows?

Eine schicke Gruppe geht an einem
Samstagabend aus und studiert die Speisekarte dieses bekannten italienischen
Restaurants. Eine Anleitung unten auf
der Karte erklärt, wie man den Aushang
zum Leuchten bringt. Wenn Paris die
Stadt des Lichts ist, warum dann nicht
auch eine Leuchtwerbung anbringen?

Pour leur virée du samedi soir, des
clients chics examinent le menu de
ce célèbre restaurant italien de Paris.
Au bas de la couverture, on explique
comment faire s'illuminer la carte. Pour
la *Ville Lumière*, il fallait bien un menu
lumineux!

RIGHT **Pigall's, c. 1926, Paris, France**

The aristocrat in formal dress has
outlasted his partially disrobed and
drunken date. The caption used in ads,
"A gentleman like me or you dines at
Pigall's," embodies the sense of abandonment experienced in 1920s Paris.

Der formell gekleidete Aristokrat hat
länger durchgehalten als sein halb ent-
kleidetes, betrunkenes Date. Die in der
Werbung verwendete Bildunterschrift
„Ein Gentleman wie ich oder Sie isst bei
Pigall's" steht für das ungezwungene
Pariser Lebensgefühl der 1920er-Jahre.

L'aristocrate bien mis n'en est pas encore
au stade atteint par sa compagne ivre
et à moitié nue. La légende publicitaire,
« Un gentleman comme vous et moi
dîne au Pigall's », exprime l'art de
vivre nonchalant dans le Paris des
années 1920.

RIGHT **Refectorium, c. 1920, Barcelona, Spain**

The embossed seal of Catalonia announces the inaugural year of a popular yet short-lived restaurant. The menu was immense—any kitchen would have been overwhelmed. Despite Albert Einstein's visit in 1923, the Refectorium went bankrupt in 1925.

Auf der geprägten katalanischen Siegelmarke steht das Eröffnungsjahr des beliebten Restaurants, das sich jedoch nicht lange gehalten hat. Die Speisekarte war immens – jede Küche wäre damit überfordert gewesen. Trotz eines Besuchs von Albert Einstein im Jahr 1923 musste das Refectorium 1925 Konkurs anmelden.

Le sceau catalan en relief annonce l'année inaugurale d'un restaurant très prisé, mais éphémère. Le menu, interminable, aurait englouti n'importe quelle cuisine. Malgré la visite d'Albert Einstein en 1923, le Refectorium fait faillite en 1925.

OPPOSITE *SS Roma*, **Navigazione Generale Italiana, 1927**

Tramonto sul Tevere

PIROSCAFO

ROMA

Fredy

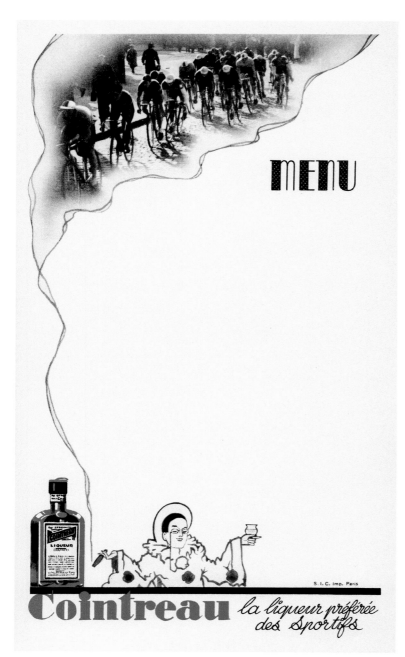

In the smoke of Pierrot's cigar, a diner sees a photograph of a Tour de France race. *Pourquoi pas?* Cointreau is the preferred liqueur of athletes.

Im Rauch von Pierrots Zigarre ist das Foto eines Tour-de-France-Rennens zu sehen. *Pourquoi pas?* Cointreau ist der Lieblingslikör von Sportlern.

La fumée du cigare de Pierrot se déploie sur une photographie du Tour de France. Et pourquoi pas? Puisque que le Cointreau est «la liqueur préférée des sportifs».

RIGHT **La Faisane, c. 1925, France**

OPPOSITE **Hôtel Claridge, 1929, Paris, France**

A banquet at the elite Claridge celebrated the novel field of medical aviation. Red Cross planes were especially necessary for the rescue of injured men serving in the colonies. After the meal, everyone was to enjoy an Aviateurs cigar, courtesy of the French tobacco monopoly.

Im elitären Claridge feierte man den Einsatz von Flugzeugen für die Medizin mit einem Bankett. Die Flieger des Roten Kreuzes wurden vor allem für die Rettung verletzter Soldaten in den Kolonien eingesetzt. Nach dem Essen gab es für jeden Gast eine Aviateurs-Zigarre, die vom französischen Tabakmonopol zur Verfügung gestellt wurde.

Un banquet donné au très select Claridge célèbre le domaine nouveau de l'aviation médicale. Les avions de la Croix-Rouge sont très utiles au sauvetage d'hommes blessés en service aux colonies. Après le repas, chacun peut apprécier un cigare Aviateurs, offert par le monopole français du tabac.

PREMIER CONGRÈS INTERNATIONAL DE L'AVIATION SANITAIRE

BANQUET

du Jeudi 16 Mai 1929, à 20 h. 30.

HOTEL CLARIDGE

THE BERKELEY
Xmas Dinner

ABOVE **Christmas dinner, The Berkeley, 1924, London, England**

OPPOSITE **Ciro's, 1925, Paris, France**

PARIS
LONDRES
DEAUVILLE
MONTE-CARLO

Ph. Rosen, Grav., Paris

Ph. ROSEN, Gr., Paris.

Les Ambassadeurs - Deauville

According to ancient legends, the
Roman ruins near Saint-Cyr-sur-Mer
were inhabited by wine-drinking nymphs.
Their vintages of choice were the red and
rosé Bandols from Provence.

Alten Legenden zufolge wurden die
römischen Ruinen bei Saint-Cyr-sur-Mer
von weintrinkenden Nymphen bewohnt.
Ihre bevorzugten Tropfen waren die
Rot- und Roséweine von Bandol aus der
Provence.

Selon les légendes antiques, les ruines
romaines situées près de Saint-Cyr-sur-
Mer étaient peuplées de nymphes buvant
du vin. Leurs crus favoris étaient les
rouges et rosés de Bandol.

Les Ambassadeurs - Deauville

TAURŒNTUM
BLANC.ROSÉ.ROUGE

MENU

TAURŒNTUM

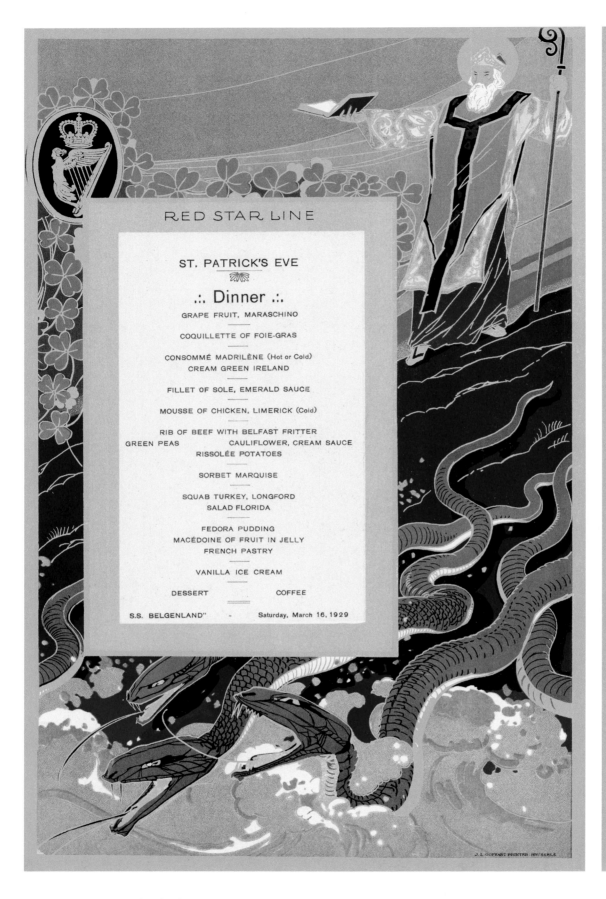

RED STAR LINE

ST. PATRICK'S EVE

.:. Dinner .:.

GRAPE FRUIT, MARASCHINO

COQUILLETTE OF FOIE-GRAS

CONSOMMÉ MADRILÈNE (Hot or Cold)
CREAM GREEN IRELAND

FILLET OF SOLE, EMERALD SAUCE

MOUSSE OF CHICKEN, LIMERICK (Cold)

RIB OF BEEF WITH BELFAST FRITTER
GREEN PEAS   CAULIFLOWER, CREAM SAUCE
RISSOLÉE POTATOES

SORBET MARQUISE

SQUAB TURKEY, LONGFORD
SALAD FLORIDA

FEDORA PUDDING
MACÉDOINE OF FRUIT IN JELLY
FRENCH PASTRY

VANILLA ICE CREAM

DESSERT   COFFEE

S.S. BELGENLAND"   -   Saturday, March 16, 1929

J. L. GOFFART PRINTER BRUSSELS.

WHERE THERE
IS NO VISION
THE PEOPLE
PER

ABOVE & OPPOSITE *SS Belgenland,*
Red Star Line, 1929

Le Perroquet

Nice

OPPOSITE Le Perroquet, c. 1929,
Nice, France

BELOW LEFT Savoy, 1929, London,
England

BELOW RIGHT Hotel Royal, 1929,
Rome, Italy

"MUMS"

Tuesday, 22nd January, 1929.

———

SAVOY RESTAURANT.   LONDON.

Hotel Royal
Rome

Le Lido
DES CHAMPS ELYSÉES
LA PLAGE DE PARIS
LES THERMES
LA MUSIQUE
LA DANSE
LE SPECTACLE

Le Lido
des Champs-Elysées
La Plage de Paris
Le premier Casino du Monde
76, Avenue des Champs-Elysées, 76
TÉLÉPHONE : Elysées 52-41 et la suite — Elysées 53-63
R. C. Seine 244.304 B
OUVERTURE à 8 h. 30 du matin
Bains de Piscine
Hammam
TARIF
Hammam
Piscine
Par carnets de 50 tickets... 15. » 12.50
— 20 — ... 17.50 15. »
— 10 — ... 20. » 17.50
Par unité .... 25. » 20. »
Bains de lumière — Massages — Leçons de natation
BAR AMÉRICAIN — BUFFET
(Tarif habituel des Bars, de 5 à 12 francs)
De 11 h. à 13 h. — L'HEURE DE L'APÉRITIF
Consommations de 5 à 12 francs
De 16 h. 30 à 19 h. 15 - Le THÉ DANSANT du LIDO
JAZZ - TANGO - ATTRACTIONS
Consommations : 25 fr. pâtisserie comprise
De 19 h. 30 à 21 h. - L'HEURE du COCKTAIL
Places assises côté Bar au tarif du Bar (5 à 12 fr.)
De 20 h. 30 à 22 h.
LE DINER DU LIDO
Avec musique et chants - PRIX FIXE : 45 fr.
De 22 h. à 3 heures
LA SOIRÉE DANSANTE
Attractions — Danses — Ballets
3 Orchestres réputés
L'heure de Venise (féerie sur l'eau)
Champagne à partir de 125 fr.
Consommations : 30 francs
(Toutes taxes comprises)
La tenue de soirée n'est pas de rigueur
L'entrée du LIDO
n'est pas payante
La consommation ou le ticket
d'hydrothérapie sont seuls
obligatoires
PHILIPS éclaire LE LIDO
Hamilton, 212, rue St-Maur
M. D. 7904

Le Lido des Champs-Élysées, 1928, Paris, France

Occupying a basement on the Champs-Élysées, an elaborate playground including a casino, pool, bars, and musical entertainment delighted Parisians as well as visitors from all parts of the world. The unusual fan-shaped program and menu reflects the essence of Paris in the 1920s.

In einem Keller an den Champs-Élysées erfreute ein kunstvoller Spielplatz mit Casino, Poolbillard, Bars und musikalischer Unterhaltung sowohl Pariser als auch Besucher aus aller Welt. Das ungewöhnliche, fächerförmige Programm und die Speisekarte spiegeln das Pariser Flair der 1920er-Jahren wider.

Abrité dans un sous-sol des Champs-Élysées, ce terrain de jeu chic comprend un casino, une piscine, des bars et des spectacles musicaux qui ravissent Parisiens et visiteurs du monde entier. L'insolite menu-programme en forme d'éventail est la quintessence du Paris des années 1920.

Restaurant Marguery, 1929, Paris, France

RESTAURANT MARGUERY

Café de Paris, c. 1929, London, England

"Coming down the stairs" was the café's sly way of suggesting the presence of the restaurant's small and intimate *cabinets particuliers*. One evening, American writer Julian Street passed a couple ascending "two by two like the animals into the Ark" into one of the "secluded and insinuating private dining rooms."

Der Name Coming Down the Stairs (Die Treppe herunterkommen) war eine versteckte Anspielung auf die kleinen, intimen *cabinets particuliers* des Restaurants. Eines Abends ging der amerikanische Schriftsteller Julian Street

an einem Paar vorbei, das „zu einem der abgeschlossenen und vieldeutigen privaten Speiseräume" hinaufstieg, „paarweise wie die Tiere auf die Arche".

La mention «Descendre les escaliers» (*Coming down the stairs*) est une façon habile d'indiquer la présence de cabinets particuliers dans ce restaurant. Un soir, l'écrivain américain Julian Street croisa un couple qui montait «deux par deux comme des animaux dans l'arche» pour gagner l'un des «salons isolés et pleins de sous-entendus».

OPPOSITE **Moët & Chandon, 1929, France**

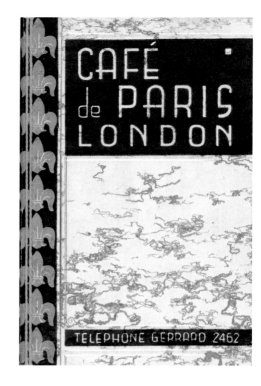

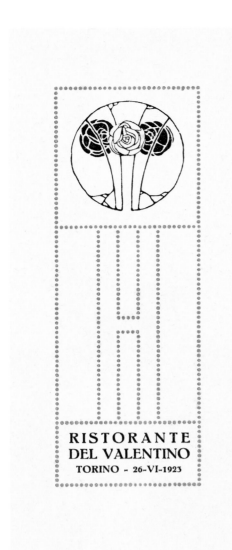

RISTORANTE
DEL VALENTINO
TORINO - 26-VI-1923

PALAIS DE LA MÉDITERRANÉE
NICE

MENU

THE CARLTON - MONTE-CARLO

VENDREDI 16 DÉCEMBRE 1927

Grand Diner de Gala

LE CÉLÈBRE ○○○○○○○○

MURRAY PILCER

○○○○ & SON ORCHESTRE

OPPOSITE **The Berkeley, c. 1926, London, England**

ABOVE LEFT **Ristorante del Valentino, 1923, Torino, Italy**

ABOVE RIGHT **Palais de la Méditerranée, 1929, Nice, France**

LEFT **The Carlton, 1927, Monte Carlo, Monaco**

Louis Icart's 1926 painting for an Ayala Champagne advertisement was recycled for a gala event at a casino-restaurant in Monte Carlo.

Das Gemälde, das Louis Icart 1926 für eine Ayala-Champagner-Werbung anfertigte, wurde bei einer Galaveranstaltung in einem Casino-Restaurant in Monte Carlo wiederverwendet.

La peinture réalisée en 1926 par Louis Icart pour une publicité du champagne Ayala ressert pour une soirée de gala dans un casino-restaurant de Monte-Carlo.

Montebello 37

OPPOSITE **Restaurant des Ambassadeurs, 1937, Paris, France**

On a July evening in 1937, executives of the *Exposition Internationale des Arts et Techniques dans la Vie Moderne* hosted a dinner for the foreign commissioners. The image of Marianne in a *tri-coloré* robe and flanked by 42 national flags hints at the guest list.

An einem Juliabend des Jahres 1937 veranstalteten die Leiter der Exposition Internationale des Arts et Techniques dans la Vie Moderne ein Abendessen für die ausländischen Vertreter. Die

Marianne ist in die Trikolore gekleidet und wird von 42 Nationalflaggen flankiert, die erkennen lassen, wer auf der Gästeliste stand.

Par un soir de juillet 1937, les organisa-teurs de *l'Exposition internationale des arts et techniques dans la vie moderne* offrent un dîner aux délégués étrangers. Cette Marianne vêtue d'une robe tricolore et flanquée des drapeaux de 42 nations donne une idée des invités.

ABOVE *SS Hansa*, **Hamburg-Amerika Line, c. 1937**

Restaurant

AUX CHAUFFEURS

19 Boul. Beaumarchais — PARIS IV

R. C. Seine 54 B 686

Tél. ARC. 96-44

Menu du DIMANCHE.

LE SOIR: POTAGE AUX LÉGUMES 60.

RADIS BEURRE 120. MUSEAU DE BOEUF 150. ANCHOIS 150. SARDINES 150. F. DE HARENG 120.
TOMATE 150. BETTERAVE 120. CONCOMBRE 150. CÉLÉRIS RÉMOULADE 140. MAQUEREAUX 3 ANE 170.
SAUCISSON À L'AIL 150. ROSETTE 170. SAUCISSE D'AUVERGNE 170. RILLETTES 150. OEUF MAI.SE 120.
AND.LLE DE VIRE 150. PÂTÉ DE CAMPAGNE 150. PÂTÉ DE LAPIN 180. LA TERRINE DU CHEF 300.
LES 6 ESCARGOTS DE BOURGOGNE 200. LES OEUFS DE SAUMON SUR TOAST 350.
LES 6 PRAIRES AU CITRON 180.

POISSONS: HOMARD À L'ARMORICAINE 850. LES 6 ÉCREVISSES AU CHABLIS 450.
LANGOUSTE MAYON.SE P.S.G. LE SAUMON GRILLÉ A LA SAUCE BÉARNAISE 470.
LA SOLE OU LA TRUITE MEUNIÈRE 450. LES QUENELLES DE BROCHET NANTUA 390.
LES COQUILLES S.T JACQUES SAUTÉES PROVENÇALE 500.

ENTRÉES: LA BOUCHÉE A LA REINE 300. LA TÊTE DE VEAU RAVIGOTTE 330.
LES OEUFS COCOTTE À LA CRÈME 280. LE PIED DE COCHON GRILLÉ P. FRITES 280.
OEUFS AU PLAT 160. OMELETTE CHAMPIGNONS 380.

LE GIGOT D'AGNEAU RÔTI AUX HARICOTS PANACHÉS 420.
LE JARRET DE PORC DEMI-SEL AUX LENTILLES 390.
LE RÂBLE DE LAPIN AU SAUVIGNON 480.

LE TOURNEDOS GRILLÉ HENRI IV 500.	LA CÔTE DE VEAU A LA BASQUAISE 480.
L'ANDOUILLETTE DE CAMPAGNE 300.	LE RIS DE VEAU BRAISÉ MADÈRE 480.
LE MIXED-GRIL VERT-PRÉ 390.	LE PIGEON RÔTI AUX PETITS-POIS 540.

LE ROGNON DE VEAU ENTIER EN COCOTTE 650.
LE 1/4 POULET RÔTI P.ES PONT-NEUF 420.

GRILLADES: CÔTES DE PORC 350. D'AGNEAU 390. CHATEAUB. 500. ENTRECÔTE-MINUTE 390.

P.ES PONT-NEUF 100	P.T SUISSE À LA CRÈME 80	FRAMBOISES MEL 3A 350. GATEAU BASQUE 300
HARICOTS VERTS 170	YAOURT 50. CANTAL 80	TARTE MIRABELLES 190. MOUSSE CHOCOLAT 130.
POISSONS NOUV.X 120	BRIE. CAMENBERT 80	G.CE VANILLE-PRALINE 100. MENDIANT. PLUM 100.
CHAMPIGNONS S.ES 180	ROQ.T 100. GRUYÈRE 80	RAISIN 120. POIRE 100. POMME 100. NOIX 90
LENTILLES 100	REBLOCHON 80	BANANE 90. CRÈME CHANTILLY 160.
SALADE 100	CRÈME FRAICHE 160	PARFAIT GLACÉ 180. CASSADE 180.

NOS VINS
RECOMMANDÉS:
LE SAUVIGNON
DE RELILLY
BEAUJOLAIS
MORGON
ET LE
ROSÉ
EN PICHET

Après le repas
un Cognac
COURVOISIER ★★★
fait honneur à qui l'offre
et plaisir à qui le boit

OPPOSITE **Restaurant Aux Chauffeurs, c. 1930, Paris, France**

The restaurant's name and illustrated vignette suggest a place favored by livery drivers and limousine chauffeurs.

Der Name des Restaurants und die illustrierte Vignette deuten auf ein Lokal hin, das bevorzugt von Taxifahrern und Limousinen-Chauffeuren aufgesucht wurde.

Le nom du restaurant et l'illustration indiquent que l'endroit est fréquenté par des cochers en livrée et des conducteurs de limousine.

RIGHT **La Coupole, 1931, Paris, France**

La Coupole was a latecomer to the café-crowded Boulevard du Montparnasse when it opened on December 20, 1927. Within a block one could already visit La Select, Le Dôme, La Rotonde, and La Closerie des Lilas, at one time Ernest Hemingway's favorite.

Mit seiner Eröffnung am 20. Dezember 1927 war La Coupole ein Nachzügler auf dem von Cafés gesäumten Boulevard du Montparnasse. Im selben Häuserblock gab es bereits La Select, Le Dôme, La Rotonde und La Closerie des Lilas, einst Ernest Hemingways Lieblingscafé.

À son ouverture, le 20 décembre 1927, La Coupole est le dernier né des nombreux cafés du boulevard du Montparnasse. Non loin de là, on peut se rendre au Select, au Dôme, à La Rotonde et à La Closerie des Lilas, le préféré d'Ernest Hemingway.

MONT-PARNASSE

Les artistes du monde entier s'inspirent à La Coupole ---!!

DINER

Couvert 3.   19 JUIN 1931

MELON la Tranche 12 ··   Beurre 1,50. Citron 1,50   1 2 Grapp Fruit 8 ··
                               Oeuf à la gelée la pièce 3 ··
                  Jambon de Parme 10 ··   Saumon fumé anglais 10 ··
        Caviar de Saumon 8 ·· Caviar pressé 12 ·· Caviar frais la cuiller 25 ··

POTAGES
Crème argentée 4 ·· Saint Germain aux croutons 4 ·· Maraichère 4 ··
        Consommé vermicelle 4 ·· Madrilène chaud et froid 4 ··

POISSONS
FILETS DE SOLE COUPOLE 12 ··
LES TRUITES DE NOTRE VIVIER AU BLEU 16 ·· BOUILLABAISSE 15 ··
Saumon froid sauce verte 10 ·· Suprême de barbue Chauchat 12 ·· Turbot mousseline 12 ··
Darne de saumon au vin du Rhin 15 ·· Merlan Déjazet 9 ·· Friture Panachée 10 ··
Ecrevisses à la nage la pièce 4 · Grenouilles Provençale 16 ·· Homard Nage 14 ··
        Homard et Langouste mayonnaise par personne 22 ··
              TRUITE A LA GELEE DE CHAMBERTIN 16 ··

ENTREES
LE QUARTIER D'AGNEAU MIREILLE 10 ··
CURRY DE VOLAILLE A LA FAÇON HINDOUE 16 ·· MEDAILLON DE RIS DE VEAU CLAMART 12 ··
Poussin en cocotte chez-soi 16 ·· Côte de veau Biarritte 12 ·· Jambon aux Epinards 10 ··
        Tournedos Persanne 15 ·· Rognons Brochette Vert-Pré 9
                   Caille Saint-Hubert 16 ··

GRILLADES & ROTIS
Entrecôte minute 12. Mutton chop, côte de porc, de mouton, de veau 12. Mixed grill 13
Pigeon rôti 24. Grain 60. Reine 75 Canard Nantais 75. Poussin 30 · Caille 16 ··
                   Carré et Selle d'Agneau

BUFFET FROID
Veau 9. Langue 9. Roastbeef 9. Jambon d'York 9 Assiette anglaise 17 ··
Terrine maison 8. Foie gras de Strasbourg 16 · Poulet froid la cuisse 16 l'aile 17

LEGUMES
ASPERGES 12 ·· Spaghetti Italienne 6 ·· Epinards au beurre 6 ··
Tomates persillées 6 ·· Haricots verts 10 ·· Artichaut vinaigrette 7 ·· Sweet Corn 7 ··
        Céleri demi glace 7 ·· Petits Pois Française 10 ·· Aubergines 7 ··
             Cêpes provençale 10 ·· Chou-fleur 6 ·· Courgettes 7 ··
                   Salade de saison 4 ··

DESSERTS
                                     Fromages 3. par personne
MELON la Tranche 12 ·· Fraises des Bois 12 ·· Fraises 10 ·· STRAWBERRY SHORT CAKE 10 ··
1/2 Grapp Fruit 8 ·· Cerises 8 ·· Cherries Pie 6 ·· Amandes vertes 6 ·· Abricot la pièce 1 ··
Ananas au kirsch 4 ·· frais 8 ·· Orange 3 ·· Pomme 8 ·· Banane 2 ·· Poire 8 ·· Pêche 8 ··
Tarte maison 4 ·· aux Fraises 5 ·· Compotes 6 ·· assorties 10 ·· Fruits rafraîchis 8 Brugnon 5 ··
Confitures de Bar-le-Duc 6 ·· Pâtisserie 2 ·· Gaufrettes bretonnes 2 Crème d'Isigny 4 ··
Pot de crème vanille, café, chocolat, caramel 5 ·· Glace Pralinée 4 ·· Parfait 8 ··
Mousse au kirsch 5. au chocolat 5 ·· Café liégeois 6 ·· Coupe Jack 6 ·· Pêche Melba 10 ··
Hot fudge 6 ·· Tranche plombière 5 ·· Banane Royale 8 ·· Fraises Melba 10 ··
                   SOUFFLE PIERROT 7 ··
                        CAFE 3 ··

Notre devise est
TOUJOURS A MIEUX
comme notre nom

AMIEUX-FRÈRES

Menu

CASSOULET DES GASTRONOMES

IMP. E & A. ROBERT FRÈRES · NANTES · PARIS

OPPOSITE **Rôtisserie de la Reine Pédauque and Café américain, c. 1930, Paris, France**

An imaginative folding die-cut advertises two different yet popular restaurants. Located just around the corner from the opera house, Café américain was the place for late suppers, rotisserie chicken, and its "Five o'Clock Artistique," a high tea happy hour that the owners called the most elegant in Paris. Rôtisserie de la Reine Pédauque, located just a few blocks away, was named after a novel by Anatole France.

Diese einfallsreiche, faltbare und gestanzte Speisekarte wirbt für zwei verschiedene, aber beliebte Restaurants. Gleich um die Ecke von der Oper lag das Café américain, das sich hervorragend für späte Abendessen, Grillhähnchen und den sogenannten Five o'Clock Artistique eignete – eine High-Tea-Happy-Hour, die den Besitzern zufolge die eleganteste in ganz Paris war. Nur wenige Straßen weiter befand sich die Rôtisserie de la Reine Pédauque, benannt nach einem Roman von Anatole France.

Ce menu découpé et dépliant fait ingénieusement la publicité de deux restaurants différents, mais également prisés. Non loin de l'Opéra, le Café américain propose des soupers tardifs, du poulet rôti et son « Five o'Clock Artistique », l'heure du thé à prix réduit, que les propriétaires présentent comme le plus élégant de Paris. À quelques rues de là, la Rôtisserie de la reine Pédauque tire son nom d'un roman d'Anatole France.

FÉDÉRATION NATIONALE
DE L'AUTOMOBILE DU CYCLE DE L'AÉRONAUTIQUE ET DES TRANSPORTS

COMITÉ D'ORGANISATION DES EXPOSITIONS INTERNATIONALES DE L'AUTOMOBILE DU CYCLE ET DES SPORTS

BANQUET
DU JEUDI 8 OCTOBRE 1931
SOUS LA PRÉSIDENCE
Mʳ PAUL DOUMER
PRÉSIDENT DE LA RÉPUBLIQUE

A L'OCCASION DE LA 25ᵉᵐᵉ EXPOSITION INTERNATIONALE DE L'AUTOMOBILE DU CYCLE ET DES SPORTS

MUSÉE PERMANENT
DES COLONIES
EXPOSITION
COLONIALE

Gueuleton de la Sureté

4ème

Desarm Tours

11 décembre 1932

Menu

Hors d'œuvres Variés
une douzaine d'Huitres
Poisson
Homard à l'Américaine
Entrée
Ris de Veau Toulousaine
Relevé
Lièvre à la Royale
Légumes
Asperges mousseline
Rôt
Fléchaise sur cresson
Salade Mimosa
Fromages
Dessert
Soufflé maison au cointr-
Champagne Martel - café
Marc 1900

Rouge Coteau du Cher 1930

Bourgueil 1928

Pommard Vieille réserve

rosé athée 1929

Vouvrié sec 1919

OPPOSITE **4ᵉ Gueuleton de la Sûreté, 1932, Tours, France**

Every December, the police force of Tours threw itself a *gueulton* (raucous) dinner, and each year a different talented cartoonist drew the distinctive, humorous menus. The common graphic theme was policemen with prisoners, including captive mice in prison stripes overseen by a large jail cat enjoying its meal.

Die Polizei von Tours gönnte sich jeden Dezember ein *gueulton*, ein rustikales Festessen, für das immer ein anderer talentierter Karikaturist eine charakteristische, humorvolle Speisekarte zeichnete. Das übliche grafische Thema waren Polizisten mit Gefangenen, etwa eine große Katze als Aufseher, die gefangene Mäuse in Streifenkleidung überwacht, während sie ihre Mahlzeit genießt.

Chaque année en décembre, la police de Tours s'offre un gueuleton et demande à un nouveau dessinateur talentueux d'illustrer le menu reconnaissable et humoristique. Le thème est toujours le même : des policiers encadrant des détenus, et des souris en tenue rayée de prisonnier dansant sous l'œil d'un gros chat qui se repaît.

BELOW LEFT **5ᵉ Gueuleton de la Sûreté, 1933, Tours, France**

BELOW RIGHT **6ᵉ Gueuleton de la Sûreté, 1934, Tours, France**

RESTAURANT
DÉGUSTATION

LA POULARDE S.t GERMAIN

7, RUE GOZLIN - PARIS-6E
TÉLÉPH.
MÉTRO : S.t GERMAIN-DES-PRÉS

ses Spécialités

Sa Cave

Menu du Bar — Couvert 40f.

Boisson { Vin rouge la Carafe 75cl - 140 frs
    d° — la 1/2 - 70 "
    Bière Spéciale 33cl - 55 "

Fines de Belon la Dz 300 - Claire la Dz 150

Filets de Harengs 80 - Sardines beurre 80
Céleri Rémoulade 80 - Filets d'Anchois 90
Jambon blanc 150 - Paté de Campagne 90

Omelette fines herbes 80 - Oeuf filat au Bacon 130
Moules marinière 100 - Escargots de Bourgogne 1/2 Dz 100

Entrecôte pommes P.tes neuf 200
Escalope de Veau aux Endives 200
Côte de mouton, Vert pré 200
1/4 de Poulet de Bresse Rôti 450

Pommes P.tes neuf 50 - Haricots verts 90
Endives meunière 90 - Salade 60

Fromage 60 - Fruits S.S.
Patisserie 70 - Glace du jour 90
Crème au Caramel 60

R. C. Seine 290.625 B

Imp. R. Dabremelle, Paris

menu

menu

MENU

offert par Le Petit Journal

"Le meilleur des digestifs : Un COGNAC MARTELL"

OPPOSITE **La Poularde St. Germain, c. 1934, Paris, France**

A stenciled menu with the traditional purple ink presented the offerings at the zinc bar of a Saint Germain bistro. The hand corrections—no *Belon* or *Claire* oysters that evening; and the *crème au caramel* as an afterthought—told the casual diner what was available.

Auf der per Matrize mit traditioneller lila Tinte vervielfältigten Speisekarte standen die Speisen, die an der Zinntheke eines Bistros in Saint-Germain gereicht wurden. Anhand der handschriftlichen Korrekturen – keine Belon- oder Claire-Austern und die *Crème au Caramel* als nachträgliche Ergänzung – wussten die Gäste, welche Gerichte verfügbar waren.

Ce menu ronéotypé à l'encre violette traditionnelle présente les plats proposés par un bistrot de Saint-Germain-des-Prés. Le client de passage sait quels sont les plats disponibles grâce aux corrections manuscrites. Ce soir-là, pas d'huîtres fines de claire ou de Belon.

ABOVE LEFT & MIDDLE **Champagne J. Massing, c. 1931, France**

ABOVE RIGHT **Le Petit Journal and Cognac Martell, c. 1930, France**

RIGHT **Swedish American Line, 1935**

POMPEI DAL FORO ITALICO

"AUGUSTUS„

LLOYD TRIESTINO

F. Masino Bessi designed a series of sports-themed Art Deco covers for the Italian steamship line. They were used on a cruise aboard the *Conte Rosso*, sailing in the prewar waters of the Mediterranean Sea.

F. Masino Bessi entwarf für die italienische Dampfschifffahrtsgesellschaft mehrere Art-déco-Titelbilder mit Sportmotiven. Sie wurden auf einer Kreuzfahrt

der *Conte Rosso* verwendet, die in der Vorkriegszeit das Mittelmeer befuhr.

F. Massino Bessi est l'auteur d'une série de menus Art déco sur le thème des sports pour cette compagnie maritime italienne. Ces menus ont servi à bord du *Conte Rosso*, qui sillonnait la Méditerranée dans l'entre-deux-guerres.

OPPOSITE **Caves Monte Crasto, 1938, Portugal**

BELOW **Relais de la Belle Aurore, c. 1935, Paris, France**

SOCIÉTÉ NATIONALE D'ACCLIMATATION DE FRANCE
198, Boulevard Saint-Germain — PARIS VII·

26ᵉ DÉJEUNER AMICAL
du Samedi 30 Mai 1931
Sous la Présidence de M. Paul MORAND

Exposition Coloniale Internationale, Paris 1931
Restaurant de l'Afrique Occidentale Française
J. FOURNIER, Concessionnaire

ABOVE **Société Nationale d'Acclimatation de France, Exposition Coloniale Internationale, 1931, Paris, France**

Edouard Mérite's fine etching of a savage hunt suggests the main course at the society's banquet: *Phacochoerus africanus* (African warthog). According to the menu, the flesh of the "highly esteemed" warthog was "thinner than that of the European boar." This amicable meal was served at Paris Colonial Exposition's *Restaurant de l'Afrique Occidentale Française*. All the dishes and ingredients originated from African or Asian colonies.

Die schöne Radierung von Edouard Mérite spielt mit ihrer Jagdszene auf den Hauptgang des Vereinsbanketts an: Phacochoerus africanus (afrikanisches Warzenschwein). Laut der Speisekarte war das Fleisch dieses „überaus beliebten" Schweins „zarter als das des europäischen Wildschweins". Die Mahlzeit wurde in geselliger Runde im Restaurant de l'Afrique Occidentale Française auf der Pariser Kolonialausstellung serviert. Alle Gerichte und Zutaten stammten aus afrikanischen oder asiatischen Kolonien.

Cette belle scène de chasse aux animaux sauvages à l'eau-forte d'Édouard Mérite annonce le plat de résistance du banquet de la société : *Phacochoerus africanus* (phacochère d'Afrique). Selon le menu, la chair de cet animal « très estimé » est « moins épaisse que celle du sanglier européen ». Ce mets sympathique fut servi au *Restaurant de l'Afrique occidentale française*, à l'Exposition coloniale de Paris. Tous les plats et ingrédients venaient des colonies françaises d'Afrique ou d'Asie.

OPPOSITE New Year's Eve dinner, Maxim's, 1937, Paris, France

Well into the 1950s, Maxim's continued to use Sem's humorous drawing of the cheerful bellboy on its menus and as the *only* image in magazine advertisements. American writer Julian Street found the "diabolic little *chasseur*," with his "bright red pillbox cap," to be "sadly funny."

Bis weit in die 1950er-Jahre hinein verwendete das Maxim's Sems humorvolle Zeichnung des fröhlichen Pagen auf seinen Speisekarten und als einziges Bild in Zeitschriftenanzeigen. Auf den amerikanischen Schriftsteller Julian Street machte der „diabolische kleine *chasseur*" mit dem „hellroten Pillbox-Hut einen traurig-komischen Eindruck".

Jusque dans les années 1950, Maxim's illustre ses menus du chasseur jovial et amusant créé par Sem. C'est même la seule image qui orne ses publicités dans les magazines. Pour l'écrivain américain Julian Street, ce «diabolique petit chasseur» avec sa «toque rouge vif» a l'air «tristement drôle».

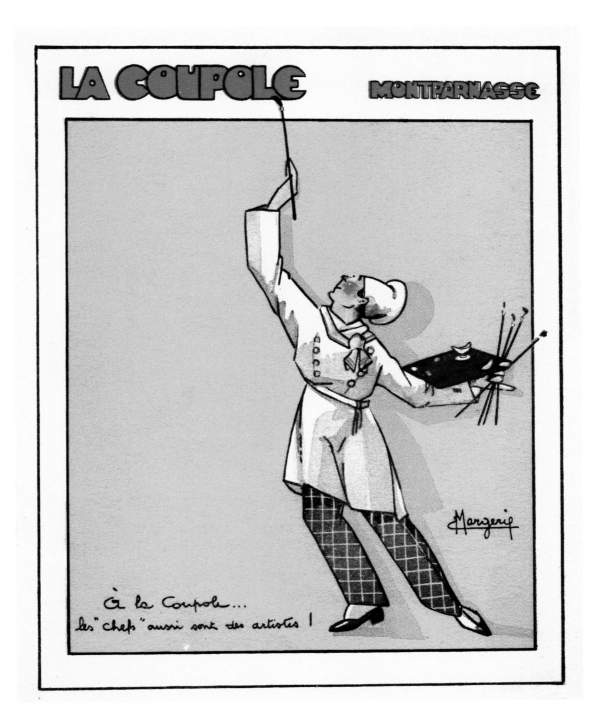

ABOVE La Coupole, 1934, Paris, France

E. Margerie created a cover that states the chef of La Coupole is also an artist. The cavernous interior, with its Art Deco details and the food served there, was often overshadowed by the popularity of the exterior terrace. In 1977 the owners reproduced Margerie's posterlike work as the cover for its 50th-anniversary souvenir.

Der Spruch auf dem von E. Margerie entworfenen Titelbild besagt, dass die Köche im La Coupole auch Künstler seien. Der riesige Innenraum mit seinen Art-déco-Details und die dort servierten Speisen wurde angesichts der beliebten Außenterrasse des Lokals oft nicht wahrgenommen. 1977 verwendeten die Besitzer Margeries plakatähnliches Werk erneut: als Titelbild für den Souvenirband zum 50. Jubiläum.

«À la Coupole, les chefs aussi sont des artistes», clame ce menu illustré par E. Margerie. La terrasse tant appréciée reléguait souvent à l'arrière-plan la vaste salle Art déco et les plats qu'on y servait. En 1977, les propriétaires reprennent cette illustration en forme d'affiche pour la couverture de leur menu-souvenir célébrant le 50e anniversaire.

OPPOSITE **Café de la Rambla, 1933, Barcelona, Spain**

A menu for a New Year's Eve dinner opens to reveal the evening's festive program. In a sign of the times, the text is in Catalan. The café was located in a section of Barcelona's famous pedestrian walkway called *La Rambla dels Ocells*, after the bird market that operated there for 150 years.

Diese Speisekarte eines Silvesterdiners enthält das festliche Programm des Abends. Der Text auf Katalanisch ist ein Zeichen der Zeit. Das Café lag auf einem Abschnitt der berühmten Flaniermeile La Rambla dels Ocells in Barcelona, benannt nach dem Vogelmarkt, der dort 150 Jahre lang seinen Standort hatte.

Ce menu d'un dîner de la Saint-Sylvestre s'ouvre sur le programme des festivités. Signe des temps, le texte est en catalan. Ce café se trouvait dans la célèbre avenue piétonne de Barcelone, la *Rambla dels Ocells*, qui tire son nom du marché aux oiseaux qui l'occupa pendant 150 ans.

A TAVOLA
BEVETE L'ACQUA DI
Nocera-Umbra
SORGENTE ANGELICA

CAFE DE LA RAMBLA

RESTAURANT

RAMBLA ESTUDIS
14 — CANUDA, 2
TELEFON 18321

31 DESEMBRE 1933
REVEILLON
DE ———— LA
— RAMBLA —

Artist Robert Roquin created a series of boldly executed sports-themed advertising menu sheets that were sponsored by the producers of the famous white wines of the Loire Valley.

Der Künstler Robert Roquin schuf eine Reihe kraftvoll gestalteter Werbespeisekarten mit Sportmotiven, die von den Herstellern der berühmten Weißweine aus dem Loiretal gesponsert wurden.

Robert Roquin est l'auteur d'une série de menus illustrés, d'une facture audacieuse, sur des thèmes sportifs. Les producteurs de célèbres vins blancs de la vallée de la Loire en sont les publicitaires.

LEFT *SS Minnetonka*, **Red Star Line, 1932**

OPPOSITE *SS Conte di Savoia*, **Italia Flotte Riunite, 1935**

A Tour in Italy *Capri*

NORMANDIE

Menu

DARAGNÈS

COMPAGNIE GÉNÉRALE TRANSATLANTIQUE
French Line

PAGE 230 *SS Normandie*, **Compagnie Générale Transatlantique, 1935**

Famous French painter and printmaker Jean-Gabriel Daragnès specifically designed a food-themed menu for the *Normandie*'s first year at sea.

Der berühmte französische Maler und Grafiker Jean-Gabriel Daragnès entwarf eigens für das erste Jahr, in dem die *Normandie* auf See war, eine Speisekarte mit kulinarischen Motiven.

Jean-Gabriel Daragnès, célèbre peintre et auteur d'estampes, est l'auteur d'un menu tout à fait gastronomique, créé spécialement pour la première année en mer du paquebot *Normandie*.

PAGE 231 **Lasserre, c. 1935, Paris, France**

A tribe of winged, bare-bottomed *petits marmitons* wreak havoc in E. Maudy's imagining of Lasserre's kitchen and the "20 chefs that you never see." French

scholar Michael Garval mused, "How might we reconcile this seeming contradiction between the spectacular ineptness of so many little chefs and the triumph of French gastronomy?"

In E. Maudys Vorstellung von Lasserres Küche und den „20 Köchen, die man nie zu Gesicht bekommt," treibt eine Gruppe geflügelter *petits marmitons* mit nackten Hintern ihr Unwesen. Der französische Gelehrte Michael Garval sinnierte dazu: „Wie lässt sich der scheinbare Widerspruch zwischen der eklatanten Unfähigkeit so vieler kleiner Köche und dem Triumph der französischen Gastronomie auflösen?"

Une tribu de petits marmitons aux fesses nues sème la pagaille dans la cuisine du restaurant Lasserre, telle que l'imagine E. Maudy, avec ses «vingt cuisiniers que vous ne voyez jamais». «Comment dépasser l'apparente contradiction entre l'incompétence spectaculaire de tous ces petits chefs et le triomphe de la gastronomie française?», se demande Michael Galvar, spécialiste du sujet.

OPPOSITE *SS Pennland*, **Red Star Line, 1936**

ABOVE **Ritz Hotel, 1933, Paris, France**

LEFT *RMS Franconia*, **Cunard White Star, 1936**

RISTORANTE

PONTE VECCHIO

FIRENZE

Night Club

LEFT **Ristorante Ponte Vecchio, c. 1938, Florence, Italy**

BELOW **Hôtel de Dieppe, c. 1935, Rouen, France**

A hotel bar just across from the town's train station offered a typical menu of cocktails, drinks, and numerous small dishes such as omelets and cheese plates.

Eine Hotelbar direkt gegenüber dem Bahnhof der Stadt hatte Cocktails, Getränke und zahlreiche kleine Gerichte wie Omeletts und Käseplatten auf ihrer typischen Speisekarte.

Le bar d'un hôtel situé en face de la gare de Dieppe propose une carte ordinaire, composée de boissons, de cocktails et de nombreux plats simples (omelette, plateau de fromages).

OPPOSITE **Restaurant Regas, 1936, Barcelona, Spain**

Simple lines delineate a busy scene at a Spanish train station before departure. Inside one finds the mimeographed menu from the station's restaurant for March 12, 1936, four months before the beginning of the Spanish Civil War.

Einfache Linien skizzieren eine geschäftige Szene auf einem katalanischen Bahnhof vor der Abfahrt eines Zuges. Im Inneren findet man die vervielfältigte Speisekarte des Bahnhofsrestaurants vom 12. März 1936, vier Monate vor Beginn des spanischen Bürgerkriegs.

En de simples traits est brossée la scène d'une gare espagnole animée, juste avant le départ d'un train. Derrière cette couverture se trouve le menu ronéotypé du restaurant de la gare, en date du 12 mars 1936, quatre mois avant le début de la guerre civile espagnole.

OLOSINAS SPAÑOLAS

Avenida Puerta del Angel, 4 ⚬ Teléfono 16737

BARCELONA

✳

Una anécdota de Luis XIV

En cierta ocasión preguntó Luis XIV de Francia, a un viejo servidor suyo:

—¿Cómo, siendo octogenario, conservas esta juvenil lozanía?

—Señor —contestó el interpelado—, desde niño que me acuesto sin cenar, más nunca sin merendar.

Los que quieran adoptar tan saludable norma, pueden escoger cada tarde entre las numerosas y selectas meriendas que se sirven en este acreditado Mesón, seguros de que no habrán de arrepentirse de ello y alcanzarán una plácida y agradable vejez.

SALVTACIÓN

Dios os gvarde, honradas gentes
qve a aqveste mesón llegáis!
Bven cobijo aqvi hallaredes
y si, en tanto reposáis,
de algo comer sois gvstosas,
bien vos podréis deleitar
con rica crema y con nata
qve fama ganado han.

Hay tortas, yemas, bizcochos,
mantecadas, dvlce pan,
chocolate mvy sabroso,
pastelón episcopal
y mil otras golosinas
qve del hispano solar
son honra y prez y apetecen
a qvien ha bven paladar.

Carta abierta

A los nuevos padres,
a los padrinos,
a los novios,
a los papás y mamás:

Han de saber Vuesas Mercedes, que mi Mesón es el lugar más adecuado para festejar aquellos acontecimientos familiares que son motivo de júbilo y alegría.

Bodas y bautizos, fiestas de Santo y cumpleaños, de Primeras Comuniones y de prometaje, pueden tener por corolario y remate un magnífico desayuno, merienda o piscolabis a base de las exquisiteces de dulcería que tanto placen a todos y que siempre tiene a vuestra disposición

EL MESONERO

El desayuno de Alfonso XII

En las cartas cruzadas entre el célebre literato y gastrónomo del siglo pasado doctor Thebussem y «Un Cocinero de S. M.» cuenta éste lo siguiente, refiriéndose al malogrado monarca Don Alfonso XII:

«Entre siete y ocho de la »mañana, a cuya hora ya ha »concluído los arreglos de su »tocado, pide chocolate. Don »Alfonso es muy afecto a este »desayuno español; lo prefiere »al café y al té de alemanes »e ingleses, y es tan de su »agrado la ardiente jícara va»ciada a fuerza de pan o de »bizcocho, que si en alguna »comida le sirvieran chocolate »en vez de ponche a la roma»na, lo tomaría distraído sin »extrañar la incongruencia».

Ya sabe, pues, el lector lo que debe hacer si quiere desayunar o merendar como un rey. Tomar el exquisito chocolate a la española que en muy variadas formas se sirve en este acreditado Mesón.

COMER DVLCES NO EMPALAGA
Y MAS SI ES OTRO QVIEN PAGA

MAS QVE AMARGAS MEDICINAS
GVSTAN BVENAS GOLOSINAS

WEIN-

KARTE

NORDDEUTSCHER LLOYD BREMEN

LEFT Vieille Cure, c. 1930, France

BELOW Chez Francis, c. 1930, Paris, France

OPPOSITE La Rioja Alta, 1939, Spain

PAGE 236 Golosinas Españolas, c. 1932, Barcelona, Spain

A well-known sit-down pastry shop offered baked sweets, ice cream, beverages, and *meriendas* (snacks). The large menu features reproductions of *Azulejos* (pictorial ceramic tiles with text), once used by Barcelona businesses for advertising. The tiles often incorporated verse. This shop's favorite was, *"Comer dulces no empalaga/Y mas si es otro quien paga"* ("Eating sweets isn't repugnant/If it is someone else who pays.")

Eine bekannte Konditorei mit Sitzgelegenheiten bot süße Backwaren, Eiscreme, Getränke und *meriendas* (Snacks) an. Auf der großen Speisekarte sind Azulejos (Keramikfliesen mit Bildern und Schrift) zu sehen, die Unternehmen in Barcelona einst als Werbung – oft mit Versen – verwendeten. Der Lieblingsspruch dieses Geschäfts lautete: „Comer dulces no empalaga / Y más si es otro quien paga" (Süßes zu essen ist nicht verwerflich / Vor allem wenn ein anderer zahlt.)

Ce célèbre salon de thé propose pâtisseries, glaces, boissons et meriendas (en-cas). Le grand menu est illustré de reproductions d'azulejos (céramiques peintes et portant des inscriptions), dont les entreprises de Barcelone se servaient pour leurs publicités, souvent rimées. Selon les vers préférés de cette pâtisserie, « *Comer dulces no empalaga/Y mas si es otro quien paga* » (« Il n'y a pas de mal à manger des choux à la crème/Tant qu'on ne les paie pas soi-même »).

PAGE 237 *SS Bremen*, Norddeutscher Lloyd Bremen, c. 1932

el mejor vino de mesa es el de la sociedad de cosecheros de vino

Menú

La Rioja Alta — Haro

8 - 9 - 35

— Almuerzo —

Entremeses variados

Arroz valenciana

Lecherillas à la financière

Langosta salsa mayonesa

Chuletas de lomo a la parrilla

Patatas lionesas

— Postres —

Helado crema vainilla

Fruta queso

LIT. Vᵈᵃ DE VALVERDE-RENTERIA

SOUVENIR DU DINER

OFFERT PAR LE PRÉSIDENT DE LA RÉPUBLIQUE

A LL. MM. LE ROI GEORGE VI

ET LA REINE ELIZABETH

le 19 Juillet 1938

RF

MENU

Consommé Rubis aux Quenelles
Crème Altesse

Médaillons de Langouste à la Marigny

Fricandeau de Dindonneau à la Rosemonde

Petits Pois de Bordeaux à la Française

Délices d'Ortolans à la Rossini
Salade Vendôme

Glace Coppélia

Corbeilles de Fruits
Dessert

VINS

Château Yquem 1923
Château Haut-Brion 1924
Chambertin 1923
Champagne Pommery brut 1928
Porto Commendador

Stern. Gr. Paris.

S. A. CHAMPAGNE POMMERY & GRENO

REIMS

LEFT **Banquet for King George VI and Queen Elizabeth of England, Palais de l'Élysée, 1938, Paris, France**

While the clouds of war were gathering during the summer of appeasement, the French president hosted a state dinner. The royal visitors were treated to standard *cuisine classique*.

Während im Sommer der Appeasement-Politik ein Krieg drohte, veranstaltete der französische Präsident ein Staatsdinner. Die königlichen Gäste wurden mit der üblichen *cuisine classique* verwöhnt.

Alors que les nuages de la guerre s'accumulent pendant l'été de l'apaisement, le président français donne un dîner d'État au cours duquel le couple royal déguste une cuisine classique.

OPPOSITE **Larue, c. 1930, Paris, France**

For many decades, Larue was *the* place. American writer Julian Street said its "excellent cuisine and wines, its cosmopolitan clientele, its Tzigany orchestra, and its florid decorations" made Larue "the sort of place one would select for a first meal in the *Ville-Lumière* after two years spent on the veldt."

Viele Jahrzehnte lang war das Larue das Lokal schlechthin. Der amerikanische Schriftsteller Julian Street beschrieb es wie folgt: „Wenn man nach zwei Jahren in der südafrikanischen Steppe zum ersten Mal wieder in der Stadt des Lichts essen gehen wollte, fiele die Wahl wegen der ausgezeichneten Gerichte und Weine, der kosmopolitischen Gäste, des Tzigany-Orchesters und der blumigen Dekoration zweifellos aufs Larue."

Pendant des décennies, le restaurant Larue est incontournable. Pour l'écrivain américain Julian Street, « sa cuisine et ses vins excellents, sa clientèle cosmopolite, son orchestre tzigane et ses décorations abondantes » en font « le genre d'endroit que l'on choisit pour son premier repas dans la Ville Lumière après deux ans d'errance dans la savane ».

RESTAURANT LARUE

27, rue Royale

F-4

OPPOSITE Chez Jenny, 1937, Paris,
France

RIGHT Restaurant Maison Rouge,
c. 1937, Strasbourg, France

BELOW LEFT Restaurant Hongrois,
1937, Paris, France

BELOW RIGHT Crêpes Gavotte, 1938,
France

COVENTRY STREET

CORNER HOUSE

BRASSERIE TARIFF

PROPRIETORS J LYONS & CO. LTD.

OPPOSITE Coventry Street Corner House, 1938, London, England

A stylish menu mirrors the Art Deco furnishings inside J. Lyons's flagship brasserie. The British chain eventually became the largest food-serving operation in the world, with over 250 shops.

Die stilvolle Speisekarte spiegelt die Art-déco-Einrichtung der Vorzeigebrasserie von J. Lyons wider. Die britische Restaurantkette entwickelte sich mit über 250 Läden zum größten Gastronomiebetrieb der Welt.

Cet élégant menu Art déco reproduit le mobilier que l'on trouve chez J. Lyons, grande brasserie londonienne. Cette chaîne britannique deviendra la plus importante du monde, avec plus de 250 restaurants sur toute la planète.

RIGHT *SS Deutschland*, Hamburg-America Line, 1937

Menu

LINGE EN LIN
BONNE MAISON

OPPOSITE Bonne Maison, c. 1938, France

Jean Facon-Marrec's expertise in designing advertising posters—from soda and perfume to men's hats and women's undergarments—is apparent in his thoughtful design, with the menu area mimicking a white linen tablecloth.

Jean Facon-Marrecs Expertise in der Gestaltung von Werbeplakaten für alle möglichen Artikel – von Limonade über Parfüm bis hin zu Herrenhüten und Damenunterwäsche – zeigt sich in diesem durchdachten Design, bei dem der Bereich für die Speisekarte einer weißen Tischdecke gleicht.

Tout le savoir-faire de Jean Facon-Marrec, dessinateur de publicités pour des boissons gazeuses, des parfums, des chapeaux pour hommes et de la lingerie féminine, est concentré dans cet astucieux dessin, où la zone réservée au menu imite une nappe blanche.

RIGHT Hôtels Splendide, Royal, and Excelsior, 1939, Aix-les-Bains, France

A few weeks before the declaration of war, Fourrures Weil introduced its latest fur creations to guests at a Provence resort.

Wenige Wochen vor Beginn des Zweiten Weltkrieges stellte Fourrures Weil den Gästen eines Resorts in der Provence seine neuesten Pelzkreationen vor.

Quelques semaines avant la déclaration de guerre, les fourrures Weil présentent leurs dernières créations dans des hôtels d'Aix-les-Bains.

Splendide - Royal - Excelsior
Aix-les-Bains

BELOW Dinner for U.S. Ambassador Joseph P. Kennedy, Claridge's, 1938, London, England

An austere design masks behind-the-scenes power struggles. In the early years of World War II, John F. Kennedy's father argued aggressively against American support to the United Kingdom.

Das strenge Design verbirgt die Macht-kämpfe, die sich hinter den Kulissen abspielten. In den frühen, überaus brutalen Jahren des Zweiten Weltkriegs trat John F. Kennedys Vater als US-Botschafter vehement gegen eine amerikanische Unterstützung Großbritanniens ein.

Ce austère menu dissimule des conflits de pouvoir ourdis en coulisses. Peu avant la Seconde Guerre mondiale, le père de John F. Kennedy était farouchement opposé au soutien américain au Royaume-Uni.

RIGHT Chez Quaglino, 1938, London, England

Nine years after its festive opening, Chez Quaglino recycled Merini's original, gilt-stamped design. The gala dinner menu for the 1938 fête was printed on silk and mounted inside. From its beginning, aristocrats favored the chic restaurant.

Neun Jahre nach seiner feierlichen Eröffnung verwendete das Chez Quaglino erneut Merinis ursprüngliches Design mit Goldprägung. Für das Fest von 1938 wurde die Galadinner-Speisekarte auf Seide gedruckt und innen eingeklebt. Seit seiner Eröffnung war das schicke Restaurant besonders bei Aristokraten beliebt.

Neuf ans après son inauguration, Chez Quaglino reprend le dessin original de Merini, estampillé à l'or. Le menu du dîner de gala de 1938 est imprimé sur soie et collé à l'intérieur. Ce restaurant chic eut d'emblée les faveurs des aristocrates.

OPPOSITE Café Bagdad, 1938, Paris, France

A Parisian nightclub known for its fashion shows and music presented a Christmas Eve dinner, which included *Salade Bethleem*. A program featuring Cuban tunes and swing numbers was rounded out by the American vaudeville performer Eddie Foy.

Ein Pariser Nachtklub, der für Modeschauen und Musik bekannt war, veranstaltete ein Abendessen an Heiligabend, bei dem auch ein *Salat Bethlehem* serviert wurde. Das Programm mit kubanischen Melodien und Swing-Stücken wurde vom amerikanischen Varietékünstler Eddie Foy abgerundet.

Célèbre pour ses défilés de mode et sa musique, ce cabaret parisien propose un dîner du 24 décembre, où l'on sert une « salade Bethléem ». L'artiste américain de music-hall Eddie Foy présente des airs cubains et des danses swing.

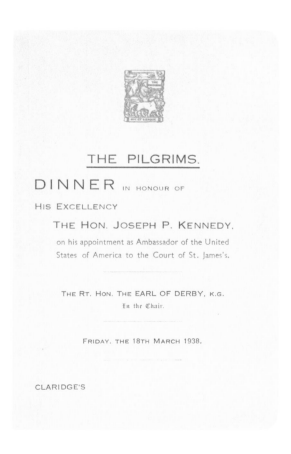

Bagdad

COMPAGNIE MARITIME BELGE (L. R.)
Société Anonyme - ANVERS.

S. S. ELISABETHVILLE
55 me. Voyage.

1ᵉ CLASSE
Mercredi
28
Janvier 1931

DINER

Potage Longchamps - Consommé Célestine

Cabillaud poché Diplomate
Pommes nouvelles

Epinards Mère Louisette

Contrefilet rôti
Haricots princesses au beurre
Pommes château

Pâtisserie

Fruits

Café   Thé

C. M. B. (L. R.)   S.S. ELISABETHVILLE
1ᵉ Classe   55ᵐᵉ Voyage

MENU

Iᴱᴿ DÉJEUNER

Fruits

Compote de prunes

Quaker Oats

Hareng fumé

Œufs : Miroir, Poché
ou brouillés Clamart

Lard grillé

Saucisson de Boulogne - Saucisson d'Anvers

Fromages : Gouda, Brie, Edam

Confiture   Marmelade

Petits pains   Toast

Café   Chocolat   Thé

Vendredi 30 Janvier 1931

OPPOSITE **Café and Restaurant
Hoftheater, 1938, Munich, Germany**

ABOVE *SS Elisabethville*, **Compagnie
Maritime Belge, 1931**

Belgian painter Charles Van Roose
created a series of colonial-themed
paintings for menu cards. Although the
accommodations were first-class, the
food—Quaker Oats *and* smoked her-
ring?—suggests otherwise.

Der belgische Maler Charles van Roose
schuf mehrere Gemälde mit Kolonialthe-
men für Speisekarten. Obwohl die
Unterkünfte erstklassig waren, scheint
das beim Essen – Haferflocken und
geräucherter Hering? – eher nicht der Fall
gewesen zu sein.

Charles Van Roose, peintre belge, est
l'auteur d'une série de menus peints, aux
thèmes coloniaux. Si les cabines sont de
première classe, les plats, qui réunissent
flocons d'avoine et hareng fumé, ne
semblent pas tenir le même rang.

Owned by the German Labour Front, the *Wilhelm Gustloff* took loyal National Socialist Party members on a "party cruise" to help vacationers maintain their "Strength Through Joy" spirit. In 1939 the ship was transferred to the German navy, and on January 30, 1945, while evacuating thousands of German personnel and refugees from Poland, a Soviet submarine torpedoed the boat, resulting in 9,300 deaths. Journalist Sarah Begley called it "the worst maritime tragedy in history."

Auf der *Wilhelm Gustloff*, die der Deutschen Arbeitsfront gehörte, unternahmen treue NSDAP-Mitglieder „Urlauberfahrten zur See", um „Kraft durch Freude" zu schöpfen. 1939 wurde das Schiff der Marine übergeben. Am 30. Januar 1945, bei der Evakuierung Tausender deutscher Zivilisten, Soldaten und Flüchtlinge aus Polen, torpedierte ein sowjetisches U-Boot das Schiff. 9.300 Menschen kamen ums Leben. Die Journalistin Sarah Begley bezeichnete das als „die schlimmste maritime Tragödie der Geschichte".

Propriété du DAF (Front allemand du travail), le *Wilhelm Gustloff* embarque à son bord des fidèles du parti nazi pour entretenir leur « force par la joie ». En 1939, le navire est intégré à la marine allemande. Alors qu'il évacue des milliers de soldats et réfugiés allemands de Pologne le 30 janvier 1945, il est torpillé par un sous-marin soviétique. 9 300 personnes périssent dans « la pire tragédie maritime de l'histoire », selon la journaliste Sarah Begley.

BELOW *SS Mexique*, **Compagnie Générale Transatlantique, 1936**

Firenze-Ponte Vecchio

Napoli-La strada di Posillipo

S. Marino

Roma-Tempio di Vesta e di Castore

PAGE 253 & THIS PAGE *SS Rex*, **Italian Line, 1939**

Vittorio Accornero de Testa's serenely colored views of Italy seem too grand for menus used on the tourist class of the *Rex*, but passengers in that class—ranked between second and third—received fine souvenirs. Gastronomically, tourist class on the most famous of the Italian liners was uninspired. By the time of this cruise in 1939, Italians were already tightening their belts. Launched in 1932, this sleek darling of the fascist regime was docked by 1940.

Vittorio Accornero de Testas farbenfrohe Darstellungen Italiens mögen etwas zu grandios für Speisekarten für die Touristen auf der *Rex* erscheinen, aber die Passagiere, die in der zweiten und dritten Klasse reisten, erhielten damit schöne Souvenirs. In gastronomischer Hinsicht war die Touristenklasse des berühmtesten italienischen Passagierschiffs eher fantasielos. Zum Zeitpunkt dieser Kreuzfahrt im Jahr 1939 schnallten die Italiener den Gürtel bereits enger. Das 1932 zu Wasser gelassene, elegante Lieblingsschiff des faschistischen Regimes wurde 1940 außer Betrieb genommen.

Ces images colorées et paisibles de l'Italie vue par Vittorio Accornero de Testa sont bien élégantes pour les menus des classes touristes du Rex. Mais ce sont de beaux souvenirs pour les passagers de ces deuxième et troisième classes, où la gastronomie n'est pas au rendez-vous, à bord du plus célèbre des paquebots italiens. À l'époque de cette croisière, en 1939, les Italiens se serrent déjà la ceinture. Lancé en 1932, ce navire racé, chéri du régime fasciste, restera à quai en 1940.

OPPOSITE *SS Nieuw Amsterdam*, **Holland-America Line, 1938**

THE TURQUOISE

PRECIOUS STONES

LEFT Trocadero Grill Room, 1937, London, England

To describe its own special brand of late dinner, the Trocadero invented a portmanteau using the French words for dinner and night, *dinuit*, and declared the dance floor the *trocaberet*.

Um seine Version eines späten Abendessens zu beschreiben, erfand das Trocadero eine Kreuzung aus den französischen Begriffen für „Abendessen" und „Nacht": *dinuit*. Die Tanzfläche erklärte es zum *trocaberet*.

Pour qualifier ses dîners de fin de soirée, le Trocadero de Londres crée des mots-valises à partir du français, *dinuit* (dîner et nuit) et *trocabaret* pour désigner sa salle de danse.

OPPOSITE Shanghai Restaurant, c. 1937, Amsterdam, Netherlands

Beyond the gilt-stamped dragon awaits a descriptive list in Chinese and Dutch of 58 dishes.

Hinter dem goldgeprägten Drachen verbirgt sich eine ausführliche Liste von 58 Gerichten in chinesischer und niederländischer Sprache.

Ce dragon estampillé à l'or défend une liste de 58 plats, en chinois et en néerlandais.

SHANGHAI

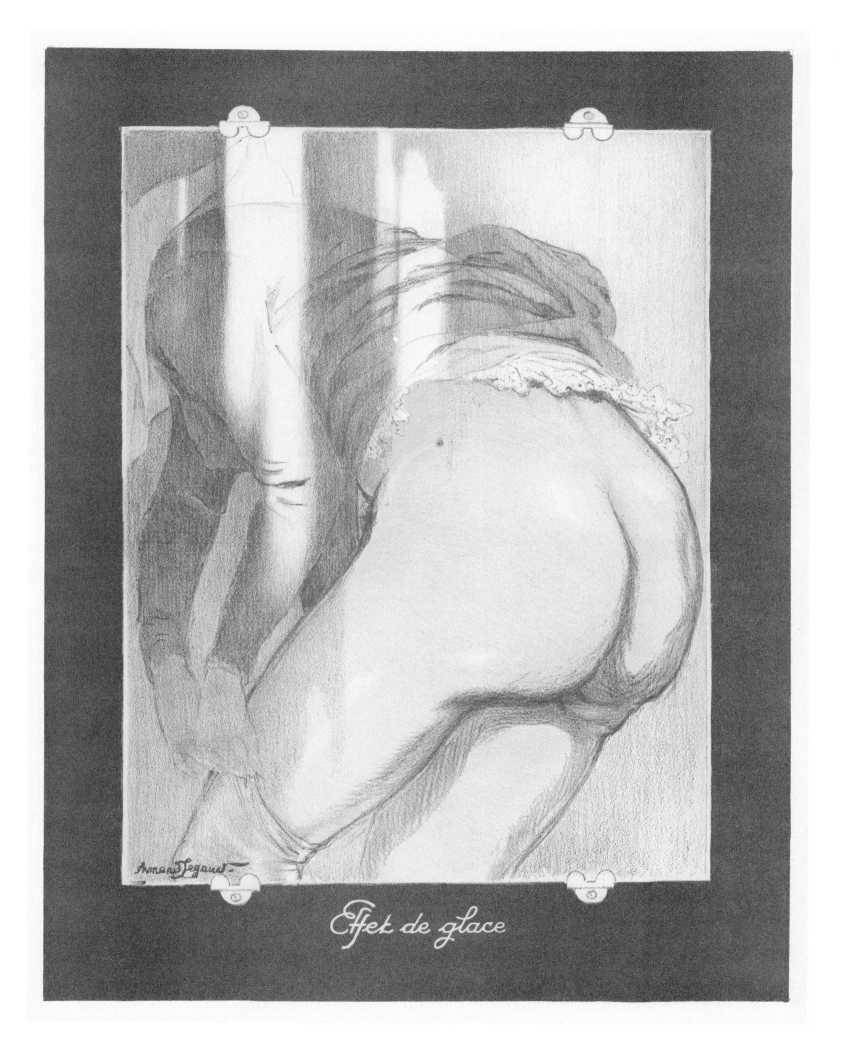

Effet de glace

MOTORLINER

diner
de
gala

kungsholm

HOFF

OPPOSITE **Banquet for Le Cornet, Restaurant du Havre, 1936, Paris, France**

Le Cornet, a male-only club consisting of wealthy, artistic, and literary-minded members, created provocative menu covers for its banquets.

Le Cornet, ein Männerklub mit wohlhabenden, künstlerisch und literarisch interessierten Mitgliedern, entwarf für seine Bankette Speisekarten mit provokanten Titelbildern.

Le Cornet, un club exclusivement masculin composé d'amateurs d'art et de littérature fortunés, a créé pour ses banquets des couvertures de menus provocantes.

ABOVE *MS Kungsholm*, **Swedish American Line, 1936**

LEFT & BELOW **Maison Prunier, c. 1938, Paris, France**

The French painters René-Yves Creston and Mathurin Méheut were both natives of Brittany and specialists in marine scenes. They were excellent choices to illustrate the origins of the seafood that appeared fresh daily at Maison Prunier restaurants and the workers who harvested the bounty.

Die französischen Maler René-Yves Creston und Mathurin Méheut kamen beide aus der Bretagne und waren auf Marinemotive spezialisiert. Niemand hätte die Herkunft der Meeresfrüchte, die jeden Tag frisch in die Restaurants des Maison Prunier geliefert wurden, und die Arbeiter, die sie ernteten, besser illustrieren können als sie.

Tous deux peintres de marines natifs de Bretagne, René-Yves Creston et Mathurin Méheut illustrent à la perfection la provenance des fruits de mer servis chaque jour dans les restaurants de la Maison Prunier, ainsi que les travailleurs qui les récoltent.

OPPOSITE **Restaurant des Ambassadeurs, Casino de Cannes, 1931, France**

RETOUR DE PÊCHE A L'ESTURGEON
« LES CALLONGES »
(CHARENTE INFÉRIEURE)

Pb, Rosen, Gr., Paris

Restaurant des Ambassadeurs
Casino de Cannes

Gᵈ CAFÉ . RESTAURANT
AUX ARMES DE LA VILLE
Ch. VALENTIN PROPRIETAIRE.

Place de l'Hôtel de Ville   66 Rue de Rivoli

ICY DANSA ESMERALDA

G.Riom

RESTAURANT AU 1ᵉʳ ÉTAGE   3 AVRIL

Couvert : 2.00

Hors-d'Œuvre   HORS D'ŒUVRE VARIES 7.00 P.Pers.(non suivis d'un plat de Viande 10.00)
HUITRES DE CLAIRES dz 8,50 ½ dz 4.50   ARMORICAINES dz 10.00 ½ dz 5.50
½ citron 0.75 Pain Bis Beurré 0.50
ESCARGOTS DE BOURGOGNE dz 10.00   PETITS GRIS dz 5.00
Croustade de Champignons 5.00 Saucisson Chaud aux Pommes à l'huile.....7.50
Terrine de Garenne.......6.00 Jambon de Pays....4.00 Jambon de Paris...3.50
Saucisson de Ménage.......3.50 Rillettes Maison..3.50 Fromage de Tête...3.50
Pâté de Campagne.......3.50 Sardines à l'huile 4.00 Thon à l'huile...4.00
CAVIAR NOIR Toast citron 20.00 Filets de Maquereaux au vin blanc.......4.00

Potages   LE POTAGE CULTIVATEUR......3.00   Consommé au Vermicelle........3.00
La Soupe à l'Oignon Gratinée.........4.00

Œufs   Omelette Chasseur..........7.50   Oeufs Poélés au jambon........7.50
Oeufs Brouillés au Fromage...........6.00

Poissons   Moules Marinière.....5.00 Quenelles Truffées Nantua 12.50
Coquille St Jacques...6.00 Filets de Sole Maison.....12.50
Raie au beurre noir...7,50 Maquereau Grillé Mtre d'Hotel 5.
Truite Meunière.....12.50 Truite du Vivier au Blau..12.50
HOMARD A L'ARMORICAINE 20.00 *Bouillabaisse* 45

Plats du Jour   LE COUSCOUS DE POULET A L'ALGÉRIENNE.......15.00
LA PIECE DE BOEUF ROTIE POMMES MOUSSELINE 9.50
LA PALETTE SALEE AUX LENTILLES..............9.50
LE JARRET DE VEAU AUX PETITS POIS...........9.50

Entrées   EMINCE DE GIGOT MADERE ET CHAMPIGNONS 9.50 Tripes Mode 8.50
Rognons Sautés au Chablis 9.50 Minute Poélée Valentin..9.50
Cote de Pré Salé Tyrolienne 9.50 Tournedos Rossini....16.00
Le 1/4 de Volaille rôtie aux Pommes Soufflées.........15.00
Choucroute Garnie 8.00 Choucroute Strasbourgeoise....12.00
FOIE GRAS A LA GELEE DE PORTO la Tranche 10.00

Grillades
(de 15 à 18 minutes)   CHATEAUBRIAND AUX POMMES SOUFFLEES............16.00
Rumpsteak 9.50 Cote de Veau 9.50 Cote de Mouton...9.50
Sauce Béarnaise sup. 2.00

Buffet Froid   Assiette Anglaise 8.50   Terrine de Garenne 6.00
Jambon de Pays.....8.00   Jambon de Paris.....7.00

Légumes Petits Pois à la Française 5.00   Endives Meunière....4.00
Cêpes à la Provençale......7.50   Lentilles..........3.50
Asperges à l'huile........8.00   Salsifis Frits.......4.00
Pâtes de Gênes au beurre...3.50   Haricots Verts.......5.00
SALADES: Endives 3.00 Laitue 4.00

Fromages   Le Plateau de Fromages 4.00   Le Véritable Munster 3.50
Creme Fraiche 3.50   Yoghourth 2.00

Entremets et Desserts   GATEAU DU JOUR: LE PUDDING DIPLOMATE 4.00
Tarte Maison 4.00 Tarte Alsacienne 4.00 Creme Caramel 4.00
Glaces Variées 4.00 Tranche Napolitaine 4.00 Parfait 4.00
Pêche Melba 7.00 Meringue Glacée 4.50 Mousse Chocolat 3.50
Crêpes Suzette au Gd Marnier 8.00 Beignets de Pommes..4.00 Banane 1.75
Gelée de Raisin 4. Mendiant 3. Ananas Frais 6.50 Poire 4. Pomme 3. Orange 3.

Poccardi

PARIS-ROME

DEJEUNER DU 21 NOVEMBRE 1938

F. 25.50

CAFE 2,-- CAFE CREME 2,25

<table>
<tr><td>

Menu Prix Fixe

DONNANT DROIT A

Couvert

Boisson

1er Plat

2e Plat

Légume ou Fromage

Dessert

BOISSONS AU CHOIX

1/2 Piémont blanc

Carafe de Chablis

1/4 coteau Toscane blanc

1/2 carafe Bordeaux blanc

1/2 carafe Bourgogne blanc

1/2 Piémont rouge

1/4 coteau Toscane rouge

1/2 carafe Bordeaux rouge

1/2 carafe Bourgogne rouge

Carafe vin de la Champagne viticole

1 bouteille de bière

1/2 Evian

1/2 Saint-Galmier

1 Santeuil naturelle

La boisson comprise dans ce repas est reprise en échange de vin supérieur pour 3.50

Contenance des carafes

Chablis	42	cl.
Champagne	42	—
1/2 Piémont	44	—
1/2 Bordeaux	34	—
1/2 Bourgogne	34	—
1/4 fiasco	47	—

DEMANDEZ

NOTRE CARTE DES VINS

CAFÉ 2— INFUSION 2.50

EN SUPPLEMENT du MENU

UN FRUIT OU UN DESSERT

3.—

</td>
<td>

1° PLAT

8 FINES CLAIRETTES "CITRON - PAIN NOIR - BEURRE"
HORS D'OEUVRE ASSORTIS (par personne, beurre compris) OU
ASSORTIMENT : JAMBON DE PARME SAUCISSON DE MILAN MORTADELLE DE BOLOGNE
BEURRE supp. 1,25 — JAMBON A LA GELEE — 2 SARDINES & BEURRE — ANCHOIS & BEURRE
FENOUILS — CAVIAR supplément 3,50 ARTICHAUT VINAIGRETTE — SAUMON FUME — THON A L'HUILE

PARMENTIER AUX CROUTONS — CONSOMME VERMICELLE — MINESTRONE GENOISE

OEUFS PLAT AUX TRUFFES DU PIEMONT — OMELETTE AU JAMBON — OEUFS COQUE

TRUITE MEUNIERE — 10 ESCARGOTS DE BOURGOGNE
RAIE AU BEURRE NOIR — FRITURE D'EPERLANS — SOLE FRITE Supp. 1.50

RISOTTO MILANAISE — SPAGHETTI NAPOLITAINE
LES PATES OU RISOTTO CUITS EXPRES supplément 1,50 — GARNITURE PASTICCIATE supplément 2,--
LES PATES, POISSONS ET OEUFS PEUVENT ETRE CHOISIS COMME 1° OU 2° PLAT

2° PLAT

OSSO BUCO AU RISOTTO
LONGE DE VEAU BRAISEE AUX CEPES
ESCALOPE MILANAISE AUX POMMES SAUTEES
ROGNONS SAUTES AU CHABLIS
PLAT DE COTE AUX LEGUMES (AVEC POULET supplément 2,--)
TRIPES GENOISE
GARNITURE DE TRUFFES BLANCHES Supp. 3.--
1/4 FAISAN SUR CROUTONS SUPP. 3.--
PERDREAU SUR CROUTONS OU AU RISOTTO POUR 2 PERS. SUR COMMANDE Supplément 10,--
CIVET DE LIEVRE AUX TAGLIATELLE SUPP. 5.--

ENTRECOTE — MUTTON CHOPP — COTE DE VEAU GRILLES POMMES FRITES

1/4 POULET ROTI FROID ET CHAUD supplément 2,50
1/2 POULET GRILLE POUR 2 PERSONNES supplément 5.--
1/4 POULET A L'ITALIENNE supplément 2.50

FROIDS : CONTREFILET MAYONNAISE — ASSIETTE ANGLAISE — FOIE GRAS A LA GELEE Supp 5,50

LÉGUMES OU FROMAGES

POMMES SAUTEES — POMMES FRITES — COURGETTES FRITES — ARTICHAUT A L'HUILE
CHOUX FLEURS MILANAISE — EPINARDS EN BRANCHES — SALADE DE SAISON
HARICOTS VERTS FRAIS AU BEURRE D'ISIGNY — PETITS POIS A LA FRANÇAISE
ASPERGES A L'HUILE supp. 2,50
SPAGHETTI A LA NAPOLITAINE A LA PLACE DES LEGUMES supp. 1,25

FROMAGES ASSORTIS — YAOURT — PETIT SUISSE — CREME D'ISIGNY

DESSERTS

Le dessert peut etre remplacé par un fromage
ENTREMETS : CREME CARAMEL — 1/2 GLACE (demandez le parfum du jour)
CASSATA SICILIENNE ET PARFAIT AU CAFE (supplément 2,--)
POIRE MELBA supp. 3.50 — PECHE MELBA Supp. 3.50

SOUPE A LA ROMAINE — TARTE MILANAISE — PETITS GATEAUX PASTA FROLLA

FRUITS : 1 MANDARINE — MENDIANT — FENOUILS - DATTES — RAISIN - POMME
1 GRAPP FRUIT supp. 1.-- — 8 NOIX FRAICHES — ORANGE — BANANE — POIRE
COUPE DE FRUITS RAFRAICHIS — ANANAS FRAIS AU KIRSCH Supp. 1.50
COMPOTES : PRUNEAUX — POIRES — PECHES
CONFITURES ASSORTIES MAITRE FRERES — MARMELADE DE POMMES

</td>
</tr>
</table>

COUPE D'ASTI VIGNOBLE UNE BOUTEILLE D'ASTI SPUMANTE POUR DEUX PERSONNES EN ECHANGE D'UN VIN Supplément 5.--
POCCARDI 2,75

CHIANTI, CHABLIS, BORDEAUX OU BOURGOGNE le verre 3.--

PAGE 262 **Aux Armes de la Ville,**
c. 1937, Paris, France

PAGE 263 **Poccardi, 1938, Paris, France**

A famous French gastronomic club
held a monthly, ritualized tasting at the
Château du Clos de Vougeot, a 16th-
century Cistercian castle in Burgundy.
The membership dressed in fancy robes
and swilled wine from silver tastevins.

Ein berühmter französischer Gastroklub
veranstaltete jeden Monat eine rituali-
sierte Weinprobe im Château du Clos
de Vougeot, einer Zisterzienserburg aus
dem 16. Jahrhundert im Burgund. Die
Mitglieder trugen fantasievolle Gewän-
der und schlürften Wein aus silbernen
Probierschalen.

Ce célèbre club œnologique organise
chaque mois une dégustation au Clos de
Vougeot, château cistercien du XVIe siècle
en Bourgogne. Ses membres se vêtent de
costumes particuliers et dégustent le vin
dans des tastevins en argent.

The Christian Democratic Party (1924–
1940) commemorated its 1938 convention
by having the menu printed on silk. The
souvenir features an image of the host
city's main coal mine, *Puits Couriot.*

Die Parti Démocrate Populaire (1924–
1940) feierte ihren Parteitag 1938, indem
sie die Speisekarte auf Seide drucken
ließ. Auf dem Souvenir ist die wichtigste
Zeche der Gastgeberstadt abgebildet, die
Puits Couriot.

Le parti démocrate populaire (1924–1940)
fête son congrès de 1938 grâce à un menu
imprimé sur soie, où est illustré le puits
Couriot, principale mine de charbon de
la ville d'accueil.

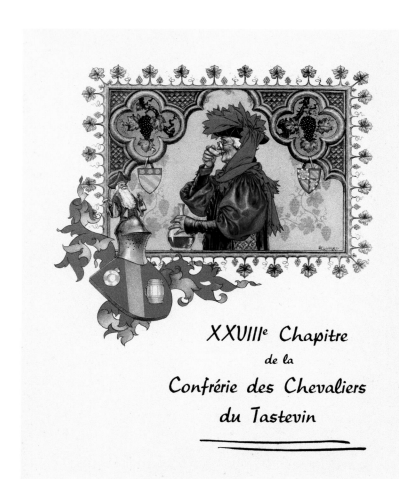

THANKSGIVING DINNER

22 NOVEMBRE 1945

OPPOSITE **Thanksgiving dinner, Hôtel Pierre, 1945, Paris, France**

BELOW **Stock menu sheet, c. 1943, Italy**

BUON APPETITO

Colazione

Auberge de la Bohème, c. 1947, Paris, France

OPPOSITE **Restaurant Viking, 1946, Copenhagen, Denmark**

When it comes to Nordic cuisine, one is either a Viking or not. Here, the specialty of the house was the hearty *Poularde Rôtie à La Viking*, which required a minimum of two persons—or one Viking.

Wenn es um nordische Küche geht, ist man entweder ein Wikinger oder eben nicht. Die Spezialität dieses Hauses war die herzhafte *Poularde Rôtie à La Viking*, die für mindestens zwei Speisende gedacht war – oder einen Wikinger.

Avec la cuisine scandinave, on est viking ou on ne l'est pas. La spécialité de cette maison est la revigorante « poularde rôtie à la Viking », pour deux personnes… ou un Viking.

RESTAURANT "VIKING"
KØBEN-HAVN

Den 18/4. 1946.

	Kr. 3.50		Kr. 3.00	
Sildeanretning:		Osteanretning:		¹/₂ Hummer efter Størrelse:

Prøv vor enestaaende Hummersalat . . Kr.

Specialitet de la Maison:	POULARDE RÔTIE À LA VIKING Kr. 8.00
	Ristet Tomat, Champignonspurée, Selleribund m. Spinat en branches, pom. saute, sce. Bearnaise, (mindst 2 Couv.) à Kr.

Supper:	Legeret Suppe Magenta Kr. 2.00	
	Klar Suppe Danois Kr. 1.75	Bouillon m/ Æg Kr. 1.50

Fiske-Specialitet:	Filet de Sole Bianco kr. 6.50
	Søtungefilet dampet i Hvidvin m/ Chalotteløg, Champignons Asparges, Erter og Fløde. (15 gr. Smør.)

Fiskeretter:

Stegt Rødspættefilet m/ Tartarsauce......4.00
Pighvarfilet Hongroise...................4.50 15gr.
Bækforel meuniere m/Champ. og Bearnaise.4.50 15gr.

Kødretter:

Spædlammesteg m/Compot og Salat...9.00
"Vikingegryden" ....5.50 15gr.
Kogt Kylling i Champignonssauce...6.50

Ægge- og Mellemretter:

Bløde Æg i Sennepssauce................2.00
Laxesalat Indienne.....................4.50
Brochette m/Fuglelever,Nyre og Champ. ..4.00 15gr.

Gemyseretter:

Champignons à la creme............5.00
Selleribunde Florentine...........2.50 logr.
Slikasparges Pompadour............4.50 25gr.

Desserter:	Karamelrand m/ Fløde Kr. 1.50	
	Pære Cardinal Kr. 2.00	Crepes Surprise Kr. 2.50 lo gr. Smør

Frisk Frugt:	Druer	Appelsin	Pære	Æble	Blommer
	Kirsebær Melon Nødder		Jordbær	Hindbær	Brombær

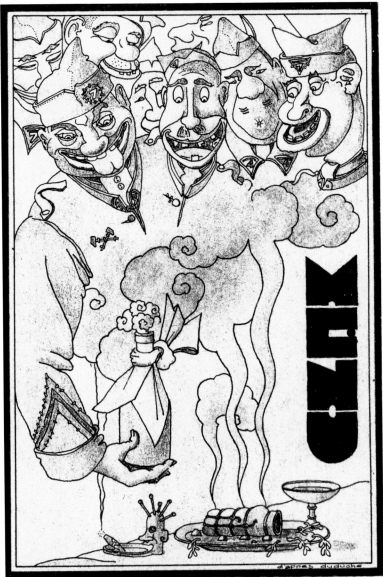

OPPOSITE & ABOVE **Stock menu cards,
c. 1945, Germany**

Charles Duchêne was a prisoner of war
in Stalag VIII-C, a German camp located
near present-day Żagań, Poland. An imaginative artist, he created a series of purple
mimeographed cards reminiscent of
underground comics. Each card mocked
the food, or lack thereof, at the POW
camp infamous for permanent malnutri-
tion and contagious diseases.

Charles Duchêne war Kriegsgefangener
im Stalag VIII-C, einem deutschen Lager
in der Nähe der heute polnischen Stadt
Żagań. Als fantasievoller Künstler schuf
er eine Reihe mimeografierter lila Karten,
die an Untergrund-Comics erinnerten.
Jede Karte spottete über das Essen – oder
dessen Nichtvorhandensein – in den
Kriegsgefangenenlagern, die für permanente Mangelernährung und ansteckende
Krankheiten berüchtigt waren.

Charles Duchêne avait été prisonnier de
guerre au Stalag VIII-C, camp allemand
situé près de l'actuelle Żagań, en Pologne.
Doté d'une grande imagination, il est
l'auteur de menus ronéotypés à l'encre
violette, semblables aux bandes dessinées
clandestines. Chaque menu raille la
nourriture servie (pas toujours) dans un
camp de prisonniers tristement célèbre
pour sa mauvaise alimentation et ses
maladies contagieuses.

Brindis monástico cantado en la comida servida

Generalísimo Don Francisco Franco,

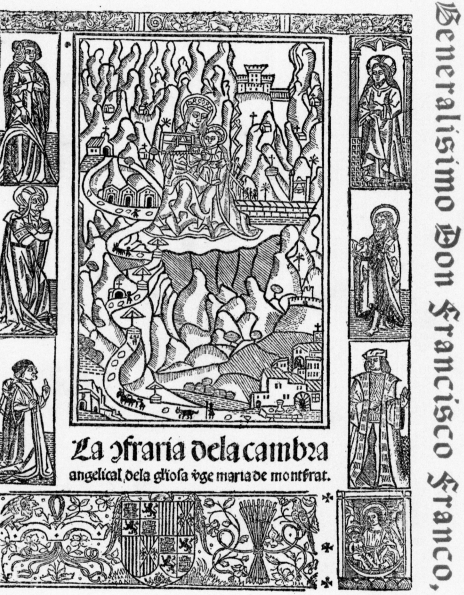

La ofraria dela cambra
angelical dela gliosa vge maria de montfrat.

en ocasión de su visita al Monasterio de Montserrat en
el III Aniversario de su liberación. Veinticinco de
enero del año mil novecientos cuarenta y dos.

On the second anniversary of the "liberation" of Spain, a quasi-canonization of "El Caudillo" was held, complete with prayers, chants, and a banquet.

Am zweiten Jahrestag der „Befreiung" Spaniens fand eine Art Heiligsprechung von „El Caudillo" inklusive Gebeten, Gesängen und einem Bankett statt.

Pour le deuxième anniversaire de la « libération » de l'Espagne est organisée une quasi-canonisation du Caudillo, avec prières, cantiques et banquet.

The Red Cross sent food packages to French soldiers imprisoned in Germany during World War II. The succinct number of items equaled "a week of nourishment."

Während des Zweiten Weltkriegs schickte das Rote Kreuz Lebensmittelpakete an französische Soldaten, die in Deutschland inhaftiert waren. Das wenige Essen war die „Verpflegung für eine Woche".

La Croix-Rouge américaine envoie des vivres aux soldats français prisonniers en Allemagne pendant la Seconde Guerre mondiale. Leur faible quantité équivaut à « une semaine d'alimentation ».

Form 1631-L
May 1941

American Red Cross
Standard Package No. 6
for
Prisoner of War
FOOD
CONTENTS:

Evaporated Milk, irradiated	1 14½ oz. can
Lunch Biscuit (hard-tack)	1 8 oz. package
Cheese	1 8 oz. package
Instant Cocoa	1 8 oz. tin
Sardines	1 15 oz. can
Pork Meat	1 12 oz. tin
Corned Beef	1 12 oz. tin
Sweet Chocolate	2 6 oz. bars
Sugar, Granulated	1 4 oz. package
Powdered orange concentrate (Vitamin C)	1 7 oz. jar
Prunes	1 16 oz. package
Instant Coffee	1 4 oz. can
Cigarettes	2 20's
Smoking Tobacco	1 2¼ oz. package

Lista

Caldo Imperial en taza

Espuma de ganso Pavía

Filetes de lenguado Yuste

Pollo en cazuela Bailén

Bomba pasta Montserrat

Pastelería

Frutas

Vinos

López Heredia Sauternes
López Heredia Graves
Siella Marfil
Cavas de Perelada
Vinos Espumosos
Licores y Moka

OPPOSITE *SS Veendam*, **Holland-America Line, 1947**

American tourists travelling first-class from New York to Rotterdam enjoyed a farewell dinner. Going the opposite direction, the ship was used exclusively for transporting postwar emigrants to America.

Für amerikanische Touristen, die in der ersten Klasse von New York nach Rotterdam reisten, gab es ein Abschiedsessen. In die andere Richtung wurde das Schiff in der Nachkriegszeit ausschließlich dafür genutzt, Auswanderer nach Amerika zu transportieren.

Les passagers américains de première classe qui vont de New York à Rotterdam ont droit à un dîner d'adieu. Au retour, le paquebot ne transporte que des émigrants qui gagnent l'Amérique après la guerre.

RIGHT **Al Giardino degli Aranci, c. 1946, Naples, Italy**

Visitors to the "Orange Garden" had to take a funicular up to the rooftop patio. There in the coffee and tea room, the garden's jazz band offered patrons "the most delightful dancing in the most charming site of Naples."

Die Besucher des „Orangengartens" mussten mit einer Standseilbahn auf die Dachterrasse fahren. In der Kaffee- und Teestube bot ihnen die hauseigene Jazz-band die „schönsten Tanzmöglichkeiten am charmantesten Ort Neapels".

Les visiteurs de ce « jardin aux oranges » montent à la terrasse par un funiculaire. Dans ce salon de thé, l'orchestre de jazz du jardin propose « les danses les plus exquises en ce lieu le plus charmant de Naples ».

In 1948 ex-Resistance fighter and trained chef Raymond Oliver bought the ancient restaurant located in the arcade of the Palais-Royal. Oliver would later make an international impact on French cooking in the kitchens of restaurants and homes.

1948 kaufte der ehemalige Résistance-Kämpfer und gelernte Koch Raymond Oliver das historische Restaurant in den Arkaden des Palais Royal. Später nahm Oliver großen Einfluss auf die französische Küche in Restaurants und Privathaushalten weltweit.

En 1948, Raymond Oliver, ancien résistant et chef professionnel, achète ce vieux restaurant du Palais-Royal. L'influence internationale d'Oliver sur la cuisine française s'exercera aussi bien dans les restaurants que chez les particuliers.

LE GRAND VÉFOUR

ABOVE La Mascotte, 1948, Paris, France

Restaurant

Dikker & Thijs

La bonne cuisine est la base du véritable bonheur

A. Escoffier

A
PREHISTORIC
REPAST

HOLLAND - AMERICA LINE

BELOW *SS Conte Grande*, "Italia" **Societá de Navigazione, 1940**

First printed in 1940 during the fascist regime, a series of menus on *Costumi Regionali d'Italia* was still being used on voyages in 1948; they are examples of folk culture transcending politics.

Die Speisekarten mit dem Titel *Costumi Regionali d'Italia* wurden erstmals 1940

während des faschistischen Regimes gedruckt, aber noch 1948 auf Fahrten verwendet. Sie stehen für eine volkstümliche Kultur, die über das Politische hinausgeht.

Imprimée pour la première fois en 1940, une série de menus sur le thème des *Costumi regionali d'Italia* a toujours cours lors des croisières de 1948. Ou comment la culture populaire transcende la politique.

OPPOSITE *SS Veendam*, **Holland-America Line, 1947**

Costume-themed events were common diversions on ocean liners, but a prehistoric dinner seemed an incongruous repast.

Mottoveranstaltungen gehörten zu den typischen Vergnügungen auf Ozeandampfern, aber ein prähistorisches Abendessen wirkte doch etwas unpassend.

Les soirées costumées sont des distractions courantes à bord des paquebots. Mais un dîner préhistorique semble bien incongru.

Costumi Regionali d'Italia

CONTE GRANDE

SARDEGNA

"ITALIA" SOCIETÀ DI NAVIGAZIONE · GENOVA

OPPOSITE Cencio, c. 1956, Milan, Italy

BELOW LEFT Luncheon for the
president of France, Guildhall, 1950,
London, England

BELOW RIGHT Lasserre, 1950, Paris,
France

In the 1930s Café Kutschera was one of the largest restaurants in Berlin. Attacked regularly by anti-Semitic thugs and the Nazi press, owner Karl Kutschera was forced to sell; then, in 1943, he and his family were sent to concentration camps. After reparations, Kutschera and his wife returned to Berlin, reopening the café under its new name, Haus Wien.

In den 1930er-Jahren war das Café Kutschera eines der größten Restaurants in Berlin. Der Besitzer Karl Kutschera wurde regelmäßig von antisemitischen Schlägern und der NS-Presse angegriffen und schließlich zum Verkauf gezwungen. 1943 wurden er und seine Familie in Konzentrationslager deportiert. Nachdem sie ihren Besitz im Rahmen der Wiedergutmachung zurückerhalten hatten, kehrten Kutschera und seine Frau nach Berlin zurück und eröffneten das Café unter dem Namen Haus Wien neu.

Dans les années 1930, le Café Kutschera est l'un des plus vastes restaurants de Berlin. Régulièrement attaqué par des malfrats antisémites et la presse nazie, son propriétaire, Karl Kutschera, doit vendre. En 1943, il est envoyé en camp de concentration avec sa famille. À la suite de réparations, il regagne Berlin avec sa femme et rouvre le restaurant sous un nouveau nom, Haus Wien.

29 MAI 1952

Banquet Annuel

des

MOTEURS CH. ROULLAND

chez Ledoyen
aux Champs Elysées

SPEISEN-KARTE

BERLINER
KINDL
BRÄU

K. JAQUET
BERLIN-STEGLITZ · SCHLOSS-STRASSE 89
TELEFON 72 45 54

RESTAURANT DE LA TOUR D'ARGENT

Aspect oriental de la Cité, Eglise de Nostre — Dame Pont de l'Hostel Dieu et partie de l'Isle Nre Dame veus de la porte S.t Bernard

Pont de l'Hostel Dieu   Palais Archiepiscopal   Tours S.t

u bord du Fleuve Seine, au cœur du vieux Paris voisine de Notre-Dame et bâtie de la même pierre de Champagne aux reflets argentés, il était une Tour... L'histoire commence à la manière d'un conte de fées. C'était en 1582, au temps du Bon Roi Henry III, des fêtes italiennes du Louvre, des pourpoints à manches ballonnées et des premières fourchettes. Oncques n'y vit on manger avec les doigts.

By 1950 the extreme popularity of La Tour d'Argent was apparent when one evening Julia Child and her husband, Paul, joined some friends there for dinner. As she recalled, "The restaurant was excellent in every way, except that it was so pricey that every guest was American."

Wie beliebt das La Tour d'Argent war, wurde spätestens 1950 offensichtlich, als dort Julia Child mit ihrem Mann Paul und einigen Freunden zu Abend aß. In ihrer Erinnerung war das Restaurant „in jeder Hinsicht ausgezeichnet, allerdings so teuer, dass alle Gäste Amerikaner waren".

Un soir de 1950, la présence à La Tour d'Argent de la grande cuisinière américaine Julia Child et de son mari, Paul, avec quelques amis témoigne de l'immense succès de cette table parisienne. « Le restaurant était parfait en tout point, sauf ses prix qui rendaient la clientèle exclusivement américaine », se souvint-elle plus tard.

RIGHT **Restaurant Excelsior, Hôtel de l'Europe, 1952, Amsterdam, Netherlands**

Located inside the Hotel de l'Europe, Restaurant Excelsior was awarded its first Michelin star in 1957. It received many more single stars until its closure in 2010.

Das im Hôtel de l'Europe gelegene Restaurant Excelsior wurde 1957 erstmals mit einem Michelin-Stern ausgezeichnet. Bis zu seiner Schließung im Jahr 2010 erhielt es den Stern noch mehrere Male.

Restaurant de l'Hôtel l'Europe, l'Excelsior reçoit en 1957 sa première étoile au *Guide Michelin*, lequel lui attribuera « une étoile » jusqu'à sa fermeture en 2010.

Hotel l'Europe
RESTAURANT EXCELSIOR

HOTEL L'EUROPE
AMSTERDAM

N. DOELENSTRAAT 2–4. AMSTERDAM–C. TEL. 34836–48406

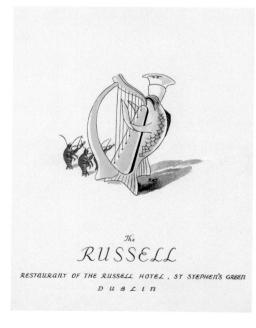

HOTEL & RESTAURANT

BOTANIQUE

PALAIS DES SPORTS ▪ **BANQUET** ▪ MARDI 11 OCTOBRE 1955

CAFÉ de la PAIX

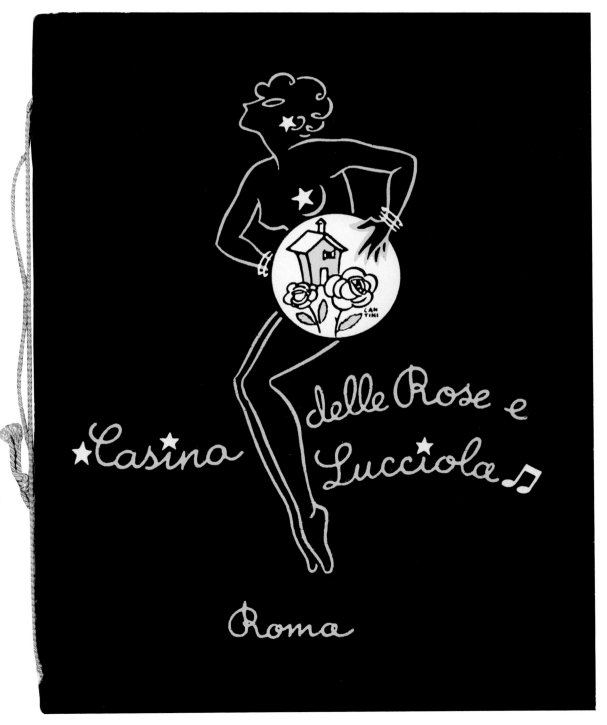

*S'il vous plaît
d'ordonner, Monsieur,
et nous laissez le soin
de flatter votre goût.*

Caviar
Saumon fumé
Cocktail de Langouste
Serge Burklé
Fines de Belon
Pamplemousse
mis en glace

POTAGES

Potage Tour d'Argent
Potage Claudius Burdel
Consommé Fabiola
Consommé
Julienne

ŒUFS

Œufs Bénédictine
Œufs en cocotte
Chanoinesse
Œufs La Rochejacquelein
Omelette à votre plaisir
Œufs en brouillade
aux truffes
Œufs Mornay

POISSONS

Filets de Sole Cardinal
Filets de Sole Caravelle *sur Commande*
Filets de Sole grillés Frédéric   **Sole du Maire en friture**
Filets de Sole Sully   **Sole en Belle Meunière**
Barbue Botticelli *sur Commande*   Croustade de Barbue Lagrené
Goujonnettes de Mostelle   **Langouste Winterthur**   **Langouste à la Mahonnaise**
Quenelles André Terrail

ENTRÉES

La Terrine de Foie Gras des Trois Empereurs
Côtes d'Agneau à la grille   **Côte de Veau Charlemagne**
Carré d'Agneau   **Côte de Veau en casserole**
Filet Tour d'Argent   Noisettes des Tournelles
Châteaubriand sauce Béarnaise
Filet sauté de Lauzières   **Tournedos Yella**
Le Filet Charolais aux quatre poivres
Rognon grillé Béarnaise   **Rognons Saint-Louis**

LÉGUMES

Petits Pois
Haricots verts
Gloire de Deuil
Champignons
à la Bordelaise
Pommes soufflées
sautées
ou allumettes

TEMPS ET SAISONS

Râble de Lièvre Goury de Champgrand
Bécasse Flambée Café Anglais
Faisan Elzear Blaze

LÉGUMES

Endives Meunière
Epinards à la crème
double
Fonds d'Artichauts
soufflés
Salade Roger
Salade Notre-Dame
Salade de l'Orbrerie

Faites nous la faveur d'ordonner par avance

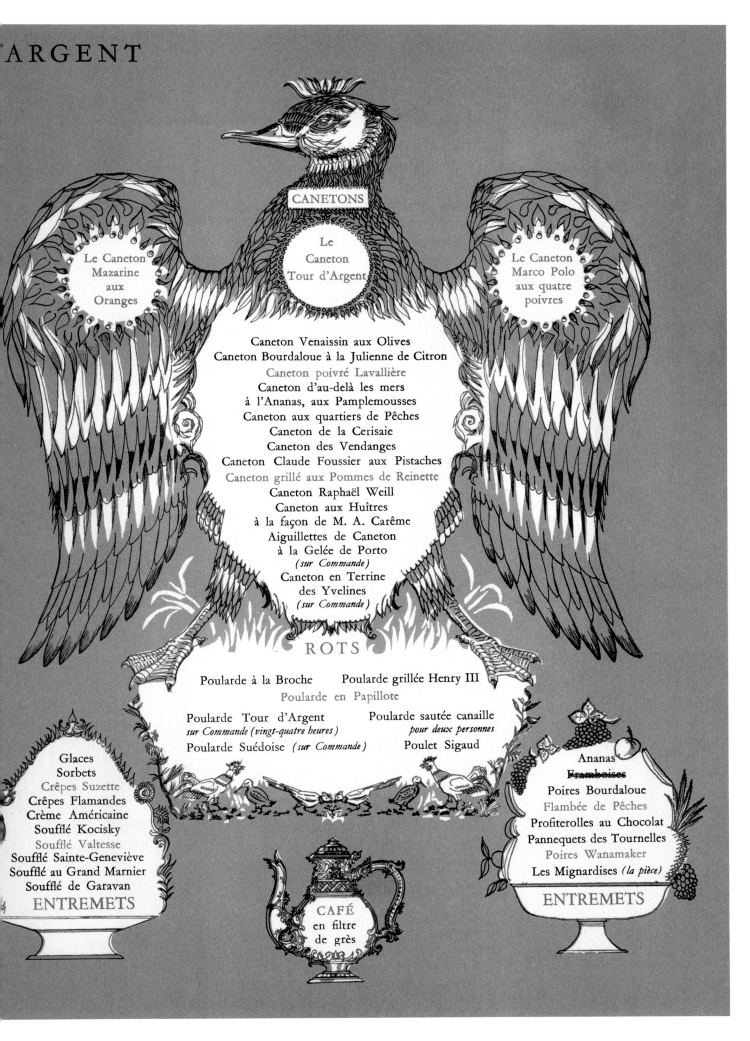

CANETONS

Le Caneton Tour d'Argent

Le Caneton Mazarine aux Oranges

Le Caneton Marco Polo aux quatre poivres

Caneton Venaissin aux Olives
Caneton Bourdaloue à la Julienne de Citron
Caneton poivré Lavallière
Caneton d'au-delà les mers
à l'Ananas, aux Pamplemousses
Caneton aux quartiers de Pêches
Caneton de la Cerisaie
Caneton des Vendanges
Caneton Claude Foussier aux Pistaches
Caneton grillé aux Pommes de Reinette
Caneton Raphaël Weill
Caneton aux Huîtres
à la façon de M. A. Carême
Aiguillettes de Caneton
à la Gelée de Porto
(sur Commande)
Caneton en Terrine
des Yvelines
(sur Commande)

ROTS

Poularde à la Broche   Poularde grillée Henry III
Poularde en Papillote

Poularde Tour d'Argent   Poularde sautée canaille
sur Commande (vingt-quatre heures)   pour deux personnes
Poularde Suédoise (sur Commande)   Poulet Sigaud

Glaces
Sorbets
Crêpes Suzette
Crêpes Flamandes
Crème Américaine
Soufflé Kocisky
Soufflé Valtesse
Soufflé Sainte-Geneviève
Soufflé au Grand Marnier
Soufflé de Garavan
ENTREMETS

Ananas
Framboises
Poires Bourdaloue
Flambée de Pêches
Profiterolles au Chocolat
Pannequets des Tournelles
Poires Wanamaker
Les Mignardises (la pièce)
ENTREMETS

CAFÉ
en filtre
de grès

ABOVE & BELOW **Negresco, 1954,
Lisbon, Portugal**

OPPOSITE **Il Capriccio, c. 1955,
Rome, Italy**

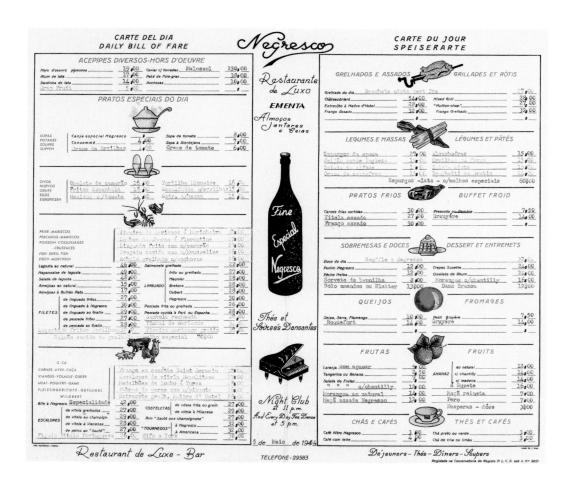

PAGES 296–297 **La Tour d'Argent,
c. 1952, Paris, France**

A pictorial menu helps diners work their
way through a meal, the centerpiece
being the famous duck dish *Le Caneton
Tour d'Argent*. Historian Stanley Karnow
wrote that the owner's "device for
numbering his innovation, *canard au
sang*, enabled him to identify precisely
which duck was eaten by luminaries."

Bei der Auswahl der Speisen half den
Gästen diese illustrierte Karte, in deren
Zentrum das berühmte Entengericht *Le
Caneton Tour d'Argent* stand. Dem Histo-
riker Stanley Karnow zufolge konnte der
Besitzer „dank der methodischen Num-
merierung seines innovativen Gerichts
Canard au sang genau nachvollziehen,
welche Ente von welcher Berühmtheit
verspeist wurde".

Ce menu illustré permet aux convives
de s'y retrouver parmi les plats proposés,
où trône le célèbre «Caneton Tour
d'Argent». Selon l'historien Stanley
Karnow, «le système de numérotation
[par le propriétaire] de son innovation,
le canard au sang, permet à celui-ci
d'identifier avec précision quel canard
a été mangé par tel ou tel dignitaire».

ABOVE **Augustiner-Gaststätten, 1959, Munich, Federal Republic of Germany**

RIGHT **Balkan-Grill, c. 1953, Vienna, Austria**

The menu suggests an international world quite fond of meat in all forms and cuts.

Das Titelbild der Speisekarte deutet auf eine Welt hin, die dem Fleisch in allen Formen und Zuschnitten sehr zugetan ist.

La couverture de ce menu présente un panorama international où règne la viande sous toutes ses formes.

GRILL"

EFON: 92-14-94

Das Abendrestaurant des internationalen Publikums
The evening restaurant of the international world
Original Balkanspezialitäten vom Spieß und Rost
Original Balkan specialities from the grill and spit

ABOVE **Frascati, 1950, Copenhagen, Denmark**

Calling itself "Paris on the town hall square in Copenhagen," an Italian restaurant in Denmark references the former Frascati on the Boulevard Montmartre.

Die Beschreibung „Paris auf dem Rathausplatz in Kopenhagen" ist eine Anspielung des italienischen Restaurants auf das ehemalige Frascati am Boulevard Montmartre.

«Paris sur la place de l'hôtel de ville de Copenhague.» Ainsi se présente ce restaurant italien de la capitale danoise, dans une allusion à l'ancien Frascati parisien du boulevard Montmartre.

RIGHT **Solmar, c. 1954, Lisbon, Portugal**

OPPOSITE **Old Swiss House, c. 1959, Lucerne, Switzerland**

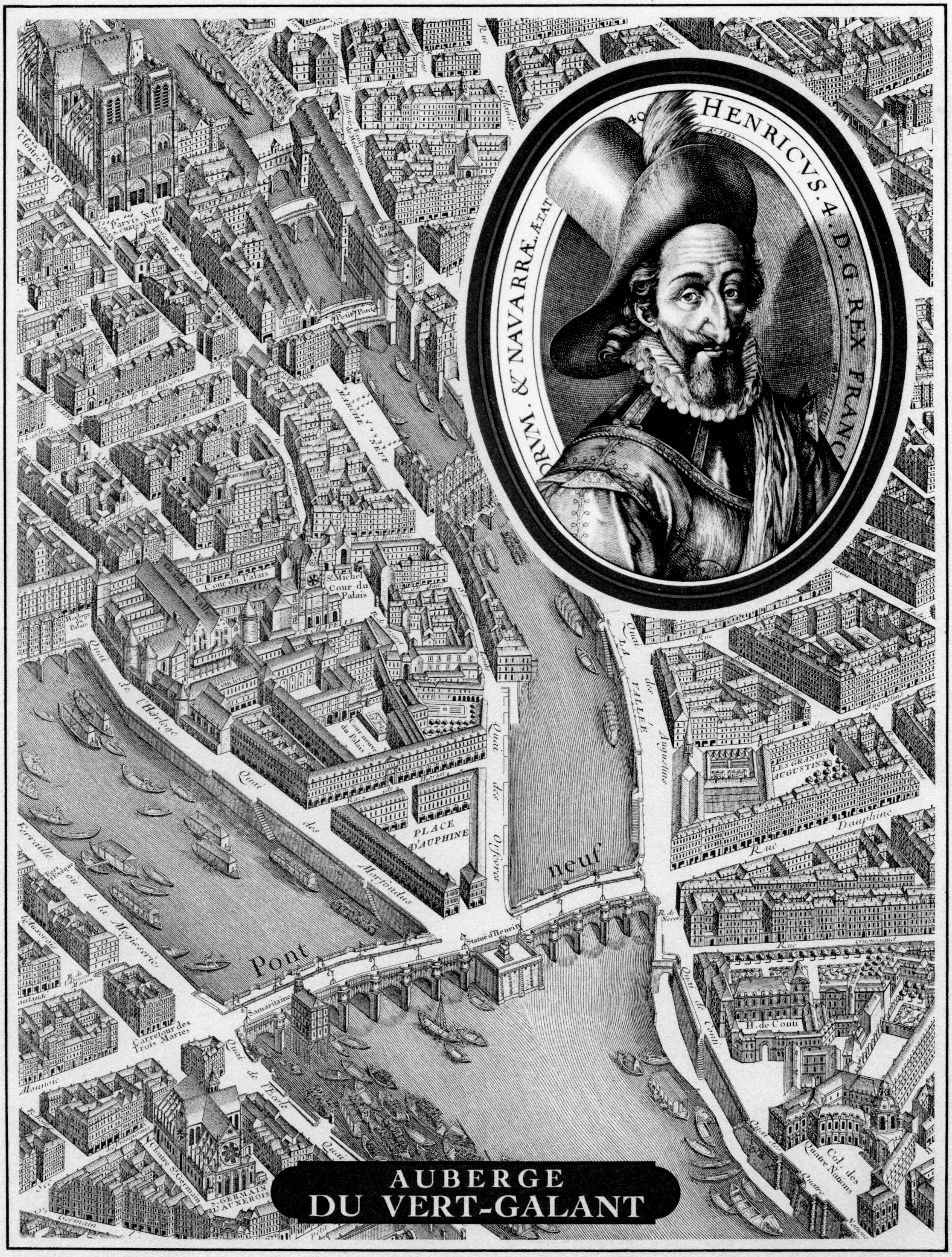
AUBERGE
DU VERT-GALANT
HENRICVS.4.D.G.REX FRANC
NAVARRÆ
PLACE DAUPHINE
Pont
neuf
Quai de l'Horloge
Quai des Morfondus
Quai des Orfevres
Quai des Augustins
Rue Dauphine
LES GRANDS AUGUSTINS
Cour du Palais
Statue d'Henri IV
Samaritaine
Carrefour des Trois Maries
Quai de l'Ecole
S. GERMAIN L'AUXEROIS
H. de Conti
Col. des Quatre Nations
Petit Pont
Quai de Conti

Located on "a charming corner in old Paris" overlooking the Seine, food essayist Waverley Root once said, "There are few pleasanter places for outdoor eating in Paris."

An einer „charmanten Ecke im alten Paris" lag dieses Restaurant mit Seine-Blick, über das der Essayist Waverley Root einmal sagte: „Es gibt in Paris kaum einen schöneren Ort, um im Freien zu essen."

De ce «charmant coin du vieux Paris» donnant sur la Seine, le critique gastronomique Waverley Root dit: «Il y a peu d'endroits plus plaisants pour manger en plein air à Paris.»

RIGHT **The May Fair Hotel Restaurant, 1954, London, England**

THE MAY FAIR HOTEL

Restaurant

BERKELEY SQUARE

Rôtisserie Périgourdine

PLACE SAINT-MICHEL   TÉL. DANTON 70-54
70-55

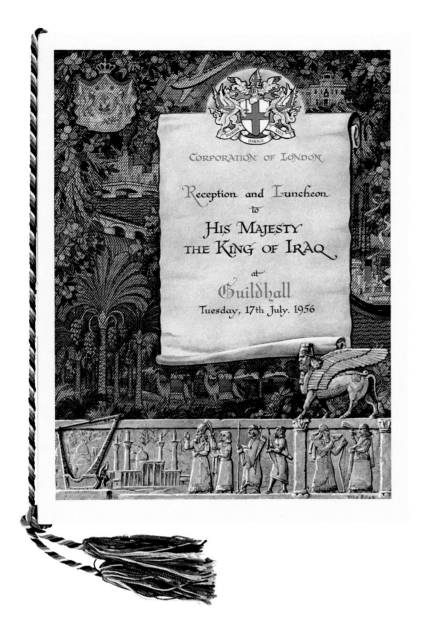

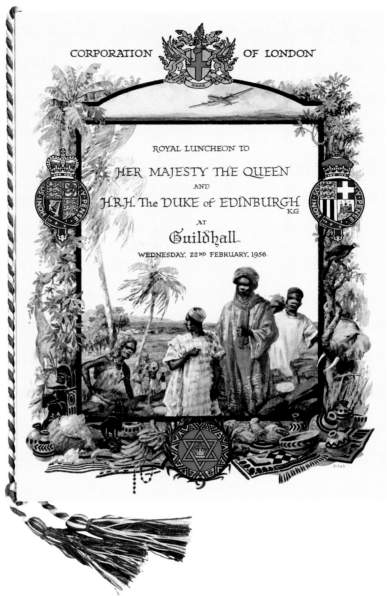

KETTNER'S

Restaurant Telephone: GERRARD 3437
Banquets   „   „   6437

ROMILLY STREET
SOHO - LONDON - W1

Pimm's
OF LONDON

Édité par G.H. RABU "*Le Cabaret*"

CHOU
de Jean Gabriel Domergue

4, avenue Franklin D. Roosevelt
Rond-Point des Champs-Élysées, Paris

N.V. Stoomvaart Maatschappij „Nederland".

BELOW LEFT **Restaurante Horcher, c. 1953, Madrid, Spain**

Despite the abundance of seafood shown in this energetic vignette, the scant bill of fare suggests the scarcity of food during the Franco era in Spain.

Trotz der vielen Meeresfrüchte, die in dieser lebhaften Skizze zu sehen sind, zeugen die wenigen aufgelisteten Speisen von der Lebensmittelknappheit, die während der Franco-Ära in Spanien herrschte.

Malgré l'abondance de fruits de mer et de poissons visible dans cette illustration dynamique, la brièveté du menu témoigne des pénuries alimentaires dans l'Espagne franquiste.

BELOW RIGHT **Schultheiss im Westend, c. 1955, Frankfurt, Federal Republic of Germany**

OPPOSITE **Ledoyen, 1953, Paris, France**

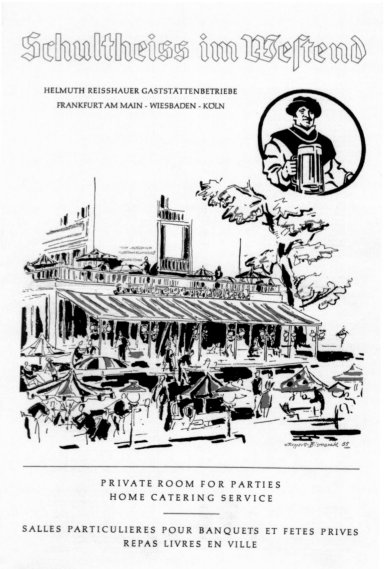

PRIVATE ROOM FOR PARTIES
HOME CATERING SERVICE

SALLES PARTICULIERES POUR BANQUETS ET FETES PRIVES
REPAS LIVRES EN VILLE

Le Restaurant Ledoyen en 1792

Ledoyen

CHAMPS - ÉLYSÉES

menu

N.V. STOOMVAART MAATSCHAPPIJ „NEDERLAND"

N.V. STOOMVAART MAATSCHAPPIJ „NEDERLAND"

de Montesquiou   Forain

SEM

PAGES 314 & 315 *MS Oranje*, Stoom-vaart Maatschappij Nederland, 1955

In a fine example of commercial work, Dutch painter Hermanus Berserik created a series of colorful seascape designs such as this one used for dinner in a second-class dining room.

Ein schönes Beispiel für kommerzielle Arbeiten ist diese Reihe farbenfroher Meereslandschaften, die der niederländische Maler Hermanus Berserik für ein Abendessen in einem Speisesaal für die zweite Klasse schuf.

Pour ces très beaux dessins commerciaux, le peintre hollandais Hermanus Berserik a réalisé plusieurs marines colorées, notamment pour ce menu d'un dîner de deuxième classe, servi à bord d'un paquebot.

OPPOSITE Maxim's, 1956, Paris, France

RIGHT & BELOW Giggi Fazi, 1959, Milan, Italy

Culinary character Giggi Fazi squeezed the life out of his caricature portrait, using it on menu covers for his restaurants in Milan, Rome, and Frascati.

Die kulinarische Persönlichkeit Giggi Fazi holte alles aus ihrem karikaturistischen Porträt heraus, indem sie es in ihren Restaurants in Mailand, Rom und Frascati auf die Titelseiten der Speisekarten brachte.

Grande figure culinaire, Giggi Fazi a mis sa caricature à toutes les sauces, y compris sur les couvertures des menus de ses restaurants de Milan, Rome et Frascati.

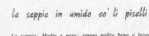

La Couronne

Jeudi 17 Mai 1956
chez LEDOYEN, aux Champs-Elysées

BANQUET ANNUEL DES **MOTEURS CH. ROULLAND**

OPPOSITE La Couronne, c. 1953,
Brussels, Belgium

ABOVE LEFT Restaurant Sundkroen,
c. 1956, Elsinore, Denmark

ABOVE RIGHT Banquet Annuel des
Moteurs Charles Roulland, Ledoyen,
1956, Paris, France

LEFT Hôtel Colombia Excelsior, 1956, Genova, Italy

BELOW Rôtisserie de la Table du Roy, c. 1950, Paris, France

OPPOSITE Weinhaus Zum Stachel, c. 1952, Würzburg, Federal Republic of Germany

banquet annuel des

MOTEURS CH. ROULLAND

jeudi 22 mai 1958

OPPOSITE **Banquet Annuel de Moteurs Charles Roulland, Ledoyen, 1958, Paris, France**

ABOVE LEFT **Banquet Annuel de Moteurs Charles Roulland, Ledoyen, 1957, Paris, France**

ABOVE RIGHT **Banquet Annuel de Moteurs Charles Roulland, Ledoyen, 1955, Paris, France**

Every spring the Vincennes-based manufacturer of electric motors threw a banquet for its workforce at Chez Ledoyen on Champs-Élysées. Each year artist Charles Lemmel drew the energetic menus that gently lampooned managers and employees alike.

Jedes Frühjahr veranstaltete der in Vincennes ansässige Hersteller von Elektromotoren für seine Belegschaft ein Bankett im Chez Ledoyen auf den Champs-Élysées. Der Künstler Charles Lemmel zeichnete dafür stets die lebhaften Titelbilder der Speisekarten, die sowohl Führungskräfte als auch Angestellte freundlich auf den Arm nahmen.

Chaque année au printemps, ce fabricant de moteurs électriques installé à Vincennes offre un banquet à ses employés chez Ledoyen, sur les Champs-Élysées. L'illustrateur Charles Lemmel est chaque fois au rendez-vous pour se moquer gentiment de la direction et des salariés sur des menus électriques !

HORS d'OEUVRES

TARTAR M. KAVIAR 4,75
Limfjords

SCRAPED RAW BEEF 4,75
with domestic caviar

HUMMERCOCKTAIL 6,50

LOBSTER COCKTAIL 6,50

FRANSKE SNEGLE .. 6,50
m. hvidløgssmør

FRENCH SNAILS ... 6,50
with garlic butter

CANAPÉ À LA
DANOISE 6,75

LIDT MEN GODT ... 7,50
på platte

TIT BITS 7,50
served on compartment plate

KOLD BORNHOLMER-
LAKS PARISIENNE 6,00
m. hummer, asparges,
tomat og carry-
mayonnaise

COLD SALMON
PARISIENNE 6,00
w. lobster, asparagus,
tomato and curried
mayonnaise

Egen import fra Doyen, Strasbourg

GÅSELEVERMOUSSE 6,75
m. trøfler (1 ds.)
brød og smør

GÅSELEVERPOSTEJ 9,75
m. trøfler, pr. couv.
brød og smør

GÅSELEVERPOSTEJ 15,75
m. trøfler (1 ds.)
brød og smør

GOOSE LIVER
MOUSSE 6,75
with truffles (1 can)
bread and butter

GOOSE LIVER PASTE 9,75
with truffles, per cover
bread and butter

CAN OF GOOSE
LIVER PASTE 15,75
with truffles (1 can)
bread and butter

ENEBÆRRØGET
WESTPHALSK
LANDSKINKE 7,50
m. flødestuvede asparges.

JUNIPER SMOKED
WESTPHALIAN
COUNTRY HAM 7,50
w. creamed asparagus.

DAGENS OPSKRIFT

Fintskåret okse-, kalve- og svinekød, løg, æbler, champignons, tomat,
carry, orange og abrikoser, med snittede mandler,
kokos og ris pilaw 8,75

CHEF'S SUGGESTION

Chopped beef, veal and pork, onions, apples, mushrooms,
tomato, curry, orange and apricots with chopped
almonds, grated coconut and rice pilaw .. 8,75

Lasserre Paris *Touchagues* 1956

LEFT **Le Restaurant Mirabelle at Maxim's, 1957, Paris, France**

Mirabelle, a London restaurant, presented its lunch specials in a cross-channel exchange at Maxim's with a lunch of English specialties such as "Steak and Kidney Pie" and "Crusted York with Peaches."

In einem Austausch über den Ärmelkanal hinweg präsentierte das Londoner Restaurant Mirabelle seine Spezialitäten im Maxim's, wo zum Mittagessen englische Speisen wie *Steak and Kidney Pie* und *Crusted York with Peaches* serviert wurden.

Le restaurant londonien Mirabelle présente ses spécialités de l'autre côté de la Manche chez Maxim's, dans un déjeuner composé de tourtes à la viande de bœuf et aux rognons ou de porc aux pêches.

BELOW LEFT **The Carlton, 1957, Brussels, Belgium**

BELOW RIGHT **Ristorante Il Tinello, 1956, Rome, Italy**

OPPOSITE **Le Grand Véfour, c. 1956, Paris, France**

In 1949 Julia Child and her husband, Paul, "unknowingly stumbled" into the Grand Véfour. Over the years it became their "old favorite."

1949 verschlug es Julia Child und ihren Mann Paul zufällig ins Grand Véfour. Im Laufe der Jahre wurde es zu ihrem „alten Lieblingsrestaurant".

En 1949, Julia Child et son mari, Paul, «tombent par hasard» sur Le Grand Véfour. Avec le temps, ce restaurant deviendra leur «cantine».

LASSERRE

SOPHIE DESMARETS — MADAME STEVE PASSEUR — GABY SYLVIA

PAGE 328 **Zum Roten Gatter, 1957, Zurich, Switzerland**

Designer Josef Müller-Brockmann's chanticleer trumpets "10 years of quality" at the inauguration of a *dîner gastronomique* prepared for festival week. Müller-Brockmann was a master of the mid-century Swiss style of graphic design.

Der Hahn des Designers Josef Müller-Brockmann trompetet „10 Jahre Qualität" bei der Eröffnung eines *dîner gastronomique*, das für die Festwoche hergerichtet wurde. Müller-Brockmann war ein Meister des Schweizer Grafikdesigns Mitte des 20. Jahrhunderts.

Josef Müller-Brockmann, maître du graphisme suisse des années 1950, a choisi un coq pour proclamer «dix années de qualité», lors de l'inauguration d'un dîner gastronomique préparé pour une semaine festive.

PAGE 329 **Italian Room, Hotel Deutsches Haus, 1956, Berchtesgaden, Federal Republic of Germany**

LEFT **Lasserre, 1954, Paris, France**

Czech-born Jan Mara drew symbolic caricatures of three French film actresses with ink lines reminiscent of American cartoonist Virgil Partch.

Der in Tschechien geborene Jan Mara zeichnete mit Tuschelinien, die an Arbeiten des amerikanischen Comiczeichners Virgil Partch erinnerten, symbolische Karikaturen von drei französischen Filmschauspielerinnen.

Dessinées à l'encre par l'artiste d'origine tchèque Jan Mara, ces caricatures allégoriques de trois actrices de cinéma françaises rappellent le style du dessinateur humoristique américain Virgil Partch.

OPPOSITE **Ristorante Oliviero, 1956, Florence, Italy**

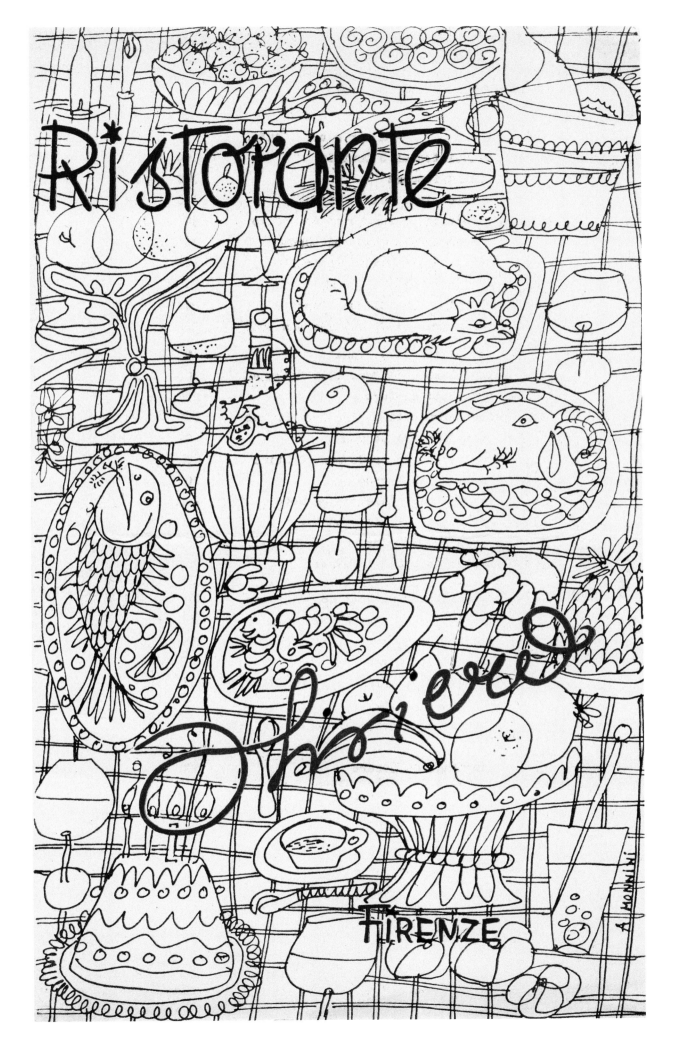

FAR LEFT **Restaurant Tsuruya, Brussels World's Fair, 1958, Brussels, Belgium**

At first glance, a Japanese restaurant at the exposition offered a timid menu of tempura, but one could search deeper and experience the beef tsukudani or sea urchin eggs.

Auf der Weltausstellung bot ein japanisches Restaurant ein auf den ersten Blick unscheinbares Tempura-Menü an, doch bei genauerem Hinsehen konnte man auch Rindfleisch-Tsukudani oder Seeigeleier entdecken.

À première vue, un restaurant japonais de l'Exposition internationale de Bruxelles se contentait d'un timide menu de tempura. Mais, en cherchant un peu, on découvrait un *tsukudani* au bœuf ou des œufs d'oursin.

LEFT **The Bacon and Egg, Lyons Corner House, 1958, London, England**

BELOW **Schnoor 2, 1958, Bremen, Federal Republic of Germany**

Au pied de cochon

Restaurant

Téléphone:
CENTRAL 11·75
" 11·76

6. rue Coquillière.

Halles centrales de Paris, entre la Bourse de Commerce et Saint Eustache...

═══ OUVERT JOUR ET NUIT ═══

NOS HORS-D'ŒUVRE

Melon glacé de Cavaillon · · · · ·	
Fond d'Artichaut vinaigrette · · ·	3,50
Pamplemousse frappé · · · · · · ·	3,—
Salade de tomates · · · · · · · · · ·	2,50
Salade de concombre · · · · · · · ·	2,50
Salade Niçoise · · · · · · · · · · · ·	4,50
Assiette de Crudités · · · · · · ·	4,50
Œuf en gelée ou mayonnaise · ·	2,50
Langoustines mayonnaise · · · · · ·	8,—
Sardine à l'huile · · · · · · · · · ·	2,50
Thon à l'huile · · · · · · · · · · · ·	3,50
Maquereau au vin blanc · · · · · ·	3,—
Assiette de Cochonnaille · · · · · ·	4,50
Médaillon foie gras truffé · · ·	13,—
Jambon de Paris · · · · · · · · · · ·	4,—
Jambon de Parme · · · · · · · · ·	8,—
Saucisson sec pur Porc · · · · · · ·	3,—
Terrine du Chef · · · · · · · · · ·	5,—
Pâté de Campagne · · · · · · · · ·	3,—
Rillettes · · · · · · · · · · · · · ·	2,50
Andouille de Vire · · · · · · · · · ·	3,—
Saumon fumé · · · · · · · · · · · ·	11,50
Caviar d'Iran avec Toast · · · · ·	15,—

NOS PLATS D'ŒUFS

Omelette aux fines Herbes · · · ·	3,—
Omelette au Fromage · · · · · · ·	3,50
Omelette au Jambon · · · · · · · ·	3,50
Œufs plat au Bacon · · · · · · · · ·	3,50

NOS POISSONS

Truite aux Amandes · · · · · · · ·	7,50
Truite du Vivier au Bleu · · · · ·	7,50
Sole Belle Meunière · · · · · · · · ·	8,—
Langouste Mayonnaise · · · · · ·	S.G.
Coquilles Saint-Jacques Provençale	8,—

NOS LÉGUMES

Salade de Saison · · · · · · · · ·	2,—
Champignons Provençale · · · · · ·	3,50
Haricots Verts · · · · · · · · · · ·	3,—
Tomates Provençale · · · · · · · ·	2,50
Pommes Allumettes · · · · · · · · ·	2,—

Couvert 1,50

Le Pied de Cochon

vous recommande

Soupe à l'Oignon gratinée · · · · ·	3,—
Grenouilles Provençale · · · · · ·	9,—
Escargots de Bourgogne, la dz. ·	6,—
Coquilles St-Jacques provençale ·	8,—
Pied de Cochon Grillé · · · · · · ·	6,—
Pied de Cochon farci Truffé · ·	6,50
Plateau grillé Saint-Antoine · · · ·	6,50
Andouillette grillée · · · · · · · ·	6,—
Saucisson chaud pur Porc · · · ·	5,50
Tête de Veau ravigote · · · · · ·	6,—
Choucroute au Riesling · · · · · · ·	6,50
Brochette de Rognons · · · · · · · ·	7,50
Rognon de Veau flambé Armagnac	11,50
Tournedos Béarnaise · · · · · · · · ·	9,—
Tournedos Rossini · · · · · · · · · ·	9,50
Steak au poivre · · · · · · · · · · ·	9,50
Entrecôte Minute · · · · · · · · · · ·	8,50

et

Ses Spécialités

Côte de Bœuf
Châteaubriant
Entrecôte à la moëlle

(2 PERS.) 20,—

NOS VIANDES

Entrecôte à la Moelle (2 p.) · · ·	20,—
Entrecôte Minute · · · · · · · · · · ·	8,50
Tournedos Béarnaise · · · · · · · · ·	9,—
Châteaubriant (2 pers.) · · · · · ·	20,—
Tournedos Rossini · · · · · · · · ·	9,50
Steak au poivre · · · · · · · · · ·	9,50
Steak Tartare · · · · · · · · · · · ·	8,50
Côte de Bœuf (2 pers.) · · · · ·	20,—
Côtes d'Agneau Vert-Pré · · ·	8,50
Côte de Porc Milanaise · · · · · ·	7,—
Côte de Veau Mandataire · · · ·	7,50
Cervelle de Veau · · · · · · · · · ·	7,50
Tripes à la Mode de Caen · ·	5,—
Boudin de Campagne grillé · ·	3,50
Saucisses de Francfort Garnies ·	3,50

NOS FROMAGES

La variété de nos Provinces · ·	3,—
Yoghourt · · · · · · · · · · · · · ·	1,—
Crème fraîche · · · · · · · · · · ·	2,—

NOS DESSERTS

Raisins, Pêches · · · · · · · · · · · ·	
Fraises des bois au sucre · · · · ·	4,50
Framboises au sucre · · · · · · ·	4,50
Ananas au Kirsch · · · · · · · · · ·	3,50
Crème Caramel · · · · · · · · · · ·	2,50
Crêpes flambées · · · · · · · · · · ·	4,50
Tarte Maison · · · · · · · · · · · ·	3,—
Coupe de Glace · · · · · · · · · · ·	2,50
Plombière "Succès des Halles" ·	4,50
Café Liégeois · · · · · · · · · · · ·	3,—
Parfait Royal · · · · · · · · · · · ·	3,—
Fraises ou Framboises Melba · ·	4,50
Pêche ou Ananas Melba · · · · ·	4,—
Coupe Saint-Eustache · · · · · · ·	4,—
Mystère du Pied de Cochon · · ·	4,50

Café Cona ou Express 1,50

Service non compris - Déjeuner 12 % - Diner-Souper 15 %
La Maison n'accepte que les Chèques certifiés

The general von Steuben

Menu

Headquarters
United States Air Forces in Europe
Wiesbaden, Germany

Although the title and Tintin-esque vignette suggest plenty of pork, the restaurant is better known for its *soupe à l'oignon gratinée*. When it opened in 1947, Au Pied de Cochon shared corners with the stock exchange, Saint-Eustache church, and, conveniently, with the meat market of Les Halles, later destroyed in 1969.

Obwohl der Titel und die an Tim und Struppi erinnernde Skizze auf viel Schweinefleisch hindeuten, war das Restaurant eher für seine *Soupe à l'oignon gratinée* bekannt. Als es 1947 eröffnet wurde, lag das Au Pied de Cochon um die Ecke von der Börse, der Kirche Saint-Eustache und praktischerweise auch vom Fleischmarkt in Les Halles, der 1969 abgerissen wurde.

Si le nom et l'illustration digne de *Tintin* mettent l'accent sur la viande de porc, la spécialité de ce restaurant est la soupe à l'oignon gratinée. Lors de son inauguration en 1947, Au pied de cochon voisinait avec la Bourse, l'église Saint-Eustache et le marché de la viande des Halles, démolies en 1969.

OPPOSITE **The General von Steuben, 1957, Wiesbaden, Federal Republic of Germany**

RIGHT **Avenida Palace Restaurant, c. 1955, Barcelona, Spain**

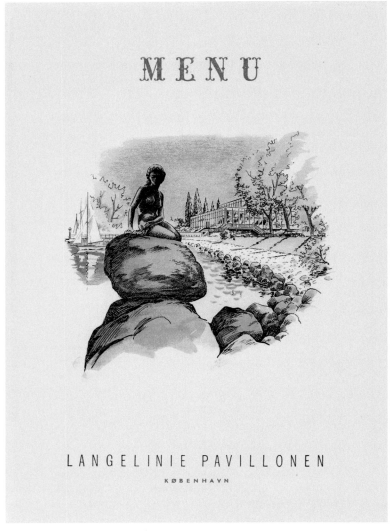

ABOVE LEFT **Hofbräuhaus am Platzl, c. 1956, Munich, Federal Republic of Germany**

ABOVE RIGHT **Langelinie Pavillonen, c. 1958, Copenhagen, Denmark**

The restaurant's newly constructed Modernist building takes a back seat to Edvard Eriksen's iconic sculpture *The Little Mermaid*, from the Hans Christian Andersen fairy tale. The new building was inaugurated in 1958.

Das neu errichtete modernistische Gebäude des Restaurants spielt neben Edvard Eriksens legendärer Skulptur *Die kleine Meerjungfrau* nach Hans Christian Andersens Märchen die zweite Rolle. Der neue Pavillon wurde 1958 eingeweiht.

Le nouveau bâtiment de style moderne de ce restaurant de Copenhague reste à l'arrière-plan de *La Petite Sirène*, la célèbre sculpture d'Edvard Eriksen, inspirée du conte de Hans Christian Andersen. Le pavillon visible au fond, il est inauguré en 1958.

OPPOSITE **Dronningen, c. 1957, Norway**

DRONNINGEN
Sommerrestaurant
SESONG   7. MAI — 3 SEPT.

The American Restaurant of the United States Pavilion

Brussels World's Fair 1958

The Brass Rail Restaurants of New York

ABOVE **The American Restaurant of the United States Pavilion, Brussels World's Fair, 1958, Brussels, Belgium**

REPUBLICA ARGENTINA

K. appeL '57

Exposicion Universal de Bruselas 1958

ABOVE **Republica Argentina, Brussels
World's Fair, 1958, Brussels, Belgium**

LEFT Ristorante Sabatini, 1956,
Florence, Italy

BELOW Giannino, 1959, Milan, Italy

OPPOSITE Fiskehusets Restaurant,
c. 1956, Copenhagen, Denmark

Giannino - Milano

FISKEHUSETS
restaurant

Gammel Strand 34 · København K · Telefoner: (01) 14 76 30 og (01) 14 79 16

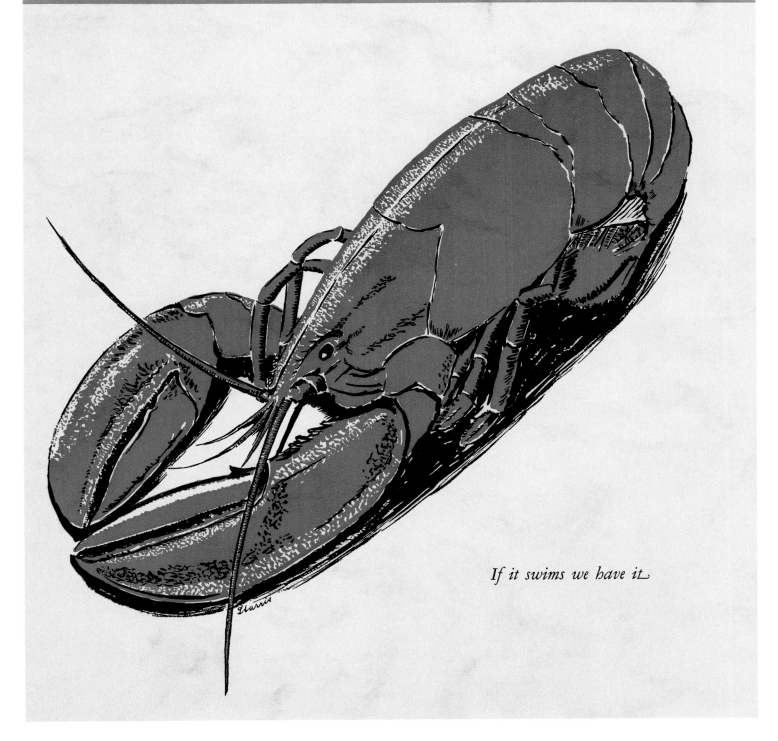

If it swims we have it

The Menus ————————————————— **343**

ristorante "21"

HOTEL MEDITERRANEO - ROMA

OPPOSITE Ristorante 21, Hotel
Mediterraneo, Rome, Italy

LEFT The Minute Room, Regent
Palace Hotel, 1959, London, England

ABOVE Independence Room, Frankfurt
Casino, 1958, Frankfurt, Federal
Republic of Germany

ABOVE **Restaurant Bellavigna, c. 1958,
Charleroi, Belgium**

SUPPEN

Bouillon nature	—.80
Bouillon mit Mark	1.50
Bouillon mit Ei	1.25
Klare Schildkrötensuppe	2.—
Real Turtle London Derry	2.50

VORSPEISEN

Rauchaal Zarter, dänischer Rauchaal	3.50
Crevetten-Cocktail Silver Star Mit Stangensellerie, an leichter Cocktailsauce	4.75
Grönländer Crevetten Mit Dill-Rahmmayonnaise oder Sauce Cocktail	4.75
Isländischer Matjes aus dem Fass Süss-sauer mariniertes Heringsfilet	2.25
Chicken Salad Florida Gebratenes Pouletfleisch mit Süssmais und Ananas	4.25
Salade de Coquilles St. Jacques Calvi Kamm-Muschelsalat, mit Peperoni, Tomaten und Oliven garniert	4.—
Bündnerfleisch und Rohschinken	4.50
Spaghetti Carbonata Mit Schinken, Pilzen, Eschalotten, Knoblauch und Oregano zubereitet	2.75

AUS UNSEREM EIGENEN RAUCHFANG

Rauchlachs Mild gesalzen, mit Toast und Butter	½ Portion Portion	4.50 7.—
Geräucherte Truthahnbrust Mit Meerrettichschaum, Toast und Butter	½ Portion Portion	3.50 6.—
Lachsforelle geräuchert Frisch geräucherte Lachsforelle mit Zitrone und Sauce Mermaid		4.25
Rauchteller Mit zarter Lachsforelle, mild gesalzenem Lachs und delikater Truthahnbrust. Dazu Toast und Butter		7.50

Während der Hauptessenszeit sind die Tische
für Gäste, die essen, reserviert.

Zuschlag 15 %
14 % für Service und Serviceleitung
1 % Wirtschaftsaufschlag

ABOVE Mövenpick, c. 1958, Zurich,
Switzerland

RIGHT Restaurant Jammet, 1958,
Dublin, Ireland

OPPOSITE BELOW Grosvenor House,
1959, London, England

AUS DEM MEER

Sole Meunière	10.50
Lemon Sole aux Amandes	6.50
Gebraten, mit Mandelsplittern bestreut	
Lemon Sole au Poivre vert	7.—
Gebratener Lemon Sole, mit frischen, grünen Pfefferkörnern	
Lemon Sole Bonne Femme	7.75
Unser Chef verwendet nur allerbesten Féchy, frische Pilze und viel Rahm, im Ofen überbacken	
Saumon étuvé au Johannisberg	9.—
Salm-Tranchen in Johannisberg gedünstet; dazu Sauce Hollandaise	
Coquilles St. Jacques Captain Kidd	8.25
Kamm-Muscheln in Curry-Rahmsauce, mit Bananen, Äpfeln und gemahlenen Haselnüssen	
Scampi au Curry	10.50
Scampi à l'Orly	9.—
In Bierteig gebacken, dazu Sauce Tartare	
Scampi Danieli	8.75
Am Spiess gebraten, mit pikanter Kräutersauce glaciert	
Scampi Fra Diavolo	9.75
Eine Zubereitung mit viel frischen Tomaten und Petersilie, südländisch gewürzt	

Dazu Beilage nach Wahl

Tafelbutter per Portion	—.25
Toast per Stück	—.15

MÖVEN-PICKEREIEN

Club-Sandwich	4.50
Toast mit Pouletfleisch, gebratenem Speck, Ei, Tomaten und Mayonnaise	
Chicken Toast Red Up	5.—
Zartes Geflügelfleisch in Whisky-Rahmsauce	
Toast Ghia	6.—
Kleine Rindsfilets an einer pikanten Kräutersauce	
Toast Louis Armstrong	4.75
Geschnetzeltes Schweinefleisch mit Champignons in Rahmsauce, garniert mit gedünsteten Tomaten und Zwiebeln	
Beefburger Sandwich	3.—
Beefburger Rossini	4.—
Steak aus reinem, gehacktem Rindfleisch, mit Mousse de Foie gras	
Taipeh Burger	4.—
Reis mit Peperoni, Tomaten, Champignons und kleinen gehackten Rindfleischstücken in Sweet-Sour Sauce	
Frischgehacktes Rindssteak	4.—
Gebraten, mit gedämpften Zwiebeln und Sauerrahm	

SNACKS

Assiette Gourmet	7.—
Eine Auswahl von Mövenpick-Delikatessen wie: Rauchaal, Rauchlachs, Riesen-crevetten, Hering, Bündnerfleisch, Spargel und dänische Leberpastete	
Beefsteak Tartare	6.50
Raffiniert und pikant zubereitet mit Toast und Butter	
Roastbeef, Sauce Tartare	5.—
Croustade Française	3.—
Champignons auf Toast mit Schinken und Käse belegt, im Ofen überbacken	
Omelette	3.50
Mit Schinken oder Champignons	
Birchermüesli	2.—
Mit Schlagrahm	+ —.50

SMØRREBRØDS

1	Crevetten mit Zitrone und Mayonnaise	4.—
2	Lachsforelle geräuchert mit Sauce Mermaid	3.50
3	Roastbeef mit Boursin	2.50
4	**Tartare Toast mit Salzgurke**	3.50
5	**Tartare Toast**	3.50
	Gebraten, mit frisch geriebenem Meerrettich	

Bei Changements der Menubeilagen Zuschlag —.50

Semmel und Brot werden separat verrechnet —.20

—.50 Couvertzuschlag, wenn 2 Personen 1 Hauptgericht teilen. Für Kinder kein Zuschlag.

HERING AUS DEM FASS

Von den über 130 Millionen Kilo Heringen, die jährlich um Island gefangen werden, haben wir uns die schönsten Qualitäten gesichert und sie mit aromatischen Kräutern, viel Liebe und Fachkenntnis so raffiniert gewürzt, dass der Hering zu einer begehrten Delikatesse bei jung und alt geworden ist.

Matjes Grönland	3.—
In süss-saurer Senfsauce mit Dill	
Feuriger Matjes	3.—
In rassiger Senfsauce mit Oliven und Peperoni	
Matjes Esbjerg	3.50
In süss-saurer Rahmsauce mit Gurken- und Apfelstreifen	
Berliner Heringssalat	3.—
Mit Äpfeln, Zwiebeln und Salzgurke	
Matjes India	3.50
Mit Cornichons, India Relish und einer pikanten Sauce	
Herings Hors d'œuvre	4.—
Eine Auswahl von 5 verschiedenen Heringssalaten	

MÖVENPICK PARADEPLATZ
8001 Zürich, Paradeplatz 4
Telefon (051) 25 52 52
Direktion: W. Doppmann
Küchenchef: D. Fellmann

WALLISER KANNE
SPEISEKARTE

CARTE DES METS
BILL OF FARE

ARMAND UND HUGO
AUFDENBLATTEN

LEFT **Walliser Kanne, c. 1958, Zermatt, Switzerland**

BELOW **Speisekarte Deutschland, Brussels World's Fair, 1958, Brussels, Belgium**

West Germany's culinary entry at Brussels World's Fair featured dishes from around the country. Without any reference to East Germany, the piece seems to suggest, "We in the West are now a complete country unto ourselves."

Der kulinarische Beitrag der Bundesrepublik auf der Brüsseler Weltausstellung umfasste Gerichte aus dem ganzen Land. Ohne jeglichen Bezug zur DDR scheint die Karte zu sagen: „Wir im Westen sind jetzt unser eigenes Land."

Le pavillon ouest-allemand de l'Exposition internationale de Bruxelles propose des mets de toute l'Allemagne, sans aucune allusion à l'Allemagne de l'Est, comme pour dire : « À l'ouest, nous formons un pays à part entière. »

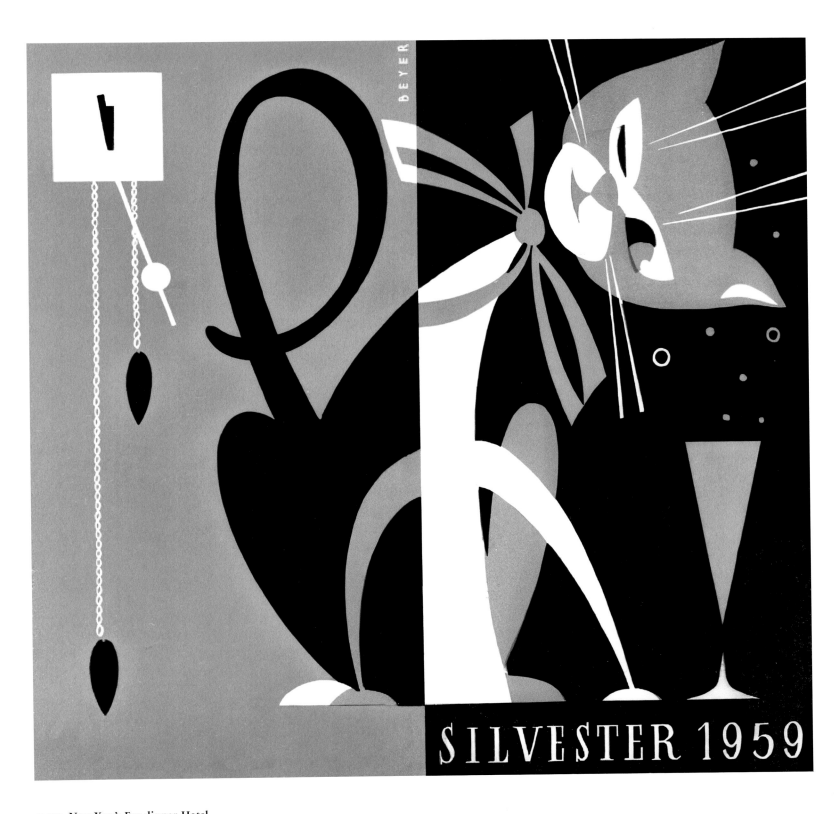

ABOVE New Year's Eve dinner, Hotel
Chemnitzer Hof, 1959, Karl-Marx-
Stadt, German Democratic Republic

CORPORATION OF LONDON

DOMINE DIRIGE NOS

Reception and Luncheon
to
HIS IMPERIAL MAJESTY
THE SHAHANSHAH OF
IRAN
at
Guildhall
Wednesday, 6th May, 1959

ABOVE **Luncheon for the shah of Iran, Guildhall, 1959, London, England**

Ellis Silas's menu for a banquet honoring the shah of Iran, with its decorative and pictorial elements, achieved the perfect balance of a Persian rug.

Ellis Silas' Titelseite einer Speisekarte für ein Bankett zu Ehren des Schahs von Persien erinnert mit ihren dekorativen und malerischen Elementen an das perfekte Gleichgewicht eines persischen Teppichs.

Avec cette couverture décorative et picturale du menu d'un banquet en l'honneur du shah d'Iran, Ellis Silas obtient l'équilibre parfait d'un tapis persan.

An East Indies restaurant in Amsterdam hinted at the city's colonial heritage. "Small tips" were offered, such as aperitifs are too sweet to drink before a meal, and beer is fine, but mineral water is preferred.

Ein ostindisches Restaurant in Amsterdam spielte auf das koloniale Erbe der Stadt an. Es gab „kleine Tipps", z. B. dass Aperitifs zu süß seien, um sie vor dem Essen zu trinken, und dass Bier in Ordnung, aber Mineralwasser besser sei.

Ce restaurant des Indes orientales à Amsterdam évoque le patrimoine colonial de la ville. On y propose «quelques astuces»: les apéritifs sont trop sucrés avant de manger, la bière est acceptée mais l'eau minérale préférée.

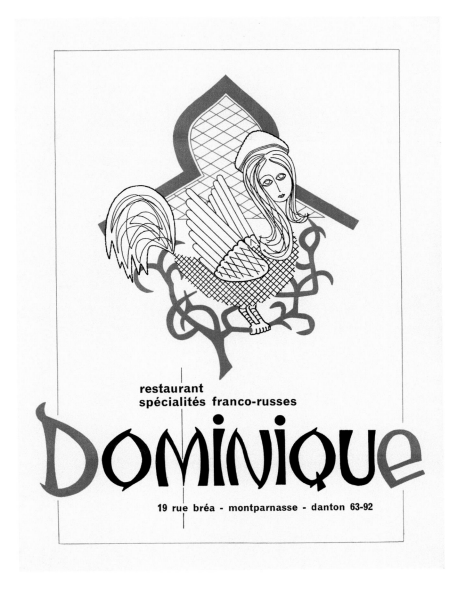

restaurant
spécialités franco-russes

DOMINIQUE

19 rue bréa - montparnasse - danton 63-92

ABOVE **Dominique, c. 1959, Paris, France**

RIJSTTAFELMENU LIDO
AMSTERDAM HOLLAND

Московский трест ресторанов

ПРЕЙСКУРАНТ

A café operated by a workers' collective, Moscow Trust Restaurants, presented a breakfast menu in four languages: English, French, German, and Russian. The most expensive item was fresh caviar.

Ein Café des Arbeiterkollektivs präsentierte eine Frühstückskarte in vier Sprachen: Englisch, Französisch, Deutsch und Russisch. Das teuerste Gericht war frischer Kaviar.

Gérés par des ouvriers, les Restaurants collectifs de Moscou proposent un menu de petit déjeuner en quatre langues : anglais, français, allemand et russe. Le mets le plus cher est un plat de caviar frais.

OPPOSITE **Bundesautobahn-Raststätte, c. 1959, Stuttgart, Federal Republic of Germany**

The closest European equivalent to the American drive-in was a service station for travelers stopping for a snack on Germany's autobahn system.

Das europäische Pendant zum amerikanischen Drive-in waren wohl die deutschen Autobahnraststätten, in denen Reisende einen Zwischenstopp einlegen und eine Kleinigkeit essen konnten.

L'équivalent approximatif du restaurant américain où l'on sert l'automobiliste au volant est, en Europe, la station-service d'une autoroute allemande.

Bundesautobahn-Raststätte
Stuttgart-Süd

Inh. *Hermann Weber*

SPEISENKARTE

Menu

Rôtisserie !

Pâté du chef

Restaurant Cattelin

STORKYRKOBRINKEN 9 · STOCKHOLM · TEL. 20 18 18   Roland Kempe 1960

Kalv vin
Tjärnd öl
Gravad
Strömming
Ost Sparris
vin
Löjrom
Filet de sole
öl
äs

Escargots
öl
vin

Pâté du chef
Paella
Espanol
Soupe à
l'oignon

Ost
vin
öl
äs
äs
vin

OPPOSITE Restaurant Cattelin, c. 1960,
Stockholm, Sweden

BELOW New Year's Eve dinner, Hotel
Chemnitzer Hof, 1960, Karl-Marx-
Stadt, German Democratic Republic

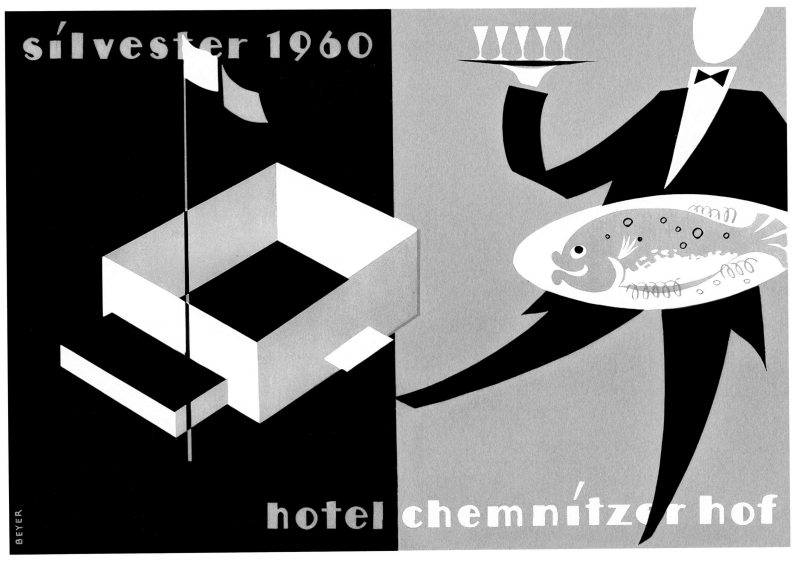

BELOW **7 Nationer, 1962, Copenhagen, Denmark**

Copenhagen's *Rådhuspladsen* (City Hall Square) seemed the ideal spot during the Cold War to open an upscale international food court. Separate dining rooms served the cuisines of Japan, Italy, Mexico, France, Denmark, and Britain, plus America's entry, the Explorer Bar.

Der Kopenhagener Rådhuspladsen (Rathausplatz) schien während des Kalten Krieges der ideale Ort für die Eröffnung eines gehobenen internationalen Food-Courts zu sein. In separaten Speisesälen wurde japanische, italienische, mexikanische, französische, dänische, britische und – in der Explorer Bar – auch amerikanische Küche serviert.

Pendant la guerre froide, la *Rådhuspladsen* (place de l'hôtel de ville) de Copenhague est le lieu idéal pour un restaurant international haut de gamme. Dans des salles différentes, on y déguste les cuisines du Japon, d'Italie, du Mexique, de France, du Danemark, de Grande-Bretagne et, dans l'Explorer Bar, d'Amérique.

OPPOSITE **Plaza Athénée, 1960, Paris, France**

CAMPARI *l'aperitivo*

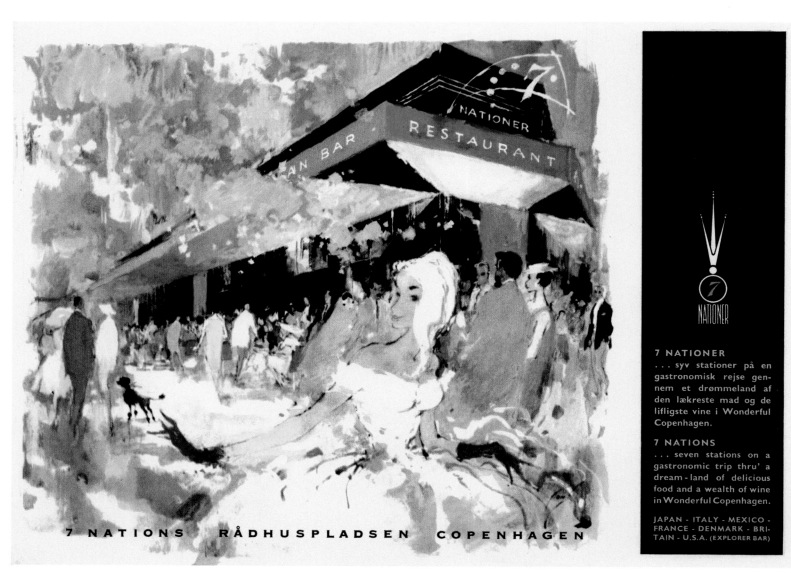

7 NATIONS   RÅDHUSPLADSEN   COPENHAGEN

7 NATIONER
... syv stationer på en gastronomisk rejse gennem et drømmeland af den lækreste mad og de lifligste vine i Wonderful Copenhagen.

7 NATIONS
... seven stations on a gastronomic trip thru' a dream-land of delicious food and a wealth of wine in Wonderful Copenhagen.

JAPAN - ITALY - MEXICO - FRANCE - DENMARK - BRITAIN - U.S.A. (EXPLORER BAR)

Frutta d'Italia A. Salietti

Grand
Hôtel de la Ville
Via Sistina, 67-71
(Trinità dei Monti)
Roma

OPPOSITE Grand Hôtel de la Ville, 1960, Rome, Italy

LEFT Europa Hotel, 1969, Mainz, Federal Republic of Germany

BELOW Bentley's, 1968, London, England

ABOVE **Rôtisserie Coq d'Or, 1965, Vienna, Austria**

RIGHT **Au Mouton de Panurge, 1961, Paris, France**

Albert Dubout's crazy cartoons of crowd scenes were once everywhere: magazine ads, dust jackets, record covers, movie posters, and more. His distinctive style was immediately recognizable, with or without his signature.

Albert Dubouts verrückte Karikaturen von Menschenmengen waren einst überall zu sehen: in Zeitschriftenanzeigen,

auf Schutzumschlägen, Plattencovern, Filmplakaten etc. Seinen Stil erkannte man sofort wieder – mit oder ohne seine Unterschrift.

À l'époque, les folles scènes de foules que dessine Albert Dubout sont partout : publicités de magazines, jaquettes, pochettes de disque, affiches de film, etc. Avec ou sans sa signature, son style est reconnaissable au premier coup d'œil.

OPPOSITE **La Rôtisserie Ardennaise, c. 1960, Brussels, Belgium**

La Rôtisserie

Ardennaise

146-148, Bd. Ad. MAX et Rue de MALINES, 26
BRUXELLES-NORD
Tél. : 17.58.17 - 17.58.18 - 17.80.71

HARRY'S BAR
FIRENZE

A la Carte MENU

U. S. Armed Forces Recreation Center

Good Morning!

Breakfast Menu

ARMED FORCES RECREATION CENTER

Berchtesgaden
Garmisch Chiemsee

ABOVE LEFT & RIGHT **U.S. Armed Forces Recreation Center, 1960, Berchtesgaden, Federal Republic of Germany**

OPPOSITE **Harry's Bar, c. 1960, Florence, Italy**

The trendy bar with an open view of the Arno River was as American as its founder, an Italian bartender. Like its famous compatriots in Venice, Paris, and New York, the Harry's in Florence ran on the fumes of alcohol—specifically award-winning cocktails.

Die angesagte Bar mit freiem Blick auf den Arno war so amerikanisch wie ihr Gründer, ein italienischer Barkeeper. Wie seine berühmten Pendants in Venedig, Paris und New York wurde das Harry's in Florenz für seine alkoholischen Kreationen geschätzt – vor allem für seine preisgekrönten Cocktails.

Ce bar chic de Florence, avec vue sur l'Arno, est aussi américain que son fondateur, un patron de bar italien. Comme ses célèbres homologues de Venise, Paris et New York, le Harry's florentin carbure aux vapeurs d'alcool de ses cocktails primés.

CAFÉ · RESTAURANT
SALON DE THÉ · SNACK

Madeleine =Tronchet

35, PLACE DE LA MADELEINE
1, RUE TRONCHET · PARIS-8ᵉ
Téléph. : ANJou 60-47 et 60-48

LEFT **Madeleine-Tronchet, 1963, Paris, France**

A simple menu for a terrace that was the Café de la Paix's rival on the Right Bank included a special one-course selection titled "Menu Touristique." It was important to know one's clientele.

Die einfache Speisekarte einer Terrasse, die mit dem Café de la Paix am Rive Droite konkurrierte, enthielt ein spezielles Ein-Gang-Menü, das menu touristique. Es war schon immer wichtig, seine Kundschaft zu kennen.

Un menu simple pour cette terrasse parisienne, concurrente du Café de la Paix sur la rive droite. Le « menu touristique » – toujours connaître sa clientèle ! – propose un seul plat.

OPPOSITE **Milchbar Ilmenau, c. 1960, Ilmenau, German Democratic Republic**

RIGHT **Milchbar Pinguin, c. 1965, Leipzig, German Democratic Republic**

East German graphic design borrowed heavily from Western sources, and this charming illustration could have easily been found at sophisticated locations on the other side of the Iron Curtain.

Das Grafikdesign der DDR war stark an westliche Quellen angelehnt. Diese charmante Illustration hätte man auch in gehobenen Lokalen auf der anderen Seite des Eisernen Vorhangs finden können.

Le graphisme est-allemand s'inspire fortement de sources occidentales. Cette jolie illustration aurait pu aussi bien se trouver dans des restaurants chics de l'autre côté du rideau de fer.

MILCHBAR

Pinguin

LEFT **The Bridge Hotel, 1961, Prestbury, England**

OPPOSITE **Le Grand Véfour, 1969, Paris, France**

BELOW LEFT & RIGHT **Lasserre, 1961, Paris, France**

Pride and anger are just two of the deadly sins often expressed by putti. Artist E. Maudy created a series of paintings for Lasserre featuring rambunctious cherubs tormenting a milkmaid.

Stolz und Zorn sind zwei der Todsünden, die oft von Putten dargestellt werden. Für das Lasserre schuf der Künstler E. Maudy eine Reihe von Gemälden, auf denen ausgelassene nackte Knaben ein Milchmädchen ärgern.

L'orgueil et la colère, deux des péchés capitaux, sont souvent représentés par des angelots. E. Maudy est l'auteur d'une série de peintures pour Lasserre, où l'on voit des angelots turbulents tourmenter une laitière.

Le Grand Véfour's neighbor and frequent customer Jean Cocteau created his harlequin-themed menu cover the same year that chef Raymond Oliver was awarded three stars from Michelin. Cocteau's dear friend Colette, who once lived upstairs, presided at her own banquette. The restaurant continued to use Cocteau's menu for decades.

Jean Cocteau, Nachbar und Stammgast des Le Grand Véfour, entwarf in dem Jahr, in dem der Küchenchef Raymond Oliver mit drei Michelin-Sternen ausgezeichnet wurde, eine Titelseite mit Harlekinmotiv. Cocteaus gute Freundin Colette, die einst im Obergeschoss gewohnte hatte, hatte hier ihren Stammplatz. Das Restaurant verwendete Cocteaus Speisekarte noch jahrzehntelang.

Voisin et habitué du Grand Véfour, Jean Cocteau a dessiné cette couverture de menu à l'effigie d'Arlequin l'année où Raymond Oliver fut récompensé par trois étoiles au *Guide Michelin*. L'écrivaine Colette, amie intime de Cocteau, y présidait sur sa banquette. Le menu signé Cocteau a servi pendant des décennies.

L'ORGUEIL

LA COLÈRE

Palais Royal

Jean Cocteau
× 1955

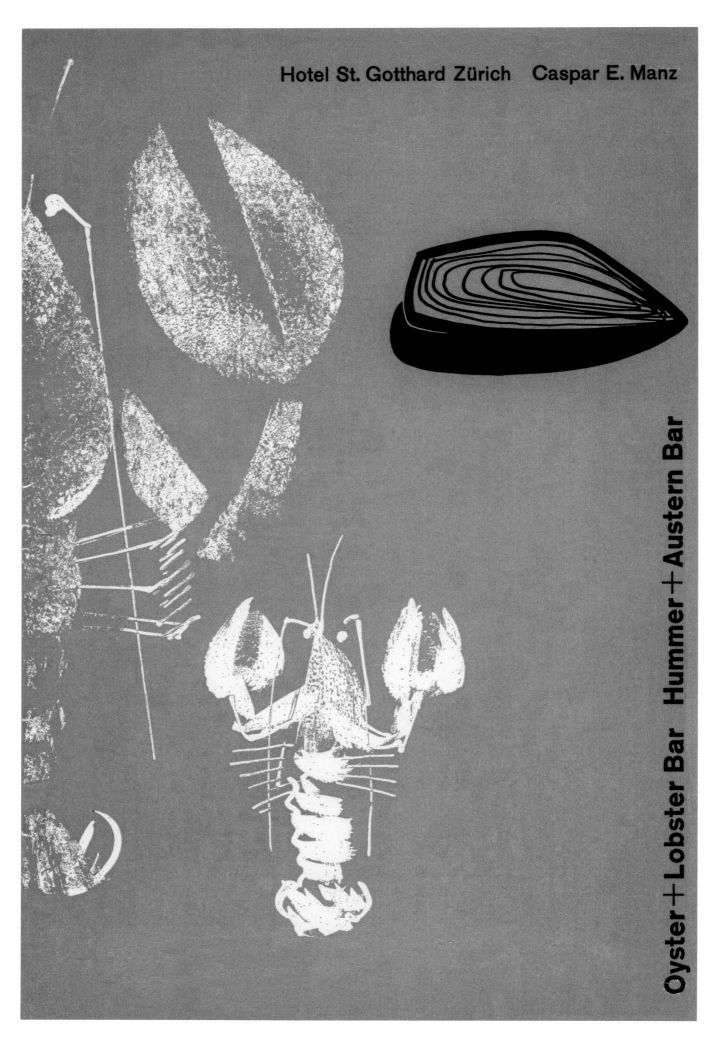

Hotel St. Gotthard Zürich   Caspar E. Manz

Oyster+Lobster Bar Hummer+Austern Bar

OPPOSITE Hotel St. Gotthard, 1962, Zurich, Switzerland

The Hummerbar, which continues to operate behind a red door, features Maine lobsters and seafood prepared in "variations of sushi and French cuisine."

Die Hummerbar, die immer noch hinter einer roten Tür betrieben wird, bietet Hummer aus Maine und Meeresfrüchte, die in „Variationen von Sushi und französischer Küche" gereicht werden.

Le Hummerbar de Zurich, dont la porte d'entrée est toujours rouge, propose du homard du Maine (nordest des États-Unis) et des fruits de mer sous forme de «sushis variés et de cuisine française».

ABOVE Restaurante Korynto, c. 1962, Madrid, Spain

RIGHT Coffee House, Hilton Hotel, c. 1962, Berlin, Federal Republic of Germany

TABLE D'HÔTE LUNCHEON

TARIFF

PROPRIETORS - J.LYONS & Cº LTD

Je vous offre mon cœur, oh mon très tendre amour,
Acceptez-le chérie, sans perdre une seconde,
Avec un doux présent qu'on apprécie toujours,
Le célèbre COINTREAU, aux quatre coins du monde.

Paul MIRVIL

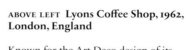

ABOVE LEFT **Lyons Coffee Shop, 1962, London, England**

Known for the Art Deco design of its coffee shops, the Lyons chain continued its graphic 1930s look beyond the mid-century.

Die Lyons-Kette, die für das Art-déco-Design ihrer Cafés bekannt war, setzte den grafischen Look der 1930er-Jahre auch nach der Jahrhundertmitte fort.

Célèbre pour le style Art déco de ses salons de thé, la chaîne Lyons a conservé le graphisme des années 1930 bien au-delà des années 1950.

ABOVE RIGHT **Disciples d'Antonin Carême, L'École Hôtelière Jean-Drouant, 1960, Paris, France**

LEFT **Savoy, 1964, London, England**

OPPOSITE **Sallingsund Færgekro, c. 1960, Nykøbing, Denmark**

Menü

Sallingsund
Færgekro

Si vous avez trouvé le service agréable --
si non, nous vous prions de nous le faire
savoir. Merci
CORTÉS

PALM BEACH
CANNES

PAGE 375 **Palm Beach Cannes,
c. 1964, Cannes, France**

BELOW **Kalastajatorppa, c. 1966,
Helsinki, Finland**

RIGHT **Helmuth Reisshauer,
c. 1962, Berlin, Federal Republic of
Germany**

Clodoaldo Cortés's Club 31 was not
a typical *Madrileño* tapas bar but a
place with a "French-inspired menu,"
which, along with his other restaurant, Jockey, became a darling of the
political and jet sets. Cortés also
directed the restaurant at the Spanish
pavilion of the 1964 New York
World's Fair.

Der Club 31 von Clodoaldo Cortés
war keine gewöhnliche Tapas-Bar
in Madrid, sondern ein Lokal mit
einer „französisch inspirierten Speisekarte", das zusammen mit seinem
anderen Restaurant, dem Jockey,
zum Liebling von Politikern und
der Schickeria wurde. Auf der New
Yorker Weltausstellung von 1964
leitete Cortés auch das Restaurant
des spanischen Pavillons.

Le Club 31 de Clodoaldo Cortés,
qui n'a rien du bar à tapas madrilène
ordinaire, propose un menu à la française. Comme son autre restaurant,
le Jockey, le Club 31 est très prisé
des milieux politiques et mondains.
Cortés dirigera aussi le restaurant
du pavillon espagnol de l'Exposition
internationale de New York.

ERKKI TANTTU · PUUPIIRROS · TRÄSNITT · WOODCUT

LASSERRE

PARIS

ÉDEN

ESPRESSO

SIÓFOK

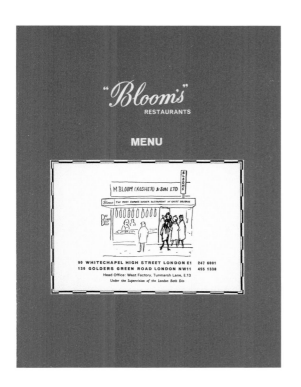

"Bloom's" RESTAURANTS

MENU

H.BLOOM (KOSHER) & SON LTD

90 WHITECHAPEL HIGH STREET LONDON E1 247 6001
130 GOLDERS GREEN ROAD LONDON NW11 455 1338
Head Office: West Factory, Tunmarsh Lane, E.13
Under the Supervision of the London Beth Din

PAGE 378 **Café de la Paix, 1965, Paris, France**

PAGE 379 **Lasserre, c. 1968, Paris, France**

OPPOSITE **Éden, 1968, Siófok, Hungary**

LEFT **Bloom's Restaurants, 1965, London, England**

At the time Bloom's claimed to be one of the few kosher restaurants in London, declaring a "rabbi and a religious supervisor on the premises every day." The restaurant, founded in 1920, also had a canning operation with the motto "Buy Bloom's Best Beef."

In den 1960er-Jahren bezeichnete sich das Bloom's als eines der wenigen koscheren Restaurants in London, wo „jeden Tag ein Rabbi und ein religiöser Aufseher vor Ort" seien. Das 1920 gegründete Restaurant führte auch einen Konservenbetrieb mit dem Slogan „Buy Bloom's Best Beef".

À cette époque, Bloom affirme être l'un des rares restaurants casher de Londres, grâce à la «présence quotidienne d'un rabbin et d'un contrôleur religieux». Fondée en 1920, cette maison est aussi une conserverie au slogan prometteur: «Au bon bœuf Bloom» (*Buy Bloom's Best Beef*).

BELOW LEFT **The Haversnack, 1966, London, England**

BELOW RIGHT **Maggi, 1965, Orselina, Switzerland**

THE
HAVERSNACK

WIMPY....

King Size pure beef Hamburger with the double filling		3/3
The Hamburger made from freshly ground 100% pure beef		1/9
Cheeseburger		2/3

TORPEDOES.....

Cheese and Tomato	1/6
Ham	1/6
Egg and Tomato	1/6
Toasted Sandwiches (various)	1/6

PASTRIES.....

Fruit Disc	1/6
Scotch Shortbread	6d
Congress Tart	8d
Eclair	1/-
Bakewell Flan	1/-
Danish Pastry	1/-
Banana Pretty	1/-

TEA 8d   MILK 11d   COFFEE 1/- HORLICKS (hot or cold) 1/- HOT CHOCOLATE 1/-

SODA FOUNTAIN

ICED DRINKS....	Corner House Orange Drink	11d
	Corner House Lemon Drink	11d
	Coca-Cola	1/-
ICE CREAM	Vanilla	10d & 1/8
	Vanilla and Strawberry (mixed)	10d & 1/8
	Chocolate Fudge Sauce	6d
ICE CREAM SODA.	Lemon	1/9
	Strawberry	1/9
SPECIAL........	Knickerbocker Glory	2/9
SUNDAES	Jelly	1/6
	Chocolate Nut	1/9
	Fruit	2/3

24366

MENU   MAGGI

LUNCH	MITTAGESSEN
Grape fruit	Grape fruit
---	---
Langue de boeuf	Rindszunge
Côte de blette	Krautstiele gedämpft
Pommes fines herbes	Petersilienkartoffeln
Salade	Salat
---	---
Pêche Melba	Pfirsich Melba

DINER	ABENDESSEN
Bouillon Vermicelles	Fidelisuppe
---	---
Cordon bleu	Cordon bleu
Pommes paysanne	Spinat à la crême
Epinards à la crême	Bauernkartoffeln
Salade	Salat
---	---
Fraises chantilly	Erdbeeren mit Rahm

Orselina, le 21 juillet 65

ABOVE & RIGHT Les Armes de
Bretagne, c. 1966, Paris, France

FRUITS DE MER

HUITRES

MOULES DE PARC
la douzaine

OURSINS
la pièce

CLAMS
la pièce

Belons 0,
les six

Spéciales 2,
les six

Claires 2,
les six

Belons 2,
les six

Spéciales Papillons,
les six

Marennes 0,
les six

Claires 4,
les six

BOUQUET ROYAL

PALOURDES
la douzaine

PRAIRES
la douzaine

*Nous nous ferons un plaisir de vous
aider dans votre choix*

ENTRÉES ET ROTS

Chateaubriand Béarnaise
pour deux personnes

Côte de bœuf à la moelle
pour deux personnes

Contrefilet grillé, maître d'hôtel

Filet de bœuf au poivre vert

Escalope de veau Viennoise

Cailles Saint-Vincent

Lamb chops vert-pré

Confit de canard Montesquiou

Coquelet

Carré d'agneau *pour deux personnes*

Faisan Beaumanoir

LÉGUMES

Fonds d'artichauts

Petits pois

Champignons sautés

Pommes sautées

Salade

Endives Meunière

Haricots verts

FROMAGES

ENTREMETS

Glaces
Sorbets
Vacherin
Tarte Tatin
Mignardises
Poire Bourdaloue
Poire Belle Hélène
Pêches flambées à la vodka

FRUITS

ENTREMETS

Ananas
Pêche Melba
Café liégeois
Gourmandise
Parfait au café
Crème caramel
Bananes flambées
au Grand Marnier
Coupe de fruits au Cherry

Café à l'Italienne
Café Melior

L'addition détaillée vous sera remise, si vous en exprimez le désir.

Service 15% non compris, perçu par le personnel.

ABOVE LEFT **Café Mosaik, 1968, Berlin, German Democratic Republic**

ABOVE RIGHT **Mitropa, 1968, Magdeburg, German Democratic Republic**

The red automobile on the dinner plate is a visual reference to the red railroad dining cars of the Mitropa catering company. Mitropa also operated restaurants at train stations, on passenger ships, and at rest stops along East German highways.

Das rote Auto auf dem Teller ist eine visuelle Anspielung auf die roten Eisenbahnspeisewagen der Bewirtungs- und Beherbergungsgesellschaft Mitropa. Sie betrieb auch Gaststätten in Bahnhöfen, Schiffsrestaurants sowie Autobahnraststätten in der DDR.

La voiture rouge qui orne l'assiette fait allusion aux wagons-restaurants de Mitropa, entreprise de restauration également présente dans les gares, sur les bateaux à passagers et les aires de repos des routes est-allemandes.

OPPOSITE **Flughafen Restaurant, c. 1967, Frankfurt, Federal Republic of Germany**

PAGE 386 **Le Coq Hardi, c. 1967, Bougival, France**

PAGE 387 **La Gran Tasca, c. 1969, Seville, Spain**

FLUGHAFEN

RESTAURANT

FRANKFURT AM MAIN

A. Steigenberger-Hotelgesellschaft KG. a. A.

LA GRAN TASCA

Parrilla

Gloire au Restaurant

Paris 14 decembre 72

C. Terechkovitch

OPPOSITE **Gloire au Restaurant, 1972,
Paris, France**

BELOW LEFT **Le Louis XIV, 1972, Paris,
France**

BELOW RIGHT **Air France, 1970, Paris,
France**

RIGHT Salle des Étoiles, Monte Carlo
Sporting Club, 1975, Monte Carlo,
Monaco

BELOW Berliner Bierstube, c. 1975,
Berlin, German Democratic Republic

OPPOSITE Zur Auster, Fish and Oyster
Restaurant, 1970, Düsseldorf, Federal
Republic of Germany

Fisch- und Austern-Spezialitäten-Restaurant
Düsseldorf · Bergerstraße 9 · Telefon 32 44 04

LEFT **Mitropa, 1970, Berlin, German Democratic Republic**

The East German dining-car company was still using Karl Schulpig's originally commissioned type font decades after its creation.

Die ursprünglich bei Karl Schulpig in Auftrag gegebene Schrift wurde noch Jahrzehnte später von der Speisewagengesellschaft der DDR verwendet.

Plusieurs décennies après sa création, la police de caractères créée par Karl Schulpig est toujours utilisée par l'entreprise de wagons-restaurants est-allemande qui la lui avait commandée.

BELOW See Restaurant, c. 1970,
Böblingen, Federal Republic of
Germany

RIGHT Hotel Neptun, 1972, Rostock,
German Democratic Republic

ABOVE **Le Relais du Café Royal, 1970, London, England**

RIGHT & OPPOSITE **Hotel Budapest, 1970, Budapest, Hungary**

Reflecting the Eastern Bloc's optimistic mood and the nascent wanderlust of its population, the restaurant, located in this new upscale hotel, offered moody menu-cover graphics and an expansive listing of comestibles.

Neben einer umfangreichen Liste von Speisen bot dieses in einem neuen Nobelhotel gelegene Restaurant Speisekarten mit modernen Grafiken, die die optimistische Stimmung des Ostblocks und die aufkommende Reiselust seiner Bevölkerung widerspiegelten.

Caractéristique de l'optimisme et de l'envie nouvelle de voyager des habitants d'Europe de l'Est, ce restaurant d'un hôtel chic de Budapest propose une carte très variée, dont les couvertures de menu sont le reflet.

CARTE
BRASSERIE

PAGE 396 **La Samaritaine, c. 1971, Paris, France**

PAGE 397 **Quinzi & Gabrieli, c. 1973, Rome, Italy**

LEFT **Tele Café, c. 1970, East Berlin, German Democratic Republic**

When completed in 1969, the Berliner Fernsehturm was considered the symbol of the Communist Party in Germany and is now an emblem of a reunited Berlin. A revolving restaurant caps the monument.

Der Berliner Fernsehturm galt bei seiner Fertigstellung 1969 als Prestigeobjekt der DDR und ist heute ein Wahrzeichen des wiedervereinigten Berlins. Das Restaurant oben im Turm dreht sich.

Achevée en 1969, la Tour de la télévision de Berlin, jadis symbole du parti communiste est-allemand, est aujourd'hui l'emblème de la réunification de la ville. Au sommet se trouve un restaurant tournant.

East German teenagers were permitted by the authorities to gather at the town hall to eat, drink, and party—but not rebelliously—at an official "Youth Dance."

Beim offiziellen „Jugendtanz" durften sich die ostdeutschen Jugendlichen im Oranienburger Rathaus versammeln, um zu essen, zu trinken und zu feiern – aber nicht zu wild.

Dans ce «dancing pour jeunes» officiel, les adolescents est-allemands sont autorisés à se réunir à la mairie de la ville pour manger, boire et faire la fête, mais sans se révolter.

ROSTANG

RESTAURANT   SASSENAGE

les frères TROISGROS

LEFT **Les Frères Troisgros, 1974, Roanne, France**

BELOW *SS France*, **Compagnie Générale Transatlantique, 1972**

For its first around-the-world cruise, the then-largest of ocean lines associated its navigational feat with Phileas Fogg's global dash as told in *Around the World in Eighty Days*. Numerous menu cover designs coincided with verses from Fogg's narrative.

Bei seiner ersten Weltumsegelung verglich der damals größte Ozeandampfer seine Navigationsleistung mit Phileas Foggs Weltumsegelung, die in Jules Vernes Roman *Reise um die Erde in 80 Tagen* erzählt wird. Die Titeldesigns zahlreicher Speisekarten stellten Szenen aus der Geschichte über Fogg dar.

Pour sa première croisière autour du monde, le *France*, le plus grand paquebot de son temps, associe cet exploit à celui de Phileas Fogg dans *Le Tour du monde en quatre-vingts jours*. De nombreuses couvertures de menu illustrent des passages de ce récit.

OPPOSITE **Rostang Restaurant, c. 1975, Sassenage, France**

Unusual for a restaurant in a small town, Rostang published its menu in a limited, numbered edition. Its culinary dynasty began here before expanding under the direction of master chef Michel Rostang.

Das Rostang veröffentlichte seine Speisekarte in einer limitierten, nummerierten Auflage, was für ein Restaurant in einer Kleinstadt ungewöhnlich war. Hier begann eine kulinarische Dynastie, die unter der Leitung von Meisterkoch Michel Rostang weiter expandierte.

Chose inhabituelle pour un restaurant de petite ville, le menu de Rostang est diffusé en édition limitée et numérotée. La dynastie culinaire est antérieure à l'expansion de cette maison sous la direction de son chef Michel Rostang.

CENTENAIRE DU VOYAGE DE PHILEAS FOGG

PAQUEBOT FRANCE
CROISIERE AUTOUR DU MONDE

COMPAGNIE GÉNÉRALE TRANSATLANTIQUE
French Line

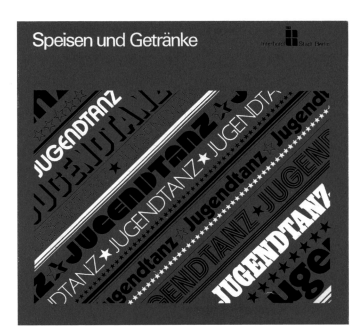

OPPOSITE Russisches Restaurant, c. 1975, Rostock, German Democratic Republic

ABOVE LEFT Hotel Neptun, c. 1975, Rostock, German Democratic Republic

ABOVE RIGHT Winterball, Interhotel, c. 1975, Berlin, German Democratic Republic

LEFT Jugendtanz, Interhotel, c. 1975, Berlin, German Democratic Republic

OPPOSITE & THIS PAGE Air France, 1974, Paris, France

On a flight from Paris to Los Angeles, first-class passengers were served identical meals but handed different menus. That year Air France had reproduced original artwork selected in a worldwide drawing competition for children organized by the United Nations Children's Emergency Fund (UNICEF). The cover artwork is by Sabeh Khalfallah, age 14, from Tunisia (opposite); Moro Domingo, age 16, Spain (above); and Parmar Jaishree, age 14, India (left).

Auf einem Flug von Paris nach Los Angeles erhielten die Erste-Klasse-Passagiere identische Mahlzeiten, doch unterschiedliche Speisekarten. In jenem Jahr verwendete Air France die Kunstwerke von Kindern, die an einem internationalen Malwettbewerb des Kinderhilfswerks der Vereinten Nationen (UNICEF) teilgenommen hatten. Die Titelbilder stammen von Sabeh Khalfallah, 14 Jahre, Tunesien (gegenüber); Moro Domingo, 16 Jahre, Spanien (oben); und Parmar Jaishree, 14 Jahre, Indien (links).

Les passagers de première classe du vol Paris-Los Angeles mangent tous la même chose, mais reçoivent des menus différents car, cette année-là, Air France les illustre de dessins d'enfants originaux, choisis lors d'un concours international organisé par l'UNICEF. Ces couvertures sont dues à Sabeh Khalfallah, 14 ans, Tunisie (page précédente) ; Moro Domingo, 16 ans, Espagne (ci-dessus) ; et Parmar Jaishree, 14 ans, Inde (ci-contre).

ABOVE **Restaurant Zinnkrug, c. 1974, Salzburg, Austria**

Form meets function in a die-cut beverage menu in the shape of a beer tankard.

Auf dieser ausgestanzten Bierkrug-Getränkekarte trifft Form auf Funktion.

Aspect et fonction sont réunis dans ce menu en forme de bock de bière.

"Ambiance de Cave"

d'après Philip

"La Bourgogne"

6, AVENUE BOSQUET
PARIS-VII*

Restaurant
CITADELLA
Étterem

OPPOSITE Restaurant Citadella, 1974, Budapest, Hungary

RIGHT Hecker's Deele, c. 1974, Berlin, Federal Republic of Germany

BELOW Hotel Luz, c. 1973, Seville, Spain

SPEISEN

HECKERS · DEELE · BERLIN

CARTA

LEFT Café Prag, 1978, Dresden, German Democratic Republic

BELOW New Year's Eve, Interhotel, 1976, Berlin, German Democratic Republic

OPPOSITE Asiatisches Restaurant, c. 1975, Rostock, German Democratic Republic

ASIATISCHES
RESTAURANT

RIGHT McDonald's, c. 1976, Switzerland

A paper tablemat is visual documentation
of how 4,000-plus franchises maintained
"constant quality." The popularity of such
fast-food places in Europe challenges the
idea of culinary superiority of the continent.

Die Papierunterlage veranschaulicht
die „konstante Qualität" von über 4.000
Franchise-Filialen. Die Beliebtheit solcher
Fast-Food-Lokale in Europa stellt die
Vorstellung von der kulinarischen Überle-
genheit des Kontinents infrage.

Ce set de table en papier témoigne
visuellement de la «qualité permanente»
de cette chaîne de plus de 4 000 restaurants.
Le succès des fast-foods en Europe remet
en cause l'idée de supériorité culinaire du
continent.

McDonald's

Le nouveau
à n

Pur boeuf de 1ère qualité

Hamburger Fr. 1.80

Cheeseburger Fr. 2.10

Big Mac

Un délicieux dessert chaud.
tendre et croustillante ... fo
compote de pommes parfu
cannelle et de
clous de girofle ...

Hamburger à "2 étages" Fr. 4.–

Chausson aux pommes

Café Fr. 1.–
Cacao chaud Fr. 1.10
Lait Fr. 1.10

Coca-Cola
Sprite - limonade
Fanta - orange   norma
Jus de pomme   grand

cDonald's
laisir de se restaurer
lleur compte

McDonald's ®

Mac le Marin

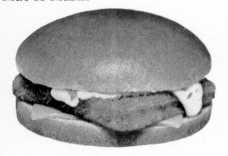

Sandwich au poisson frit Fr. 2.–

Le Quart

Fr. 3.70
Portion "royale" de hamburger

Le Quart au fromage Fr. 4.30

A EMPORTER !

. . . .

Pour vos soirées télé ou
si vous êtes en retard. . .
ou si vous n'avez pas envie
de faire la cuisine
mais de faire des économies. . .

Pommes Frites

Normal Fr. 1.10
Grand cornet Fr. 1.60

Mac Shake (frappé glacé)

Chocolat/Vanille/Fraise/Mocca Fr. 2.–

Bière Fr. 1.40

McDonald's
c'est la garantie d'une qualité
constante et d'un service
expérimenté apprécié
journellement par les
consommateurs des
4000 restaurants McDonald's
dans le monde.
McDonald's vous offre
toujours davantage.

McDonald's
Switzerland ®

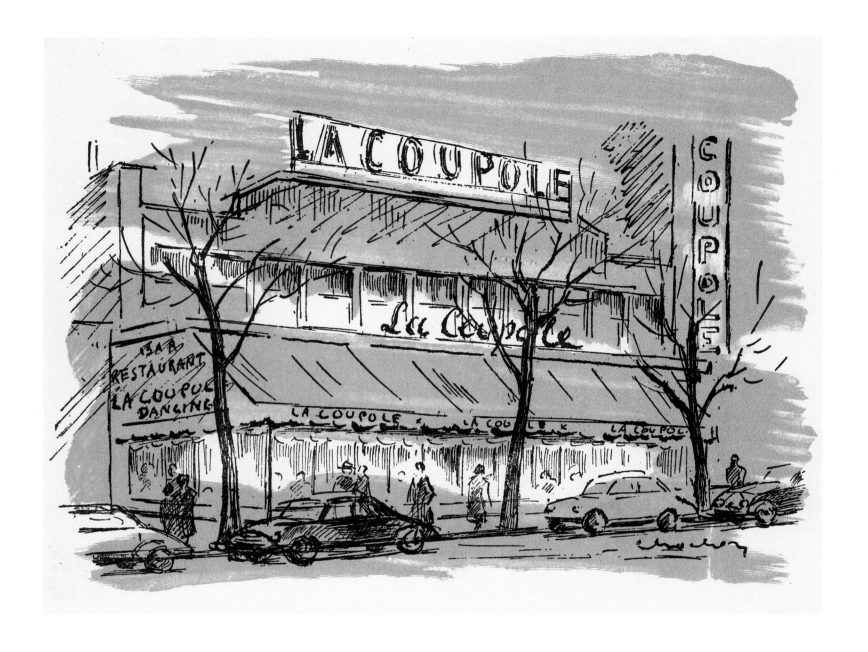

ABOVE La Coupole, 1979, Paris, France

The landmark La Coupole café enjoyed immense popularity well into the 1970s, shining as a hub of late-night activity much as it had in the 1930s.

Das berühmte Café La Coupole erfreute sich bis weit in die 1970er-Jahre hinein großer Beliebtheit und war schon in den 1930er-Jahren ein Hotspot des Pariser Nachtlebens.

Au cœur de la vie nocturne parisienne, ce célèbre restaurant connaît encore dans les années 1970 l'immense succès qui est le sien depuis les années 1930.

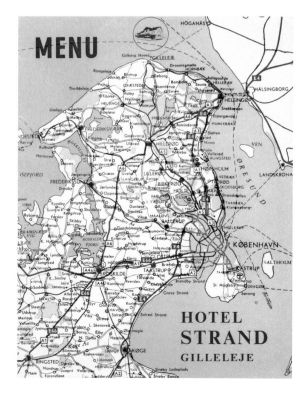

THE
OLD PALACE,
HATFIELD HOUSE,
County of HERTFORD
ENGLAND

OPPOSITE The Old Palace, Hatfield House, c. 1981, Hatfield, England

T R O I S G R O S

À la famille Troisgros, qui, composé avec les parfums de la terre, mille et un repas oniriques.

ENOTECA
PINCHIORRI

ABOVE **Les Frères Troisgros, c. 1983, Roanne, France**

The patriarchs of the Troisgros family, brothers Pierre and Jean, were culinary innovators who promoted nouvelle cuisine, propelling their restaurant to the status of one of the best restaurants in the world.

Die Brüder Pierre und Jean, die von den Patriarchen der Familie Troisgros beaufsichtigt wurden, waren kulinarische Innovatoren, die die Nouvelle Cuisine propagierten und ihr Restaurant zu einem der besten der Welt machten.

Sous l'œil des patriarches de la famille Troigros, les frères Pierre et Jean innovent avec la nouvelle cuisine et propulsent leur table parmi les meilleurs restaurants du monde.

LEFT **Enoteca Pinchiorri, 1984, Florence, Italy**

OPPOSITE **Tanzbar Kosmos, 1982, Karl-Marx-Stadt, German Democratic Republic**

TANZBAR KOSMOS

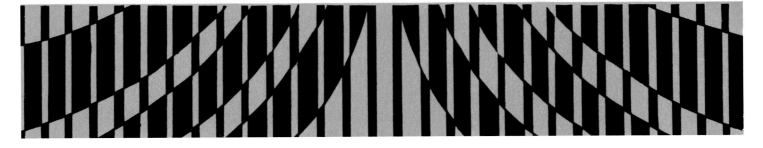

il terzo sesso

Pour
maintenir l'Esprit
de la Grande Cuisine
Française et Régionale en
sauvegardant les plats saisonniers
Jean et Pierre Troisgros ont
recréé pour votre plaisir
l'ordonnance des Menus
d'Antan

PAGE 422 Le Paname, c. 1982, Paris, France

PAGE 423 Papa Giovanni, 1984, Rome, Italy

LEFT Les Frères Troisgros, 1985, Roanne, France

RIGHT Dinner for the Gorbachevs, United States Embassy, 1988, Moscow, Soviet Union

The U.S. ambassador invited Russia's first couple into his official residence and to an uninspired dinner. It concluded with frozen custard and dry cookies.

Der US-Botschafter lud das russische Präsidentenpaar zu einem fantasielosen Abendessen in seine offizielle Residenz ein. Es endete mit gefrorenem Pudding und trockenen Keksen.

L'ambassadeur des États-Unis invite M. et Mme Gorbatchev dans sa résidence officielle pour un dîner sans inspiration, qui s'achève par une mousse au chocolat et des gâteaux secs.

BELOW Dinner for the royal wedding, The Dorchester, 1981, London, England

BELOW RIGHT Lameloise, c. 1984, Chagny, France

DINNER
Honoring
His Excellency
The General Secretary of the Central Committee of the Communist Party of the Soviet Union and Mrs. Gorbachev

Lobster Bisque
Sesame Sticks

Supreme of Chicken
with Truffle Sauce
Cherry Tomatoes with Fleurons
Carrot Soufflé and June Peas

Mixed Green Salad
Brie Cheese

Frozen Chocolate Mousse
Vanilla Sauce
Petits Fours Sec

LA CREMA *Reserve Chardonnay 1986*
CHALONE *Pinot Noir 1981*
SCHARFFENBERGER *Summit Cuvée 1984*

SPASO HOUSE
MOSCOW
Tuesday, May 31, 1988

IN CELEBRATION
OF THE MARRIAGE OF
THE PRINCE of WALES
&
LADY DIANA SPENCER

Royal Wedding Week
July 1981

The Dorchester

Lameloise

Ταβέρνα

"ΚΑΛΟΚΑΙΡΙΝΟΣ,,
ΑΝΤΩΝΗΣ ΓΑΛΑΝΟΠΟΥΛΟΣ & ΥΙΟΣ
ΟΔΟΣ ΚΕΚΡΟΠΟΣ 10 - ΤΗΛ. 32.32.054

ΠΛΑΚΑ - ΑΘΗΝΑΙ

L'Auberge du Père Bise

PAGE 426 **Kalokerinos Tavern, 1984, Athens, Greece**

PAGE 427 **L'Auberge du Père Bise, 1985, Talloires-Montmin, France**

Marguerite Bise, the founder's daughter-in-law, made L'Auberge du Pere Bise's excellent cuisine famous, giving rise to its reputation as one of the best restaurants in France. In 1951 Bise became the third woman to obtain a Michelin three-star rating.

Marguerite Bise, die Schwiegertochter des Gründers des L'Auberge du Père Bise, machte die ausgezeichnete Küche des Lokals berühmt und begründete seinen Ruf als eines der besten Restaurants in Frankreich. 1951 war Bise die dritte Frau, die mit drei Michelin-Sternen ausgezeichnet wurde.

Belle-fille du fondateur de L'Auberge du Père Bise, Marguerite Bise fait, par l'excellence de sa cuisine, la réputation de ce restaurant, l'un des meilleurs de France. En 1951, elle devient la troisième femme à obtenir trois étoiles au *Guide Michelin*.

ABOVE LEFT **Les Crayeres, c. 1985, Reims, France**

ABOVE RIGHT **Lucas Carton, 1989, Paris, France**

RIGHT **Cazaudehore La Forestiere, c. 1985, Saint-Germain-en-Laye, France**

OPPOSITE **Mövenpick, c. 1985, Zurich, Switzerland**

LONDON

ESTABLISHED LONDON JUNE 14th 1971

♲ RECYCLED PAPER

OPPOSITE **Kubanisches Restaurant, c. 1985, Rostock, German Democratic Republic**

ABOVE **Hard Rock Café, c. 1984, London, England**

American entrepreneur Peter Morton, heeding his instincts that young Brits craved casual food from across the pond, served a winning combination of hamburgers and rock and roll.

Sein Instinkt sagte dem amerikanischen Unternehmer Peter Morton, dass junge Briten Lust auf amerikanisches Essen in ungezwungener Atmosphäre hätten, weshalb er ihnen eine gelungene Kombination aus Hamburgern und Rock 'n' Roll bot.

Sentant que les jeunes Britanniques ont envie des plats simples d'outre-Atlantique, le chef d'entreprise américain Peter Morton leur propose une carte qui mêle avec bonheur hamburgers et rock.

RIGHT **Café Schauspielhaus, c. 1985, German Democratic Republic**

RIGHT Hotel Kosmos, c. 1985, Erfurt, German Democratic Republic

Located in the state of Thuringia, a popular tourist destination, the hotel was a prized stop along with its numerous restaurants, which were equally teeming with customers. The menu's minimal graphics include an awkwardly placed logo on a photo of the cosmos.

Dieses Hotel in der beliebten Urlaubs-region Thüringen war ein begehrter Anlaufpunkt, ebenso wie seine zahlreichen Restaurants, in denen es von Kunden nur so wimmelte. Auf der minimalistischen Grafik der Speisekarten ist ein ungeschickt platziertes Logo auf einem Foto des Kosmos zu sehen.

Dans le *land* est-allemand de Thuringe, prisé des touristes, cet hôtel est une étape obligée, avec ses multiples restaurants et ses clients non moins nombreux. Sur cette couverture de menu au graphisme minimaliste, l'emplacement du logo dans une image du cosmos est mal choisi.

PAGE 434 **Les Terrasses de Lyon, c. 1989, Lyon, France**

PAGE 435 **Lasserre, c. 1988, Paris, France**

HOTEL
KOSMOS

Les Terrasses de Lyon

Hilaire

OPPOSITE **La Brasserie Bofinger, 1993, Paris, France**

RIGHT **Au Fer Rouge, c. 1991, Colmar, France**

Patrick Fulgraff

HOME MADE SOUP OF THE DAY *served with freshly baked roll £2.75*

GARLIC BREAD *Full size pizza base, fresh garlic* £2.75

Also available:

GARLIC BREAD PROVENÇALE *with fresh garlic and tomato £2.75*

BAKED GOAT'S CHEESE *in sesame on grilled sundried tomato Ciabatta, roast pepper salad, tomato chutney £6.50*

CHARGRILLED SKEWERED SEASONAL VEGETABLES *served on basmati rice, braised puy lentils green olive tapenade £6.50*

ROAST VEGETABLE FETA AND FILO PARCELS *served on a spicey bean cassoulet £6.50*

CAESAR SALAD *with smoked bacon, cos lettuce, anchovies, croutons, fresh parmesan, olives £5.99*

GREEK SALAD, *with herbed olives, feta cheese, cos & iceberg lettuce, tomato, cucumber, fresh oregano and a lemon olive oil dressing £5.99*

SALAD NIÇOISE - *very filling salad including tuna, mixed leaves, tomatoes, beans, potatoes, cucumber, onion, olives, capers, hard boiled egg and vinaigrette dressing £5.99*

SCOTCH SMOKED SALMON ON RYE *with cream cheese, dill gherkin, olives & seasonal salad £5.99*

CUMBRIAN HAM SALAD *home roasted at Salts, served with potato salad, coleslaw, mixed leaves and orange syrup £5.99*

NORTH YORKSHIRE SMOKED CHICKEN SALAD *tossed in a light mayonnaise with frisée, tiny bacon pieces, croutons & orange segments £5.99*

ROAST SQUASH AND WILD MUSHROOM *risotto cakes marinated green bean and roast tomato salad with a dried fruit, nut and chilli salsa £6.99*

CHINESE CHICKEN *and sticky rice pancakes with a fresh coriander, chinese leaf salad, lime chilli jam £6.99*

GRILLED SCOTTISH SALMON FILLET *wild organic rocket, roast tomato salad, potato and caper fritters, humous £7.50*

BRAISED LAMB SHANK *with thyme potato, parsnip and beans, herb gravy, green olive tapenade £7.50*

CUMBERLAND SAUSAGE *first class sausage grilled and served with braised red cabbage, mashed potato and a delicious sauce, very filling £5.99*

SALT BURGER *home-made with 100% minced chuck steak and our own blend of spices, chargrilled and served in a bun with gherkin & tomato relish, coleslaw & potato salad £5.99*

CONFIT OF DUCK LEG *served with leek and parsley polenta and watercress and apple salad £7.50*

CHARGRILLED ENGLISH RIB EYE STEAK *served with sauté potatoes, herb butter mixed salad £8.00*

FRESH SPINACH AND RICOTTA RAVIOLI *served with a light tomato sauce, parmesan £6.50*

PASTA *with pan fried salami, tomato and herb sauce fresh parmesan £5.99*

PASTA *and potato with roast pepper, mushrooms, green beans, fresh rosemary, chilli and garlic £5.99*

SALTS' PIZZAS -

CHARGRILLED SEASONAL VEGETABLE *pizza with or without mozzarella £5.99*

TOMATO AND MOZZARELLA *with fresh ripped basil £5.50*

SPICY PEPPERONI *with mozzarella and chilli £5.99*

SALTS HOME ROASTED HAM *with mozzarella and olive £5.99*

SMOKED CHICKEN *and roast mushroom £5.99*

SHREDDED DUCK *with bok choi and hoi sin £6.50*

CONFIT OF CHICKEN *with feta and green olive £6.50*

SIDE ORDERS *mixed seasonal salad - home-made potato salad - home-made coleslaw and sliced gherkin - mini Caesar salad - mini Greek salad - sauté potatoes - cherry tomato, feta, cucumber, orange and mint salad - Salts homemade humous with toasted pitta - green olive tapenade with warm sour dough bread - green and black olives marinated in olive oil, garlic, peppers and red onion £2.99.*

Roll and butter 50p

We hope you enjoy your meal, service charge is not included

salts
diner
menu

CH 93.

dal Pescatore

PAGE 438 Salts Diner, 1993, Shipley, England

David Hockney drew the template for a menu that could allow changes within the area illuminated by an overhead lamp. Thus, while the descriptions and prices change, the art remains.

David Hockney zeichnete die Vorlage für eine Speisekarte, auf der man innerhalb des von einer Deckenlampe beleuchteten Bereichs Änderungen vornehmen konnte. Während sich die Beschreibungen und Preise stetig änderten, blieb die Kunst dieselbe.

Le peintre David Hockney est l'auteur de ce menu où les plats figurant dans la zone éclairée par la lampe peuvent être modifiés à loisir. Si la carte et les prix changent, l'œuvre d'art reste la même.

PAGE 439 Dal Pescatore, 1997, Mantua, Italy

Dal Pescatore has been in the Santini family since 1925. In 1996 Michelin awarded the trattoria three stars. The Santinis have held on to them for decades.

Das Dal Pescatore befindet sich seit 1925 im Besitz der Familie Santini. Im Jahr 1996 verlieh Michelin der Trattoria drei Sterne, die die Santinis seit Jahrzehnten erfolgreich verteidigen.

Ce restaurant de Mantoue appartient à la famille Santini depuis 1925. En 1996, il reçoit trois étoiles au *Guide Michelin* et ne les a jamais perdues depuis.

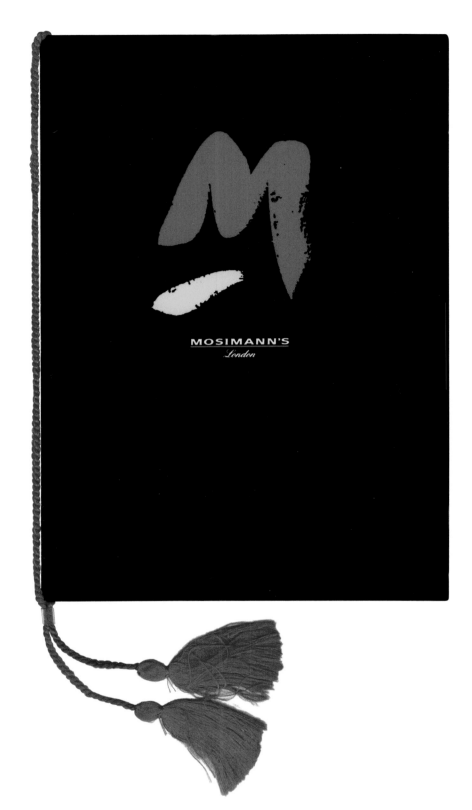

ABOVE An evening with Anton Mosimann, La Chaumiere, 1993, London, England

LEFT Restaurant Michel Chabran, 1997, Pont-de-l'Isère, France

OPPOSITE Lasserre, 1998, Paris, France

PAGE 442 Ombremont, c. 1992, Le Bourget-du-Lac, France

PAGE 443 The Canteen, 1995, London, England

PAGE 444 Le Grill, 1992, Reims, France

PAGE 445 La Table du Gourmet, 1997, Riquewihr, France

THE CANTEEN

Jean - Luc Brendel

Index

Imprint

A hearty thanks goes to Benedikt Taschen for his continued support and friendship. His innate taste and decision-making reflect his ability to produce the best books in the world. And a tip of the hat goes to Marlene Taschen for her enthusiasm and guidance throughout the project.

As usual, I am indebted to the generosity of collectors and institutions who made material for this volume available, especially Marc Selvaggio, Henry Voigt, Justin Jampol and the Wende Museum, The Culinary Institute of America/ Hyde Park, the Los Angeles Public Library, and our anonymous donor who continues to be gracious and overly generous with his collection. The menus from my collection reflect innumerable purchases from a variety of flea market dealers and antiquarian book and ephemera merchants to whom I am grateful for continuing to unearth multitudinous historical treasures.

The TASCHEN team in Cologne is to be feted for their consistent and valuable contributions in constructing this volume, including Marion Boschka, Ute Wachendorf, and, of course, our eternally positive Editorial Director Mahros Allamezade. A special mention goes to Kathrin Murr, whose even temperament, dedication, and 24-7 availability made her work the glue that bound the project.

In Los Angeles, Nemuel DePaula's work provided an initial template for the book, while Ryan Mungia devoted countless hours to perfecting the layout and kept me on course to complete the project. All the while, he has continued to be the director of my vast collections, ensuring they are organized and preserved.

A special mention goes out to the incomparable Steven Heller, who consistently provides sterling essays (before their due date!) on whatever subject matter he is given, while Marc Selvaggio, under a compressed schedule, applied his acute knowledge to the exquisite captions.

—Jim Heimann, Executive Editor, TASCHEN America

Collector's note: While all the menus in this book retain their original character and integrity, some of the menus have been altered for production and design considerations.

All images are from the Jim Heimann Collection unless otherwise noted. Any omissions for copy or credit will be given in future editions if such copyright holders contact the publisher. Additional images were provided courtesy of the following individuals and institutions: Courtesy of The Culinary Institute of America Menu Collection, Conrad N. Hilton Library, Hyde Park, N.Y. 15, 20, 22, 24, 38, 41, 53 top, 58 top, 60, 77 left, 90 bottom, 100 left, 114, 115, 171, 192, 204, 223, 224, 225, 247, 256, 276 right, 277, 278 right, 283 right, 289, 290 bottom, 299, 300–301, 309, 312 left, 317 top, 325, 326 top, 328, 332, 339, 340, 344, 347, 348 bottom, 349 bottom, 350 right, 353, 359, 360, 361 bottom, 367 top, 371 right, 372 top right and bottom, 381, 389 left, 394 left, 396, 397, 406, 414 top, Los Angeles Public Library Special Collections 233 bottom, 292, 312 right, 326 bottom right, 329, 334, 345, 364, 365, 389 right, 394 right, 395, 404, 405, 416, 419, 420 bottom, 423, 424, 425 left, 428 bottom, 431 left, 436, 437, 439, 440, 442, 443, 444, 445 Marc Selvaggio Collection 74 top, 272, 273 bottom Henry Voigt Collection 58 bottom, 64, 70, 77 right, 78 top, 111, 127, 154, 174, 175, Courtesy of The Wende Museum 31, 33, 351, 357, 366, 367 bottom, 384, 390 bottom, 392, 393 right, 398, 399, 402, 403, 410, 411, 421, 430, 431 right, 432–433

Text © Steven Heller (introduction)
Text © Marc Selvaggio (captions)

EACH AND EVERY TASCHEN BOOK PLANTS A SEED!
TASCHEN is a carbon neutral publisher. Each year, we offset our annual carbon emissions with carbon credits at the Instituto Terra, a reforestation program in Minas Gerais, Brazil, founded by Lélia and Sebastião Salgado. To find out more about this ecological partnership, please check: www.taschen.com/ zerocarbon
Inspiration: unlimited.
Carbon footprint: zero.

To stay informed about TASCHEN and our upcoming titles, please subscribe to our free magazine at www.taschen.com/magazine, follow us on Instagram and Facebook, or e-mail your questions to contact@taschen.com.

© 2022 TASCHEN GmbH
Hohenzollernring 53,
D–50672 Köln
www.taschen.com

German translation: Svenja Tengs, Berlin
French translation: Jean-François Cornu, France

Printed in Italy
ISBN 978-3-8365-7873-8

TANZBAR KOSMOS

Berliner Bierstube

N.V. STOOMVAART MAATSCHAPPIJ „NEDERLAND"

Notre devise est
TOUJOURS A MIEUX
comme notre nom

Menu

SWEDISH AMERICAN LINE

WINES
COCKTAILS
& DRINKS
ETC. ETC.
FROM THE
KUNGSHOLM bar

DÉSILINE Tonique
Stomachique
Digestive

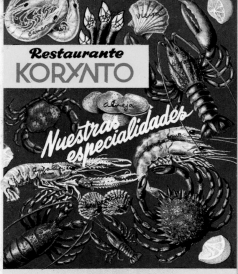

Restaurante KORYNTO
Nuestras especialidades

PRECIADOS, 46 • TELEFONOS 2320038 • 2319046 • 2215965 • MADRID

Norddeutscher Lloyd
Bremen.

Algier, Moschee Abder-Rahman.

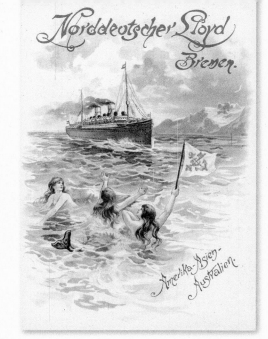

Norddeutscher Lloyd
Bremen.

Amerika-Asien-Australien

LES CHEFS-D'ŒUVRE
ÉPHÉMÈRES

PARIS
LONDON
DEAUVILLE
MONTE-CARLO

RESTAURANT DES AMBASSADEURS

BERLINER
KINDL
BRÄU

K. JAQUET
BERLIN-STEGLITZ • SCHLOSS-STRASSE 89
TELEFON 72 45 54

HOTEL
LUTETIA